Shelley's Annus Mirabilis

Shelley's Annus Mirabilis

THE MATURING OF AN EPIC VISION
by STUART CURRAN

HUNTINGTON LIBRARY
SAN MARINO, CALIFORNIA
1975

7-3-75   BT 2626

To the memory of
EARL REEVES WASSERMAN

◦◯◦

The splendours of the firmament of time
May be eclipsed, but are extinguished not.

The Sceptics held a middle path between the Dog-matists and Academicians, the former of whom boasted that they had attained the truth, while the latter denied that any attainable truth existed: the Sceptics, how-ever, without asserting or denying its existence, pro-fessed to be modestly and anxiously in search of it; as St. Augustine expresses it, in his liberal tract against the Manichæans, "nemo nostrum dicat jam se invenisse veritatem; sic eam quæramus quasi ab utrisque nescia-tur." From this habit of impartial investigation, and the necessity which they imposed upon themselves, of studying not only every system of philosophy, but every art and science, which pretended to lay its basis in truth, they necessarily took a wider range of erudition, and were more travelled in the regions of philosophy than those whom conviction or bigotry had domesticated in any particular system. It required all the learning of dogmatism to overthrow the dog-matism of learning; and the Sceptics, in this respect, resembled that ancient incendiary, who stole from the altar the fire with which he destroyed the temple.

THOMAS MOORE, Preface to
The Sceptic: A Philosophical Satire (1809)

CONTENTS

ILLUSTRATIONS

PREFACE

THE HUNTINGTON LIBRARY AND ART GALLERY, whose collections like its gardens harmonize the climates and cultures of the world, has seemed to more than one reader a reasonable microcosm of paradise. The genesis of this book coincides with my first visit to San Marino, where I found my particular Edenic bower in the three Shelley notebooks that crown the Library's superb holdings on this poet. Although they were ably deciphered at the beginning of the century by that paragon of gentleman-scholars, H. Buxton Forman, they offered a temptation—a necessary ingredient of any Eden—I could not resist. As I strained my eyesight no less than my wits to penetrate the scrawls of ink and pencil, I came to appreciate what the printed word conceals, that mysterious logic of quick inspiration and disquieted revision by which literary masterpieces move from fragmentary conception into the poised clarity of art. Two of the three Huntington notebooks are largely devoted to that period traditionally known as Shelley's *annus mirabilis*, that miraculous period of little over a year—from the early autumn of 1818 to the beginning of 1820—when, having left England forever, the poet discovered his genius in the fertile warmth of Italy and produced a series of works which, for diversity and brilliance, have seldom been matched by any writer.

If the Huntington notebooks record a rare genius fulfilling itself in abundance, by their very nature they raise the questions that this study has sought to examine and through its investigation answer. For, what is clear from the proximity of poetic conceptions that a reader generally approaches as wholly separate works of art is that Shelley himself was engaged in literary endeavors he saw as intrinsically related. The activities of a single month, mid-August to mid-September of 1819, stood for me as revelatory of a mental latitude never fully explored by earlier commentary. To read in the notebooks and correspondence of this period is to be surprised by remarkable simultaneity. Finishing *The Cenci,* Shelley is strongly moved by news of the event that swept all England with forebodings of civil war, the attack on the unarmed citizenry assembled at Manchester to protest a depressed economy and unresponsive government, the Peterloo Massacre—so strongly moved as to write his stirring exordium to the populace, *The Mask of Anarchy.* Yet at the same time, as with another and more finely strung mind, he is revising parts of the three acts of *Prometheus Unbound* already composed in the preceding months and drafting the conception of the cosmic celebration with which, as Act IV of that unsurpassed exercise of his genius, he was to draw the miraculous year to a close.[1] The sudden burst of genius one is prepared for. But this strenuous vitality points to an outlook more methodical, if still able to assimilate events of the moment, a vision so capacious that such events assume an ordered existence within a larger conceptual structure.

To experience through the notebooks the living evidence of Shelley's genius has resurrected with a new intensity some questions that insistently demanded answers beyond the range of my previous study, *Shelley's "Cenci": Scorpions Ringed with Fire.* The purpose of this book is to focus in large perspective the extraordinary versatility of Shelley's miraculous year, to justify within an encompassing framework the seeming contradictions in tone, idea, and purpose that such diversity necessarily accrues. And beyond seeking the wholeness of Shelley's vision, I have been prompted, as anyone who loves his art must be, to wonder what produced this intensity of creative activity and how it related to the comparatively meager effusions of his English apprenticeship. To some extent the events of Shelley's life provide answers: Italy, that country he called the "Paradise of exiles," so alive in its natural and human resources, cannot but have been responsible for the enlivening of his genius, as it was for activating Byron's. And it can be no accident that the fruition of Shelley's abilities coincides with his first marked experience of human mortality, the succumbing of his daughter Clara in late summer of 1818, gratuitously attenuated by his infant William's sudden death in June the next year. A new and urgent maturity conjoined with an eye newly awakened to the fecundity of life to produce a poetry more responsive at once to the sorrows and to the possibilities of human existence.

But a further event occurred within this crucial year of Shelley's awakening, one not so easily documented from the surface of the records, yet to which the notebooks stand as insistent testimonial. Unsure of his talents in England, Shelley distanced himself from his friends and allegiances, and after a hiatus of inactivity, as curious in its way as the flowering that followed, committed himself to a fully conceived vocation. The extent of that commitment his readers glean only from the high tonalities of *A Defence of Poetry*. The profession to which he dedicated himself upon graduating from his English apprenticeship had little to do with mere versification, though a fine craft was its basis. To engage in poetry, as Shelley conceived it, was to build upon the stability of one's craft a comprehensive vision of human life and aspiration. In his paradise of exiles Shelley was to renew the quest of those he considered the exemplary poets of western culture, Dante and Milton, to resolve the crucial problem of western thought, the justification of evil within so much potentiality for good. Amid my own Edenic bower, conscious of those examples, it would have been impossible for me not to feel the weight of their conceptions on Shelley.

For Shelley to place himself in this noble line of succession demanded more than the adolescent nerve he had once amply demonstrated. Almost from the start he had attached himself to the line of visionary poets who write a canon rather than an idle succession of individual flights of fancy, and in large measure the creativity of 1819 represents his discovery of the unique balances that would define the Shelleyan canon. Preferring a different emblem, no doubt, he must have appreciated the parallel voiced by Wordsworth in his prefatory remarks to *The Excursion*, between the creation of his canon and the construc-

xv

tion of a cathedral. To build such a structure is a deliberate act of faith whose purposes are not introverted, obscurantist, or narrowly aesthetic, but public, educational, visionary. If one reads the successive prefaces Shelley wrote for his volumes of poetry, one is struck by a voice far removed from the delicate timbres venerated as Shelleyan in the later years of the nineteenth century. It is a strong, commanding voice, assured in its social no less than its poetic values, conveying a sense of purpose, of responsibility. The poet conceived by these prose utterances fulfills a critical position in society, testing its values against past history and future possibility, shaping coherence out of temporal fragmentations, reminding his readers of the complexities as well as the verities of human life. His mission is epic.

The first requirement of an epic vision is that it be encyclopedic, and Shelley was more qualified than any of his contemporaries—with the exception of Coleridge, who found that his "abstruse research" robbed his poetry of its life—to represent the wholeness of his culture's knowledge within the canon he was shaping. A master of seven languages, who in his teens translated half of Pliny's enormous *Natural History* to whet his Latin, presents a comprehensive challenge to his student. His reading was wide and deep, arcane and popular; he was as excited by the first forays into modern physics as by the ancient wisdom of the Greek tragedians. The journal that Mary kept almost, one feels, as a public duty after she and Shelley met in 1814, records the course of study on which she and her husband embarked year after year. And yet one glance at the pretentious array of authors to whom Shelley alluded in the notes to *Queen Mab* in 1813, or at the list of skeptical philosophers he jotted as he was writing the fragmentary *Treatise on Morals* is enough to suggest the limitations of Mary's reading list. Doubtless it is true, as James Rieger once remarked to me, that Shelley could scarcely have toured Italy with the British Museum on his back. But he had a prodigious memory, as his cousin Thomas Medwin emphasizes in his biography, and on occasion had access to Byron's sizable reference library or to the books of such friends as Maria Gisborne and Mrs. Mason. One conceives him, too, in the several years before he left England building his strength for later exertions in the vibrant company of Peacock and Hogg, Hunt and Godwin. Especially in the environment of Marlow, with the learned Peacock a short distance away, Shelley's education did not end at home. There is some reason to believe that the initial ideas for the poetic keystone of the *annus mirabilis, Prometheus Unbound,* came to Shelley as early as 1817. Quite clearly in June and July of that year he was systematically doing research on the setting he was to use: in Aeschylus, in Arrian's account of Alexander's expedition into India, and in the contemporary traveler of the orient, Mountstuart Elphinstone. In addition, several of the characters of the drama—like Demogorgon—can be traced directly to Peacock's library. One suspects that Shelley's conversations with Peacock, either in his library or during their long, rambling walks, were seldom about the weather.

I emphasize such sources of Shelley's knowledge because my study, especially in its second chapter, assumes that Shelley had knowledge of major cultural movements of his time, which Peacock clearly shared, but whose authors are largely unrecorded by his or Mary's references. Three writers in particular recur in the annotations as authorities, mostly because Shelley's conceptions seem so frequently similar to theirs that one can suggest his knowledge of them from the circumstantial evidence: Thomas Maurice (1754-1824), author of *Indian Antiquities* and *The History of Hindostan,* George Stanley Faber (1773-1854), whose principal work *The Origin of Pagan Idolatry* was published in 1816, and Francis Wilford (ca. 1760-1822), a protegé of Sir William Jones and frequent contributor to the major organ of the orientalists, *Asiatic Researches.* Interestingly enough, both Maurice and Faber matriculated at University College, Oxford, from which Shelley was expelled in 1811, the former with a B.A. in 1778 and an M.A. in 1808, the latter with a B.A. in 1793. In the preface to *Indian Antiquities* (1: 49-50) Maurice commends his former teachers at Oxford for their encouragement and gives particular thanks for the support, financial as well as moral, of Dr. Wetherell, then Master of University College. The connections with Shelley of the second distinguished alumnus of University College are more substantial. Faber was for some time a member of the Durham clergy and well acquainted with the family of Thomas Jefferson Hogg. When Hogg and Shelley selected University College as the dissemination point for subverting the Anglican orthodoxy, Faber became one of those self-sacrificing divines with whom they engaged in nefarious correspondence. He appears also to have interceded with Hogg's parents to treat their scapegrace son tolerantly, and thus earned the grudging, if condescending, respect of the expelled elite. The subscription list for *The Origin of Pagan Idolatry* includes Hogg's father, as well as the intriguing entry, "---- Peacock, Esq. Norton." It would be a strange coincidence that Norton, a mere village, should house a Peacock, for by this point Hogg was closer to Peacock than to the mutual friend who introduced them, and was a resident of Norton House, the family estate. In the Regency Wilford had become rather famous: Thomas Moore, for example, routinely cites "Wilford's learned Essays on the Sacred Isles of the West" in the notes to *Lalla Rookh* (1817, p. 233). That Peacock entered the India House in 1819 does not, of course, predicate a long and detailed familiarity with oriental scholarship, but the author of *Palmyra* and *Ahrimanes* would surely have known, if he did not possess, the *Asiatic Researches*.

However far-flung its sources, Shelley's learning was prodigious but never merely antiquarian or an end in itself, always subordinate to the sense of mission that directed his life and art. A virtuoso craftsman as well, he used his technical mastery in the same way, to revivify the past for a new age. His knowledge of the classical decorum of the poetic genres is unmatched by his contemporaries, but he touches no convention that he does not alter irrevocably. The achievement of the *annus mirabilis,* in which Shelley moved through form after form, writing economic analysis with his left hand and a sublime mythological drama with his right, testifies to a unified sensibility that sees all aspects of human endeavor, from the mundane to the sublime, to be inextricably related. In seeking to comprehend the harmonious vision to which these works in their integrity pertain, a critic sets himself a challenge akin to that of the poet, that of discerning a whole so capacious that it nurtures the integrity of the parts it subsumes. If the structures I emphasize derive from the array of masterpieces of little over a year in Shelley's life, in tracing the development from his earlier endeavors I have sought to ascertain the seeds responsible for this sudden flowering. And although the poems of the last two years of his career are beyond my purview, yet I trust that this study also has implications for their reading. In a number of cases—one thinks of *Epipsychidion* especially—Shelley became more introverted, examining the fundamental nature of reality, of human thought and art, within a vortex of skepticism that allowed him progressively fewer premises on which to stand. And yet, there are the ringing affirmations of *A Defence of Poetry*, the shrewd propaganda of *Hellas*, during these same years. If one strain of Shelley's temperament draws him to ethereal projections, another is fully committed to the betterment of this world. That Shelley was capable of squarely confronting the destructiveness of experience in his last poem, *The Triumph of Life*, does not testify to suicidal inclinations or mutually cancelling impulses, but rather to a fundamental honesty large enough to take human realities, not dogmas, as the ground of art. The whole he conceives is thus tentative, constantly enlarging, as was the structure of his life. At the moment of his death Shelley was on a verge of a new career, preparing from a sanctuary beyond threat of imprisonment to inaugurate a journal, *The Liberal*, in which to flay a reactionary English government with enlightened social views and great poetry. It is that unified commitment and the largeness of vision it supports that makes Shelley's early death so momentous a loss to the future culture of the English-speaking world. No other of such youth had so much left to say. Still, what he did say in his comparatively brief life has been sufficient to command the enthusiasm and to expand the intellect of this student for many years—for many more years, I fondly hope. Shelley is the last of the English Renaissance poets and among the first of its modern ones, and, like the Dante he venerated in the *Defence of Poetry*, his work has become a "bridge thrown over the stream of time." From that span the horizons are large indeed.

Research for this volume has been a commitment of some years' standing, and I am grateful for the aid from a number of sources that has steadily advanced it toward completion. I began work under the auspices of a summer grant from the American Philosophical Society and continued under a National Endowment for the Humanities Junior Fellowship and two separate grants from the Henry E. Huntington Library, with supplemental aid from the Graduate School of the University of Wisconsin. To judge the resources of the Huntington Library more worthy of celebration than its accomplished and loving staff would require a discrimination beyond my capacity, and my gratitude is as full as it is indiscriminate. I have also been fortunate to have enjoyed a long period of residence at the Library of Congress, an institution of extraordinary depth for a project of this kind and deserving of a recognition in our national life it seldom receives. My research has also been materially furthered at the Folger and Newberry Libraries, the Carl Pforzheimer Library, the New York Public Library, and the libraries of Harvard College, Yale University, and the University of California at Los Angeles. The willingness of all these institutions to extend their welcome and resources to a visiting scholar I deeply appreciate. The illustrations accompanying the text come mainly from the collections of the Huntington Library, but in several instances I am grateful to other institutions for permission to reproduce their materials: to the Widener Collection of Renaissance Bronzes, the National Gallery of Art, Washington, D.C.; to the Newberry Library, Chicago; to the Library of Congress; and to the British Museum. Several of my friends and fellow scholars have been unfailing in their kindness to me: Donald Reiman was always willing to take time from his busy schedules to answer queries; Kamal Verma gave my conclusions the benefit of his extensive knowledge of both Shelley and Eastern cultures; and Donald Howard deserted his Chaucerian pilgrimage for several days to read the manuscript with dispatch and customary sensitivity. Joseph Wittreich's attentive perusal was but the last of his many contributions to the intellectual life of this author and this book. Finally, I should like to thank Vincent Newton for the repeated, crucial loan of his typewriter and to acknowledge that for patience, good cheer, and reasonable accuracy in typing I am wearily obliged to myself.

San Marino, California
25 June 1974

Standard reference works recurring in the text have been abbreviated as follows:

Clairmont Journals	*The Journals of Claire Clairmont*, ed. Marion Kingston Stocking (Cambridge, Mass.: Harvard Univ. Press, 1968).
Letters	*The Letters of Percy Bysshe Shelley*, ed. Frederick L. Jones (Oxford: Clarendon Press, 1964).
Mary Shelley's Journal	*Mary Shelley's Journal*, ed. Frederick L. Jones (Norman: Univ. of Oklahoma Press, 1947).
Peacock, *Works*	*The Works of Thomas Love Peacock*, ed. H. F. B. Brett-Smith and C. E. Jones (London: Constable, and New York: Gabriel Wells, 1924-34).
Shelley, *Prose*	*The Works of Percy Bysshe Shelley*, ed. Roger Ingpen and Walter E. Peck (London: Ernest Benn, and New York: Charles Scribner, 1926-30), Vols. 5-7.

For citations from Shelley's poetry the Oxford Standard Edition edited by Thomas Hutchinson has been relied upon, except in the case of *Prometheus Unbound*, which is quoted from the text of Lawrence Zillman, *Shelley's "Prometheus Unbound": The Text and the Drafts. Toward a Modern Definitive Edition* (New Haven and London: Yale Univ. Press, 1968). Standard editions have also been used for quotations from other English poets, and the Loeb Library has similarly served for classical authors, cited by customary reference number and, where applicable, the translator and page. Unless otherwise indicated, translations are the author's.

Shelley's Annus Mirabilis

1

EPIC VENTURES

I should not think of devoting less than 20 years to an Epic
Poem. Ten to collect materials and warm my mind with universal science. I would be a tolerable Mathematician, I would
thoroughly know Mechanics, Hydrostatics, Optics, and As-
tronomy, Botany, Metallurgy, Fossilism, Chemistry, Geology,
Anatomy, Medicine—then the *mind of man*—then the *minds
of men*—in all Travels, Voyages and Histories. So I would
spend ten years—the next five to the composition of the poem
—and the last five to the correction of it.
   —Coleridge, Letter to Joseph Cottle, April 1797

I would not that you should immediately apply yourself to the
composition of an Epic Poem . . . I hope for no more than that
you should, from some moment when the clearness of your
own mind makes evident to you the 'truth of things,' feel that
you are chosen out from all other men to some greater enterprise of thought; and that all your studies should, from that
moment, tend towards that enterprise alone: that your affec-
tions, that all worldly hopes this world may have left you,
should link themselves to this design. *What* it should be, I am
not qualified to say. In a more presumptuous mood, I recom-
mended the Revolution of France as a theme involving pictures
of all that is best qualified to interest and to instruct mankind.
   —Shelley, Letter to Lord Byron, 29 September 1816

As the Dover packet left the quay on the stormy afternoon
of March 12, 1818, it is unlikely that Shelley had much opportunity for studied reflections on the celebrated cliffs of his
homeland. The sole distraction from the heavy winter seas
was the wife of a Colonel Hare, who, having apparently taken

on the sins of the entire company, was, as Claire Clairmont wryly noted, "much frightened & repeated the Lord's Prayer in her Distress. every now & then requesting her Servant to go on with it as she was prevented by Sickness."[1] Shelley himself had ample cause for concern as the protector of two women not yet legally adults, his infants Clara and William, and Allegra, the offspring of Claire's romantic attachment with the melancholy Lord Byron. Of the young, eccentric, and hopeful family that embarked that day at Dover, only Mary and Claire would return, both chastened, with their lives darkened to a fitful world of memories—Mary after the death of her children and husband; and Claire, whose child likewise succumbed to the Italian climate, after employing herself as a lonely governess in Vienna, suffering expulsion for her links with the revolutionary Shelley, and pursuing her unhappy trade amid the vicious winters and imperial tempers of Moscow. Obsessed with escaping a disordered and difficult existence, however, they little intimated the tragedies of the near future. Shelley left behind obloquy and scorn, a fortune he could not touch, constant demands on his time and annuity by friends incapable of managing their own affairs, a climate disastrous to health, two children remanded to more suitable guardianship than could be anticipated from the author of *Queen Mab*, and several books of poems poorly received. "We are all very well & in excellent spirits," he wrote Leigh Hunt from Calais. "Motion has always this effect upon the blood, even when the mind knows that there are causes for dejection."[2]

The day Shelley left England in 1818 he was only a few months younger than Keats at his death; but he had written little of comparable magnitude: one long poem, *Alastor*, two short pieces in an elevated mode—the *Hymn to Intellectual Beauty* and *Mont Blanc*—and a small collection of lyrics, of which only *To Constantia* evidences unquestionable mastery.[3] That Shelley frequently should have expressed dissatisfaction with his own accomplishment, or that he should have felt himself obscured by the greatness of Byron when the two met at Lake Geneva in 1816 and again in Venice in 1818, is wholly understandable. Moreover, it is just. The highly uneven achievement of Shelley's English period had been, in balance, little better than the verse of his young contemporaries, Leigh Hunt and Thomas Love Peacock. His schooling by these friends and fellow poets, if far more significant to his later successes than critics have been wont to acknowledge, was, like most education, beyond a certain point inhibiting to Shelley's native gifts. In forsaking England, he carried with him Hunt's technical facility and Peacock's heterodox learning. He left behind the tendencies toward triviality in the one and over-exacting classicism in the other. In a very real sense Shelley's destiny lay with Lord Byron. The Geneva meeting had prompted the most perfect of his poems to date. That in Venice would inaugurate the miraculous year in which Shelley was to emulate and then surpass the acknowledged genius of contemporary English poetry. Withdrawing at the age of twenty-five from the comfortable periphery of London's literary life, Shelley came of age.

For many poets preliminary successes, however portentous of a future course they may be, are less significant to actual development than are ambitious failures. Tracing Endymion through convoluted paths and frequently losing him in a luxurious vegetation hastily transplanted from the conservatory, Keats nonetheless taught himself the craft of poetry. Conversely, Robert Southey put his considerable talent to such facile use in *Joan of Arc* and *Thalaba* that, encouraged by dazzled bluestockings, he became blind to his inadequacies and courted the willing hand of oblivion. Shelley's success on a small scale had not insured an equal mastery of the great themes that compelled his most ambitious work. If massive failure always presaged radical improvement, *Queen Mab* and *The Revolt of Islam*, the major poems Shelley left behind him at Dover, would have been cause for great encouragement. But since the only favorable notices Shelley received until some months after he left England were those of Hunt, his literary future looked bleak.[4] *Queen Mab*, to be sure, had earned him youthful notoriety, the instant enmity of largely conservative reviews, and added strains on his family. In his epigraph he had vowed with Archimedes that, given a place to stand, he would move the universe; but, in truth, he had touched few minds and shaken no empires but his own. *The Revolt of Islam*, newly born from the press despite Godwin's severe censure, was the logical enlargement of the often ingenuous scheme of *Queen Mab*.[5] If Shelley did not deserve the scandal-mongering in which the *Quarterly Review* indulged its spleen in 1819, its critical distaste for the epic was defensible. History records fewer kind words for this poem than for *Queen Mab*: it was destined, as Medwin recalls, "to line many a trunk and furnish wrappers for the grocer."[6] In 1829 there still remained enough copies of the original edition for John Brooks, a publisher associated with the followers of Robert Owen, to reenlist the forgotten warrior in the battle for reform.

And yet, with characteristically impetuous energy, Shelley had invested his hardest labors on the composition of these major efforts in behalf of universal enlightenment. Their failure to affect the climate of reaction driving England toward a second civil war could only have been a heart-rending disappointment to one who earnestly sought to avert the cataclysm he saw perilously imminent. That the first poem was too strident and the second too tedious hardly alters the purposes for which Shelley launched them on an indifferent public. Nor can it alter the faith that compelled Shelley to assume such unlikely vehicles for transformation of the fundamental fabric of English society. It is easy to cavil at *Queen Mab* and *The Revolt of Islam*, but that a poet of Shelley's years should have produced two poems of epic pretension is indicative both of his culture and of his conception of the poet's place in it. Even more, it is indicative of the nature of epic pretension in the Romantic period.

I

The thirty-five year span by which we generally denote the period of English Romanticism saw the greatest outpouring of epic poems in modern literary history: epic, indeed, is the major genre of the time.[7] Partly this is a reaction against the sterility of the genre in the eighteenth century, an attempt to prove that, with or without the accepted rules promulgated by Le Bossu and his imitators over a century before, the literary form that took precedence over all others could be relevant to a contemporary world. Epic was a fever of the time. Charles Lamb, for instance, exhorted Coleridge in January, 1797, to put himself under the contagious influence of Southey:

> Coleridge, I want you to write an Epic poem. Nothing short of it can satisfy the vast capacity of true poetic genius. Having one great End to direct all your poetical faculties to, and on which to lay out your hopes, your ambition, will shew you to what you are equal. By the sacred energies of Milton, by the dainty sweet and soothing phantasies of honeytongued Spenser, I adjure you to attempt the Epic.[8]

The major impetus to this revival, considered as a purely literary event, was William Hayley's *Essay on Epic Poetry*, a poem in five heroic epistles that combined a discriminating appreciation of past achievements with overt disparagement of the pedants who refused their credentials to all but Homer and Virgil on the grounds that later epics did not comply with their rules. From our vantage point what Hayley demonstrated at great length seems a belaboring of the obvious, but he opened for his time the apertures of an ancient and musty edifice to salutary winds of change. Coleridge, in a letter to Southey, applauds Hayley's *Essay* as a treatise "almost every literary man speaks of with pleasure & gratitude."[9] And Southey himself emphasizes the germinal character of Hayley's work: "A greater effect was produced upon the rising generation of scholars, by the Notes to his Essay on Epic poetry, than by any other contemporary work, the Relics of Ancient Poetry alone excepted."[10] Since one of Hayley's contributions was to suggest the rich sources of epic material in Eastern mythologies, its effect on Southey is manifest.

In their attempt to resuscitate what they considered the central spirit of English poetry from the moribund verse of the Augustan age, the early Romantics saw an enemy with which

Spenser and Milton were never forced to contend. The place of heroic poetry, trammeled by rigid convention and false standards of taste, had in the preceding half-century been surrendered without skirmish to the epic in prose, as Fielding defined the novel. An *Epigoniad* or *Leonidas* could find its way into select libraries by subscription, but Richardson and Fielding were actually reaping pecuniary rewards from their efforts. If the scramble for *Pamela* was offensive to refined tastes—and few enough of them—it irrevocably altered literary history. By the end of the century half the governesses in England were, like the later Miss Prism, secretly at work on a three-decker fantasy of amorous adventure and romantic intrigue. It was against this phenomenon that Hayley wrote his plea for the spirit, not the conventional form, of epic poetry; and against it, too, that Southey mounted the offensive of "an epic every spring."[11] That the battle for supremacy was won not by Dickens, Thackeray, and Eliot, but by Walter Scott, suggests that historical destiny, rather than numbers or enthusiasm, tipped the balance. Ultimately, it was a philosophical struggle between the partisans of Berkeley and of Locke. To a modern civilization whose strength is conceived upon the immutability of external reality, it comes as no surprise that the real world emerged victorious; but every Romantic poet who wrote an epic—and all the major ones did—defended a post-Miltonic conception of the genre as the repository of their culture's highest, if often least observed, spiritual truths. The most vociferous in this respect were Blake, Shelley, and Keats. Wordsworth's place among their idealist ranks was reserved for the publication of *The Prelude* in 1850 and *The Recluse* in 1888. His contemporary contribution to the development of the epic—more noteworthy from the point of genre than content—was *The Excursion*, whose locus is the natural world in painstaking detail. Byron's two poems of epic scope set the terms of the contest in remarkable clarity. The troubled broil of internal and external realities in *Childe Harold's Pilgrimage* is resolved through the comic perspective of *Don Juan*, where the contradictory, absurd, but unavoidable reality of the world is fully embraced, and where the only spiritual essence that endures is man's capacity to survive his own ruin.

The Romantic epic, however cognizant of the modes and conventions of Homer and Virgil, does not return to them either for motivation or ideology. Its fountainhead is Milton, and, unlike that of the Victorians or, indeed, many modern critics, the Romantic conception of Milton is profoundly political.[12] Not only was he a central figure in establishing the first republic in the modern world (this to a generation present at the second such attempt), but his epic poems were radically subversive of the secular state. Southey, as pompous laureate of Regency reaction, might well have reconsidered his early enthusiasm for Hayley's *Essay on Epic Poetry,* for nowhere is the post-Miltonic emphasis more apparent.[13] Hayley attacks Virgil not simply for his imitation of Homer, nor because he furnished Le Bossu the means by which to codify his rules, but because his muse became a "Slave of State" (II, 227). Lucan, on the other hand, is celebrated as Freedom's bard (II, 237-38), and Ariosto, as "Born every law of System to disown, / And rule by Fancy's boundless power alone" (III, 155-56). The true subject for a revitalized epic poetry in England is the foundation of British liberty and the imaginative genius by which it has been accomplished. Hayley proves himself a confirmed Buff-and-Blue Whig in his aesthetic; but his successors, having watched that splintering of the Whig party by which Charles Fox became almost the lone voice from the wilderness willing to champion the French Revolution, also witnessed the august political foundation Hayley praised under serious jeopardy from the fanaticism of Pitt and the mindless degeneracy of the court. The poets who followed Hayley's admonition were understandably less susceptible to the platitudes of liberalism he enjoined upon them. They would agree that "Poesy. . .[was] fair Freedom's friend" (I, 276, 278), but might well wonder where in England or in France another was to be found.

Virgil and Spenser had made epic poetry a handmaiden to empire. The Miltonic tradition posited at its base spiritual premises "more Heroic" than the mundane needs of the state.[14] In the Romantic period heroic verses in support of the crowned heads of Europe, not to mention the variously addled ones of the extant Hanoverians, would seem unimaginable had not Southey, upon becoming laureate, endeavored to write them.[15] Even so, it is a remarkable fact that every epic or quasi-epic poem of any merit during this period follows the Miltonic tradition by which the noblest of genres became also the most politically radical.[16] Landor's *Gebir* celebrates a hero who refuses to do battle. Southey's *Joan of Arc*, with Coleridge's assistance, not only pays homage to Mary Wollstonecraft in its choice of heroic figure, but celebrates one of the greatest leaders in French liberation from English rule at a time when England was once again at war with France. For all the exoticism of *Thalaba* and *The Curse of Kehama*, both epics center upon an apocalyptic battle between the forces of good and evil: the former—simple, loving souls steeled by Miltonic virtues—bring down all the kingdoms of the earth. Although Kehama suffers from Napoleonic hubris, his Indian origin might just as easily approximate the economic colossus of the British Empire. Wordsworth's political vision, to be sure, is more apparently conservative, but it is radically so. The dual political allegiance, so forcefully demonstrated in the French scenes of *The Prelude*, admits no synthesis, but rather a negation. In the clash of empires individual imaginative vision is decimated: its eternal enemy is the state. Wordsworth's withdrawal to the Lake District, where the state seldom intrudes, bears with it the messianic responsibility of altering the politics of the world by educating minds away from merely political solutions. But the state does intrude upon Cumberland; and the only point after the opening of *The Excursion* where Wordsworth's poetry regains its former vatic fire, in Books VIII and IX, is his virulent denunciation of the woe wreaked on his pastoral community by industrialism acting in the specious name of progress.

The foundation laid by the first generation of Romantics supports the even more radical assumptions of the second. Surveying the manifold ruin of empires, *Childe Harold's Pilgrimage*, *Queen Mab*, and *Hyperion* quietly negate the rationale for the twenty years of war aimed at subduing one empire only to supplant it with others. The highest of destinies in *Endymion* is an imaginative vision for whose sake a Prince of Latmos abdicates his throne against the sensible objections of that English womanhood embodied in his sister. Byron, having documented the insubstantiality of love, glory, empire—"I have stood upon Achilles' tomb, / And heard Troy doubted; Time will doubt of Rome" (*Don Juan*, IV, 101)—turns his epic vision upon what counts for the civilized life and finds it just as lacking in permanent value. The only comparable vision is what can be gleaned from the fragments of Peacock's *Ahrimanes*, where the Power of Evil holds the world in total thrall. The triumph of life then becomes, as Shelley saw, one of death; and only "the sacred few" remain unscathed. This is something more than traditional English pessimism reasserting itself in response to fruitless war and peace. It is part of a larger vision that profoundly questions the nature of man's relationship to his society and concludes, in one sense or another, that the only society conducive to individual spiritual integrity is that of Milton's saints. All else is composed, as Blake would say, of "Single vision and Newton's sleep."[17]

The only Romantic epic to attempt a traditional justification of the nature of the universe is Wordsworth's *Excursion*, whose Christian piety and quietism seem less than adequate to resolve the dark issues it raises. The abrogation of the great chain of being— brought to its definitive climax with the French Revolution, though clearly presaged throughout the preceding century—demanded an epic theodicy beyond the limitations of orthodox Christianity. Except for *The Excursion*, none of the Romantic epics offers a literal theodicy, since there is a quiet understanding among them, broken only by Shelley's impatience with such understandings, that a transcendent deity will not be invoked. It is clear, too, that with the fear of anarchy in France and repression at home, and with the Napoleonic Wars sapping the lives and fortunes of Europe, justification of the status quo would be outrageous to intellectual integrity. But the legacy of Milton, teaching that epic poetry is "doctrinal and exemplary to a Nation," again illuminated the poet's role in a sick and reactionary society.[18] If whatever was was wrong, the highest duty of those possessed of imaginative vision was to justify what should be—not by numbering the streaks in a vitiating reality, but by projecting the ideal and leading the way to its attainment. If it was no longer possible to justify the ways of God to man, the panoramic vision of epic poetry must at last justify man himself.

II

In March of 1791, as the first issues of Paine's *Rights of Man* went on the streets, Thomas Holcroft, an abettor of the publication, joyfully greeted his fellow-conspirator William Godwin: "Hey, for the New Jerusalem! The Millenium! And peace and eternal beatitude be unto the soul of Thomas Paine."[19] Twenty years later, when Shelley greeted Godwin as if risen from the dead, "a luminary too dazzling for the darkness which surrounds him," the original millenarians were either themselves dead, in exile, or, like Godwin, Whiggish shadows of their former selves.[20] The Holy Alliance and Napoleon Buonaparte's failure to distinguish his will to power from the destiny of the French nation had transformed the mental struggle against the Antichrist into a quarter-century clash of arms whose issue could only be the rightful seat of the Great Whore. For twenty years the despairing Spectre of Los "kept the Divine Vision in time of trouble" (*Jerusalem* 44:15), while violence and backsliding deepened the moral crisis of Albion. Shelley, reared in placid wealth in an English country house, kept his own faith.

It was the Godwin of 1791 that Shelley hoped to find alive in 1812, when he excitedly introduced himself. And though Godwin was suitably flattered by Shelley's attentions, he quickly cast himself in an avuncular role, reproving the burning haste of youth, cautioning restraint and dispassionate intellection. But Shelley, dismissed from Oxford into existential freedom, had hoisted the banner of the apocalyptic church militant of the 1790s. A godless crusade it was, but otherwise it reproduced with fidelity the tone, the excitement, and the mental exertion of the early revolutionary days. Shelley, one must remember, was England's first great poet born after the Revolution. To the older generation, however exciting in prospect, the grandiose social experiment had failed. To Shelley it was, like Godwin, an accomplished fact: that it had not succeeded was not to deny that it had been.

It is possible that a vision of reality so obstinately ideal indicates, as Shelley's common-sense critics have asserted, a woefully defective understanding of history. But it is more probable that Shelley's ability in his isolated, late adolescence to reillume the light that had failed European culture represents, as Kenneth Cameron has suggested, the "visionary penetration. . . of a man rising on a wave of a titanic historical struggle to see deep and far, farther and deeper in essentials than many later and more particularized thinkers."[21] The fruit of that vision is *Queen Mab*, despite its faults one of the most remarkable documents of cultural, as well as literary, Romanticism. Its rhetoric derives from vituperative radical tracts, its style from enlightenment didacticism, and its conceptions from Volney, Sir William Jones, and Peacock.[22] For all its redolence of a slightly out-dated vernacular, however, it is far more than a late-enlightenment curiosity. The most openly libertarian of Romantic epics, *Queen Mab*'s true forbears are Langland's *Piers Plowman*, of which it is likely that Shelley was ignorant, and Milton's *Paradise Regained*, twin pillars of an authentic English tradition, the epic of social vision. Its revival in Shelley's hands came by way of the conventionally pious meditations of Edward Young's *Night Thoughts*, whose scope Shelley enlarged and, to put it mildly, revolutionized. He was neither the first nor the last of the English Romantics to adopt the nine-book meditative structure of Young's confrontation with human frailty, but all in all he may have been the most successful. Blake's *Four Zoas* manifestly lacks the coherence of *Queen Mab*; Wordsworth's *Excursion* lacks its energy and intellectual daring.[23]

Young begins *Night Thoughts* with a reluctant awakening from deathlike sleep and continues for book after book to counsel the frivolous Lorenzo to emulate the embalmed state of his friend Philander. Morbidly ascetic as this Christian piety is, Shelley recasts it in *Queen Mab* partly, one feels, because, in placing the only meaningful reality in the communication of man and God, Young gives validity to a reactionary social system that does not assuage, but intensifies, the fallen condition of humanity. A truly universal vision would attempt to align ultimate harmonies with human life, not to divorce the two. Thus, Shelley's poem begins not by an act of awakening, but by a deeper, more imaginative sleeping, and it continues by defining Young's absolutes of death and time as conditional. What is absolute is the iniquity of capitalist imperialism, thriving on war, on superstition, and on oppression, dehumanizing and debasing man: "The harmony and happiness of man / Yields to the wealth of nations" (V. 79-80). Shelley transforms Young's conventional humility into an indictment of the principle of self as the essential cause of the social cancers destroying the vitality of the body politic. The social vision of *Queen Mab* may be annoying in its stridency, but it is also admirable in its unity. It is little wonder that Friedrich Engels began a translation or that Karl Marx lamented Shelley's early death; *Queen Mab* was called the "Bible of Chartism," because like that movement it sought not to accrue separate grievances against a resistant social system, but to define the basic principles responsible for perpetuating it, as well as those human virtues by which it could be replaced.[24]

Shelley's ideology in *Queen Mab* stems from French enlightenment principles, but his poetic conception bears the unmistakable stamp of English Romanticism. *Queen Mab* is customarily discussed as if it were a prose tract, and one must suppose that it has been read more for its notes than its symbolism. But the comprehensive social vision is itself subsumed within an abiding metaphor from which the poem derives its title. The ascent of the dreaming Ianthe in the chariot of the fairy queen is a movement into the imagination, which is itself "in its changeless purity" (I. 182) the essential spiritual nature of man. It took a succession of angels to initiate Adam to past, present, and future. Here, though the tour is nominally under the authority of Queen Mab, it takes place within the mind of Ianthe. Like the powers who illuminate the sleeping mind in Fuseli's engraving for Erasmus Darwin's *Temple of Nature*—a work whose assertion of the unity of human and natural spheres left a lasting stamp on Shelley's conceptions—the fairy queen opens the portals to a kind of collective unconscious in which Ianthe comprehends the immutable truths of humanity.

Such a sleep is truly regenerative. On an individual level its boon is to lend coherence to one's social analysis and determination to one's resolves. Were so visionary a sleep to occur universally, the result would be apocalyptic, as the poem portends. To further that end, the imaginative dreamer translates his vision into poems like *Queen Mab*. Dreams beget dreams: poems, even those published in 250 copies, change the world. The basic metaphor of the dream-vision both ties together and explicates further ramifications of the poem. If one can equate the renovating power of imaginative vision within the psyche to the way in which the initiated poet then revitalizes his community, the result is a continuum linking all men in spirit. Shelley pursues the metaphor even further, in what, with self-conscious parody, he calls, "the great chain of nature" (II. 108). The principle that motivates this poem is the distinguishing force of every Ianthe, or flower, the compulsion to bloom. This "secret Strength of things," as Shelley explains it in *Mont Blanc*, not only "governs thought," but is universal in nature— "to the infinite dome / Of heaven is as a law" (*Mont Blanc*, 139-41). *Queen Mab* envisions a commonalty of spirit and matter created through "Nature's unchanging harmony" (II. 257), which, in this nineteenth-century Pythagorean view, is indeed the harmony of the spheres. Conservation of energy is a historical and a spiritual truth, as well as a physical law (II. 211-24). Atomic principles "produce the laws / Ruling [man's] moral state" (II. 236-37), as well as the laws governing the planets (III. 226-40). Queen Mab's chariot, ascending to imaginative truth within Ianthe's mind, is self-evidently a comet spreading its "fiery track" (I. 227) through the void. The first two notes Shelley

THE POWER OF FANCY IN DREAMS.

So holy transports in the cloysters shade
Play round thy toils, visionary maid;
Charmd oer thy bed celestial voices sing,
And Seraphs hover on enamourd wing.

1. Henry Fuseli, "The Power of Fancy in Dreams." Erasmus Darwin,
The Temple of Nature (London, 1803)

16

appended to *Queen Mab* are not political, but astronomical: the imaginative structure of his vision - the internal reality of Ianthe's searching mind - is everywhere buttressed with the solidity of scientific law.

The heaven painted by Shelley under the rubric of Queen Mab's palace seems a deliberate embodiment of the imaginative paradise of Coleridge's *Kubla Khan*.

> As Heaven, low resting on the wave, it spread
> Its floors of flashing light,
> Its vast and azure dome,
> Its fertile golden islands
> Floating on a silver sea.
> (*Q.M.* II. 31-35)[25]

But the dichotomy Coleridge envisions between earthly and conceptual paradises is illusory to Shelley. The liberated mind, ascending and descending "the great chain of nature," mediates between heaven and earth, spirit and matter. Queen Mab, Shelley's imaginative agent, is in his later revision of the poem "the Daemon of the World," a mediator between time and eternity whose presence will be constant in the regenerated world. The eighth canto ends with such a depiction of utopian harmony activated by mind:

> ... every shape and mode of matter lends
> Its force to the omnipotence of mind,
> Which from its dark mine drags the gem of truth
> To decorate its Paradise of peace.
> (VIII. 235-38)

In the regenerated world mind is omnipotent, at last even denying time its habitual victories (IX. 34-37).

To concentrate thus on the metaphorical aspects of *Queen Mab* allows us to see beyond its overt didacticism. It encompasses anathemas against the reigning and corrupt establishments of the earth, but it moves continuously to transcend them. In this sense it has much in common with the develop-

17

ment of *Paradise Regained*, which moves by means of the dialectic between Christ and Satan to a universal perspective dwarfing but always subsuming the antitheses that accumulate. Christ progresses toward his divine ministry through a series of imaginative discriminations that culminate in the blazing self-knowledge in which he assumes the godhead and casts off the Satanic principle. Metaphorically, at least, this is true of Ianthe as well. Shelley designed his poem not merely to distinguish and attack abuses of power, but to frame "a picture of the manners, simplicity and delights of a perfect state of society; tho still earthly." "The Past, the Present, & the Future are the grand & comprehensive topics" he sought to encompass in an encyclopedic and essentially epic form.[26]

That Shelley met with less than success in his venture is of less moment than the scale of the undertaking itself. But the terms of the failure are significant to the development of his subsequent career. It is true enough that Shelley's haranguing of the iniquitous rather deafens us to the placid tonalities of his utopia. But the problems of *Queen Mab* do not reduce simply to matters of balance and tone. There are serious metaphysical faults undermining the confident surface of the poem. Shelley borrows Young's Christian duality of flesh and spirit (I. 139-56) to support a metaphor that eventually denies the separation of matter from soul. His use of Dalton's atomic theory upholds the proto-Marxist dialectical materialism by which Necessity works its gradual way, and yet Shelley's utopia, unlike Blake's, dissolves the contraries that produce it. Not only is there one law for the lion and the kid, which Blake defines as oppression, in Shelley's paradise (VIII. 124-28), but so close is the affinity between microcosm and macrocosm that the earth helpfully rights her axis and the seasons consequently disappear. Similarly, Shelley's claims for the omnipotence of mind are seriously threatened by the French Necessitarianism he embraces, a problem that Marxism later would have to confront as well. Shelley's belief in "consentaneous love" (VIII. 108) as the motive force of life, metaphorically implicit in the dedicatory sonnet to Harriet that begins the poem and in

18

Henry's vigil with which it ends, is similarly threatened by his determinism. Shelley's realistic attack on the drudgery of the industrial age, where men become "Scarce living pulleys of a dead machine, / Mere wheels of work and articles of trade" (V. 76-77), is compelling; yet the next canto turns it topsy-turvy. This Necessity directing every atom to act "as it must and ought to act" (VI. 173) presides over a human universe with the same mechanical metaphor, "Apportioning with irresistible law / The place each spring of its machine shall fill" (VI. 163-64). Shelley is caught not by his own ignorance so much as by the assumptions of his philosophical model. Deism shares, after all, basically the same Christian construction that had engendered the prolonged, schismatic debate over free will and determinism in the early church. Necessity is merely another term for Milton's God: as long as you follow its dictates, you have free will. Edward Young, as an Anglican divine, had learned his juggling act from a curriculum polished over centuries and naturally understood that the basic beneficence of the power that transcends human life rests on the premise that whatever is is right. Shelley, barely able to find an honest man in a position of power and, metaphorically at least, committed to educating the evil out of their sins, justifies the very evil he attacks as well as his individual powerlessness before it in the name of venerable Necessity. It worked no better for Shelley than for Holbach, Priestley, and Godwin. The great philosophical Necessitarian of the eighteenth century was Jonathan Edwards, and Shelley should have known as much.

The inner contradictions that belie the confident assurance of Shelley's natural theodicy arise mainly from his philosophical heritage; but they depend on an analysis of evil with which he could not rest content. Notwithstanding his revolutionary allegiances, the Napoleonic wars were the historical backdrop of his entire youth. The gradualism he advocated for the alleviation of England's social ills, while evidence of his capacity to transcend the short views of his contemporaries, nonetheless simply begged the most pressing question of his age: why the French Revolution, mounted so confidently on a natural dialectical edifice, had transformed itself into a debacle of monumental proportions. Shelley was aware of the insufficiency of *Queen Mab* as a total view. In correspondence with Elizabeth Hitchener early in 1812, he mentions that he has "for the present postponed" its completion, turning instead to the now-lost novel, *Hubert Cauvin*, whose purpose was to "exhibit the cause of the failure of the French Revolution, and the state of morals and opinions in France during the latter years of its monarchy."[27] Though he apparently never completed his novel, the composition of *Queen Mab* itself seems to have compelled Shelley toward grounding its materials in an immediate historical reality. That desire was equally strong five years later. Informing Byron of his latest venture in the fall of 1817, he shrewdly remarked the defects of his early epic: "It is in the same style and for the same object as 'Queen Mab', but interwoven with a story of human passion, and composed with more attention to the refinement of language and the connexion of its parts."[28] Thus Shelley characterizes his second epic, *Laon and Cythna* (*The Revolt of Islam*), an even more ambitious poem than *Queen Mab*, in which he undoubtedly remedied the faults of the earlier work and extended its vision, but in which he simultaneously lost its considerable strength.

Alastor, although ostensibly a poem retreating from a large social vision to contemplate the existential experience of poetic inspiration, in many respects serves as a bridge between *Queen Mab* and *The Revolt of Islam*. The three poems continually experiment in deploying common elements of imagery and symbolism within a narrative structure, and each concentrates to some degree on the effects of a universal imaginative vision upon an individual's life. Already in *Queen Mab* Shelley demonstrates his awareness of the hazards of the imagination which he takes as the major theme of *Alastor*. There is in *Queen Mab* a second dream-vision within Ianthe's own, the first of the internalized repetitions that become a hallmark of Shelleyan structure. Ahasuerus, the Wandering Jew, overwhelming the seventh canto of the poem, endangers both the structures and themes that up to this point have been integrated. He seems a barbarous excrescence, an angry young man in death-defying senility, anathematizing like the poet, but against evils he sees as locked into the universal design. Nowhere in Shelley's indictment are the evils of Christianity so patently demonstrated. Ahasuerus is an icon of sublime futility, a figure of Satanic energy who, as Faulkner might say, is his own battleground; he is a Sisyphus victimized by his own delusions and thus inextricably bound to the tyranny he berates. His vision is a parody of the central imaginative metaphor of the poem, manacling him to an unending struggle with chimeras of his own creation. His disturbance of Shelley's otherwise implacable certainties testifies to the underlying honesty of Shelley's search for visionary truth. Ahasuerus has adopted the Holy Ghost as his guide rather than Queen Mab, an error in judgment no less honest than disastrous.

The poet of *Alastor* is pursued by a similar demon of his own creation, not a mediator between eternal and temporal truths, but an autocratic force demanding that they be forever divorced. When Peacock gave Shelley his title, he probably added a lesson in Greek grammatical niceties. An *alastor* is not only a *kakodaimon,* an avenging deity goading his victims to their strict deserts; he is also the cursed man who suffers from that divine vengeance. Both Jehovah and Ahasuerus are defined by the one term, a situation conveyed overtly in *Alastor,* where the impalpable vision that entices the poet to his eventual death is the perfect ideal of his own mind.[29] In the reflecting pools that unify the poem's landscape, the wandering poet continually sees himself: his journey inward admits of no egress but the irony of death. In both *Queen Mab* and *Alastor* Shelley deliberately conveys dual allegiances. The integrity of the wanderer's vision, his unwillingness to compromise his ideals in an easy acceptance of the status quo, these attract Shelley. But he shows himself to be no fool. The wrongheaded intensity of these figures may steal our admiration, but narcissistic solipsism, visionary or mundane, is the very essence of the selfish principle that corrupts human society.

Because of this recognition, it is no mere evangelical sense

2. Henry Fuseli, "Queen Mab" (1814). Collection Carl Laszlo, Basel

of duty that prompts Queen Mab to forsake the splendors of her palace to visit spirits on earth.

> ... were it virtue's only meed, to dwell
> In a celestial palace, all resigned
> To pleasurable impulses, immured
> Within the prison of itself, the will
> Of changeless nature would be unfulfilled.
> Learn to make others happy.
>
> (II. 59-64)

The survey of the world follows this utterance, and it is no accident that in the first extended portrayal, a disguised rendering of the Prince Regent, Mab's lines are echoed. The King is "immured / Within a splendid prison" (III. 90-91), fearful of slumber because he is granted "Not one moment / Of dreamless sleep" (III. 66-67). In contrast, Ianthe's dreams are regenerative because she possesses in full the virtues celebrated at both the beginning and end of the poem:

> Soul of Ianthe! thou,
> Judged alone worthy of the envied boon,
> That waits the good and the sincere; that waits
> Those who have struggled, and with resolute will
> Vanquished earth's pride and meanness, burst the chains,
> The icy chains of custom, and have shone
> The day-stars of their age.
>
> (I. 122-28)

> ... bravely bearing on, thy will
> Is destined an eternal war to wage
> With tyranny and falsehood, and uproot
> The germs of misery from the human heart.
> Thine is the hand whose piety would soothe
> The thorny pillow of unhappy crime,
> Whose impotence an easy pardon gains,
> Watching its wanderings as a friend's disease:
> Thine is the brow whose mildness would defy
> Its fiercest rage, and brave its sternest will,
> When fenced by power and master of the world.
> Thou art sincere and good; of resolute mind,
> Free from heart-withering custom's cold control,
> Of passion lofty, pure and unsubdued.

23

Earth's pride and meanness could not vanquish thee,
And therefore art thou worthy of the boon
Which thou hast now received.

(IX. 189-205)

Ianthe is vouchsafed her vision because she is capable of discerning that it has no integral meaning beyond a human reality. She dreams not to perpetuate fantasy, but to return with a renewed sense of mental unity to her lover and to the potential paradise of the earth. Her vision is pure, unlike those of Ahasuerus or the poet of *Alastor*, because her own fulfillment is inseparable from that of humankind. Her mental journey through the self culminates in a humanitarianism not attained by visionaries who refuse those natural claims binding them to the earth.

Despite its assertion of a social, as opposed to a solely spiritual, reality, *Queen Mab* through its basic metaphorical structure remains an austere vision of history and society, detaching itself from the local and temporal wherever possible in order to achieve breadth. Its human claims notwithstanding, it is not a very human poem. Seeking in *The Revolt of Islam* to rectify its faults, Shelley shifted the focus of his vision away from a metaphorical internalization to "a story of human passion in its most universal character, diversified with moving and romantic adventures, and appealing, in contempt of all artificial opinions or institutions, to the common sympathies of every human breast" (Preface, *The Revolt of Islam*). Indicative of the alteration is a contrasting emphasis in the frame-narrative, whose purposes are otherwise similar to those of the frame in *Queen Mab*. Whereas in the earlier poem the "thin and misty form" (I. 109) of Queen Mab arrives in an "aethereal car" (I. 65) drawn by "Celestial coursers" (I. 60) with "filmy pennons" (I. 61)—"not an earthly pageant" (I. 84) in the least—*The Revolt of Islam* begins by portraying the woman who is to lead the poet to the Temple of the Spirit weeping passionately. Her life history, full of suffering and hope, gains an almost manic—perhaps mantic—intensity: her recital is an overture

24

giving synoptic voice not merely to the themes, but to the emotive keys of the ensuing story of Laon and Cythna.

In recasting his epic vision, Shelley's emphasis is, of course, greatly different: the social analysis that forms so much of the substance of *Queen Mab* is condensed into Cythna's speech to the sailors. But the dedicatory poem to Mary neatly, rather too neatly, balances the sonnet to Harriet that began *Queen Mab*. Though surrounded by strong emotions and a number of heaving bosoms, the reader is soon within a familiar "boat of rare device" (I. 325) on his way to a Coleridgean paradise, an islanded dome, from which Eternity will judge the productions of time. If the symbolism is more ornate than in *Queen Mab*, a result, one supposes, of Shelley's having landscaped a good part of Asia in *Alastor*, it is also for the most part still carefully restricted to the first and last cantos. But unlike *Queen Mab* Shelley here manages—somewhat fitfully, it is true—to reintroduce his symbolic vocabulary within the texture of the poem: so, the Hermit's cave of the third canto, or the marble pyramid reared by the Federation in Canto V, are reverberations of the topographical and architectural symbols of the opening canto.

The process through which Ianthe is educated is replicated in the finest section of *The Revolt of Islam*, in the account of Cythna's imprisonment and self-education, her discovering within her "One mind, the type of all, the moveless wave / Whose calm reflects all moving things that are" (VII. 3104-05). If this is a more realistic depiction of how one discerns universal truths through internal analysis, it is far from the only educational model in the poem. Shelley has shifted his emphasis from the conspiritorial interlockings of church, state, and commerce to the process by which one comes to distinguish them and to discover true values with which to counter them. We have described to us Laon's education as a youth, his re-education with the Hermit, and his educating by word, deed, and reputation the peoples of Argolis and of the Golden City. Cythna's history is similarly detailed, as is that of the Woman in Canto I and even that of Cythna's child in Canto XII. This concentration helps to explain Shelley's otherwise gratuitous and self-indulgent account of his own adolescent alienation and studiousness in the dedicatory stanzas to Mary, as well as his celebration of her illustrious parentage. Further, it underlines the significance of Shelley's romanticized summary of his credentials as epic poet in the preface. The "education peculiarly fitted for a poet" that he has pursued is encyclopedic, balancing a regimen in the library with active experience among all classes of men. If the poet is to be an orator in the ancient sense, a spokesman for truth to the mind and heart, his education must be balanced, synthesized and a foundation for further synthesis, not fragmented and conducive only to analytical dissection.[30] The educational programs of *The Revolt of Islam* all stem from this Renaissance ideal of wholeness, combining the active and contemplative lives. They are a silent rebuke to the learned poet in *Alastor*, who rejects the truths of experience and with them his human obligations. In *The Revolt of Islam* the commitment is to fullness of experience, both mental and physical, and even from the perspective of eternity, Laon does not look back on his efforts, in the manner of Troilus, as trivial or inadequate. To Shelley's eyes his hero has already lived his life from the perspective of eternity.

Whatever its underlying inconsistencies, *Queen Mab* relates a finished vision. *The Revolt of Islam*, on the other hand, is concerned with how that vision is to be attained. Its narrative structure is meant to illustrate, as Shelley's prefatory remarks indicate, "the growth and progress of individual mind aspiring after excellence." The achievement is something less than that of Wordsworth's *Prelude*, but the similarity in aim is interesting. Wordsworth wrote that extraordinary poem, at least in its original form, as an attempt to analyze the spiritual crisis of his time and to teach his readers how it might be surmounted, indeed, how paradise could be found on earth despite the failures of the French Revolution. Though Shelley is not didactic in his aims, he does wish to rekindle the ideals "of liberty and justice . . . faith and hope in something good" (Preface), obscured but not destroyed in the violence of his generation. His narrative is an exposition of failure, of heroic efforts defeated and of heroes destroyed. The life-long commitments of Laon and Cythna expire at an inquisitorial stake. But their truth survives them: the seeds they have sown, as Shelley intimates in the long first draft of the *Ode to the West Wind* that ends Cythna's monologue, must germinate. This epic, a recasting of the joyful toppling of ancient hierarchies and their subsequent restitution by the Holy Alliance, originally bore the subtitle "A Vision of the Nineteenth Century." It looks ahead, not back, acknowledging setbacks, refusing either to gloss over the magnitude of the failure or to surrender to the inevitability of defeat. The experiential education of the poem is to lead us to "the wisdom of a high despair" (XII. 4700), much like that of the narrator at the end of *Alastor:* humanity with energy, commitment, and pure intentions may have been inadequate to the imperatives it confronts, but to acknowledge this should mature one's idealism, not ravage it.

And yet, the justification of failure can, as Browning frequently proved, be a shallow panacea. An organic congruity exists between the failure of Shelley's revolutionaries and of his poem. *The Revolt of Islam* is the watershed in Shelley's career: his most ambitious undertaking in point of length is in intellecual depth and emotional force his least successful poem; but it too plants the seeds of future growth. Throughout his preface Shelley is more than customarily humble. He seems as conscious as Keats in the prefatory note to *Endymion* of a flawed achievement, yet rather than revise the poem pursues its immediate publication. History, perhaps, explains this curious behavior, as well as substantiates the thrust of Shelley's prefatory remarks. Shelley began his poem the year after Waterloo and after his summer expedition to Geneva had, as he notes in the summary of his experience, taken him through "the theatre of the more visible ravages of tyranny and war; cities and villages reduced to scattered groups of black and roofless houses, and the naked inhabitants sitting famished upon their desolated thresholds." This was the physical aftermath of the Napoleonic Wars. In 1815, too, the Congress of Vienna, rounding up the available royal survivors from a quarter-century of exile, restored the Bourbon line to the French and Spanish thrones. With a destitute Europe at peace, and stability, albeit more veneer than substance, reclaimed, it was time for all parties, even radicals, to begin the process of reconstruction. Shelley's role is that of propagandist: to "awaken the feelings," to restore the "thirst for a happier condition of moral and political society." He writes a narrative not a didactic poem, but it is enlisted "in the cause of a liberal and comprehensive morality" (Preface).

Shelley's successes in the poem are structural; his failings are conceptual. The poem moves in a circle, balancing the poet's journey to the Temple of the Spirit in Canto I with that of Laon, Cythna, and her child in Canto XII.[31] Laon's release and education in Canto IV balance the account of Cythna's education and release in Canto VII. And indeed, Cantos IV through VI, in which we follow Laon's career, are duplicated by Cythna's monologue in Canto VII through IX. In essence, the poem begins again at mid-point and moves backward through its materials, portraying Laon and Cythna as adults in the same isolated but loving contentment they had shared as children, reproducing the capture of Laon from Canto III in Canto XI, returning us at last to the paradise we gained in Canto I. If through this process we are continually led to see likenesses between Laon and Cythna, between their task and that of the poet, more interesting are the symbolic contrasts that it allows. The libertarians of Canto V, in perfect health and happiness, blessed with the bounty of nature, rear in one night a great marble pyramid as an altar on which to consecrate their fraternal devotion to liberty. In Canto X, on the other hand, the famished, diseased, and superstitious subjects of the restored tyrant raise an ugly funeral pyre to offer the lives of Laon and Cythna as expiation to divine wrath. On the first pyramid Laon and Cythna reawaken their childhood love: on the second they are put to death. Such contrasts stress the Manichean antithesis of the poem: the forces of love and of hate are in exact opposition. Finally, there is a clear parallel between the sexual consummation of the lovers in Canto VI and their attainment of paradise in Canto XII. The paradise is a metaphorical extension of human love, which

Shelley asserts in the last line of his preface to the poem "is celebrated everywhere as the sole law which should govern the moral world."

These structural parallels and antitheses, designed to underpin the ideology of the poem, suggest a maturer Shelley than does the uncharacteristic mode. His generic reconstruction of *Night Thoughts* in the writing of *Queen Mab* is a minor intellectual triumph, but he had no such success using Southey as his model in *The Revolt of Islam* because he does not desire to transcend the form, only to exploit it.[32] If one's purpose is to touch the chords of a common humanity, a vehicle proven so successful as Southey's epic-romance form had its obvious appeal. But after the historical epic of *Joan of Arc* Southey no longer sought to achieve overt political ends in a protracted form, but fashioned romantic adventures out of exotic mythologies, suppressing all urges to verisimilitude. Shelley binds himself to the same mode for political purposes. Beyond the first canto he rejects allegory, by which he could possibly have fused his formal and ideological claims: the result is the poem's tenuous hold on reality. Outside of the frame-narrative, it is never so fantastic as to be utterly beyond the bounds of belief, but it is never so realistic as to qualify for an actual representation of reality. With Southeyan machinery—black chargers, wonderful eagles, mad crones—rumbling throughout the poem, Shelley sets in motion a political epic of radical vision.

The claims of Shelley's ideology are ultimately antithetical to the generic properties in which he envelops them. The bloody battle scenes, designed to shock a doubting Thomas into political awareness, sit uncomfortably next to avowals of pacifism. The fraternity of the world's peoples is not consonant with the suspect hero-worship by which Laon and Cythna are deified: had Shelley cast an eye toward St. Helena, he might have recalled the excesses to which such an abandonment of republican principles had led the French. And it is likewise more than curious that an epic that would dismantle the churches, eradicate the notion of a transcendent deity, and raise its altar to liberated humanity, should have eleven of its twelve cantos narrated from a realm suspiciously like heaven. That it is presided over by Lucifer is Shelley's personal touch, but its denizens are nonetheless the Elect of a new Calvinism, which is simply the old Calvinism turned on end and morally rearmed. That Shelley was not aware that his commercialism had betrayed his ideology may mitigate the intellectual effrontery, but cannot salvage his poem.

The art of *The Revolt of Islam* is an art of propaganda, sacrificing intellectual depth for the sake of emotional commitment, inflating its human prototypes until their natural ambiguities disappear. But such figures are no longer human; they are caricatures, mere roles brought out of stock to be enacted before Southey's backdrop. The epic lacks the dialectic it presupposes: it creates not contraries but antitheses. The Manichean framework, depicted in the emblematic struggle between serpent and eagle in Canto I and then carefully explicated by the Woman who has watched it, is absolute and eternal. Only in the portrayal of the fanatic Iberian priest is there subtlety of psychological insight: "fear of God did in his bosom breed / A jealous hate of man, an unreposing need" (X. 4097-98). For the rest, the liberticide armies pour down from "the unresting fountains / Of darkness in the North" (XI. 4236-37) in waves that neither time nor education seem capable of stopping. On the deepest level the virtues the poem extols are denied by its events. It may be true, as Shelley asserts, that "Love is celebrated everywhere as the sole law which should govern the moral world," but in its heroic dimensions the poem is virtually devoid of compassion.

Shelley's sense of his own failure is justifiable. But it is a failure caused by more than his willingness to sacrifice political ideals to the demands of his genre. Shelley committed himself to the taxing length of *The Revolt of Islam* in order to remedy the outstanding flaw in *Queen Mab*, the abruptness with which his vision of a corrupt present gave way to a utopian future. That transition demanded legislative skills that the as yet unacknowledged poet simply lacked. But in focusing on the means by which evil is to be transformed into good in *The Re-*

30

volt of Islam, Shelley does little more than expand to tedious
length the analysis of *Queen Mab.* There it is claimed,

> Some eminent in virtue shall start up,
>> Even in perversest time:
> The truths of their pure lips, that never die,
> Shall bind the scorpion falsehood with a wreath
>> Of ever-living flame,
> Until the monster sting itself to death.
>> (VI. 33-38)

In the ninth canto the image is repeated. Shelley supposes that
as the world degenerated, crime became more and more blatant,
until finally Falsehood, "done by her own venemous sting to
death, / . . . left the moral world without a law" (IX. 45-46).
As the Manichean forces are intensified in *The Revolt of Islam,*
Shelley expands this portrayal of evil. The tyrannical forces,
descending upon the Golden City, literally uncreate it:

> Five days they slew
> Among the wasted fields; the sixth saw gore
> Stream through the city; on the seventh, the dew
> Of slaughter became stiff, and there was peace anew.
>> (X. 3888-91)

Such an unnatural sabbath produces first plague, then, as the
corruption grows, famine. The liberticides seek to evade their
responsibility for their own peril through the sacrifice of Laon
and Cythna, but as the gruesome catalog of the late cantos
mounts, it is clear that Shelley intends to depict unintended but
effective mass suicide. The basic compulsion of evil is to destroy: at last it destroys itself. Such an apocalypse has its dramatic points, but it is by the same token rather too easy to stage.
It also suggests that the true function of those who love liberty
is to martyr themselves, provoking the forces of evil to begin
the unnatural chain reaction that ravages everything in its path,
including its perpetrators. The will that is the agent of revolution seems finally to have only a negative capacity, furthering
the destruction of the social fabric wrought by tyranny, but

unable by itself to reverse the deterioration. Of what use, then, are the educational models of the poem? They have value certainly on a personal fantasy level, but it takes more than a structural parallelism equating Shelley and his wife, Godwin and Mary Wollstonecraft, Laon and Cythna, and Lucifer and Venus to produce a regeneration on earth.[33] Without a consistent philosophy, without a vision recognizably humane in its dimensions, such equations are merely the rhetorical indulgence of Shelley's wishful thinking.

Diverse in purpose and mode as *Queen Mab* and *The Revolt of Islam* are, their ambitions force their author into a structural and ideological cul-de-sac, where inner contradictions and rival values perpetrate chaos in the name of encyclopedic form. That Shelley is capable of dealing with the large issues he raises is clear from his prose tracts, not to mention the sophisticated and astute Preface to *The Revolt of Islam*. His recurring problem is formal: the structures of *Night Thoughts* and of *Thalaba* are foreign to his design and probably to his temperament, limiting him on the one hand to a perspective too detached and didactic and, on the other hand, to one whose shallow narrative must be constantly infused with ritualistic poses in an effort to achieve depth. Both forms—the internalized journey of Ianthe and the externalized narrative of heroic adventures—had in common a tendency to constrict Shelley's characteristic desire to make inner and outer realities congruous and reflective. But more serious than this is a fatal compulsion to separate the sheep from the goats and have done with the historical complexities that had brought an entire generation to the verge of despair. Shelley was to overcome this urge only by acknowledging that in the French Revolution the sheep had transformed themselves into goats through following this very tendency to its logical and bloody conclusion. The formal problem Shelley solved by a sleight-of-hand that makes it seem simple but conceals profound literary intuitions. Abandoning the epic form on which he had invested his greatest labors, Shelley set to work in a variety of genres to create the vision that was its substance.

2

THE KEY TO ALL MYTHOLOGIES

. . . the fatal time approacheth, in which these [evil gods] shall be destroyed by Famine and Pestilence, and Arimanius utterly destroyed, and the Earth made even and smooth; There shall be one Life and one City (or common Society) of all men living, and one Language.
—Thomas Stanley, *The History of the Chaldaick Philosophy* (1701)

The roads southeast of Calais were bad, and they got worse. The normal effects of late winter, compounded by years of neglect under the tedious burden of Europe's armies, made travel unpleasant and difficult. To pass the time, Shelley, who had lost his taste for sensational novels, beguiled his fellow travelers by reading aloud from Augustus Wilhelm Schlegel's *Course of Lectures on Dramatic Art and Literature*. The choice, if unusual, was significant, and not simply because of Schlegel's veneration for the Greeks, for Shakespeare, and for Calderón, the dramatists who form Shelley's pantheon in *A Defence of Poetry*. It was Schlegel who in his introductory lecture first defined Romanticism, distinguishing between a classical devotion to the senses and the world and the romantic craving for an ideal realm:

> The Grecian idea of humanity consisted in a perfect concord and proportion between all the powers,—a natural harmony. The moderns. . . have arrived at the consciousness of the internal discord which renders such an idea impossible; and hence the endeavour of their poetry is to reconcile these two worlds between which we find ourselves divided, and to melt them indissolubly into one another.[1]

Such a passage could stand as an epigraph for Shelley's life work: it must have struck him with peculiar force. Up to this

33

time he had published scarcely a poem that did not stretch the normal boundaries of reality with the vague compulsions of eternity. These compulsions destroy the poet of *Alastor*, even as they sustain the votive singer's tenuous faith in the *Hymn to Intellectual Beauty*. The bard of *Queen Mab* and *The Revolt of Islam*, willfully blind to such perilous ambiguity, yokes ideal and reality violently together, resolving incongruities amid the confident assurances of inner space. Yet, as a whole the poems of Shelley's English period undermine certainty, achieving unity only in their quest for it. Individually, they reflect the very fragmentation, the inadequacy of any single solution, that Shelley sought to escape.

Schlegel not only comprehended a sensibility that, more than any other English Romantic, Shelley possessed, but, without himself noting the link, delineated an archetypal emblem of the very struggle to reconcile dual commitments that defined Romanticism for him: "an image of human nature itself: endowed with a miserable foresight and bound down to a narrow existence, without an ally, and with nothing to oppose to the combined and inexorable powers of nature, but an unshaken will and the consciousness of her own elevated claims." This could be a description of the poet of *Alastor* or of *Epipsychidion*, but it is Prometheus that Schlegel thus characterizes, who is made to suffer by the powers of the earth for a disobedience that "consists in nothing but the attempt to give perfection to the human race."[2] An archetypal revolutionary and the exact embodiment of the romantic sensibility, he endures a physical suffering incidental to a sublime spiritual failure. The duality steadfastly refuses success to his labor to reconcile earthly life with ideal perfection. Schlegel points to the magnitude of that defeat: "The other poems of the Greek tragedians are single tragedies; but this may be called tragedy itself."[3] And yet, the original Aeschylean trilogy was, like the *Oresteia*, ultimately comic, moving from an initial representation of tragic agony to a calm conceived not in despair, but in a regained wholeness of vision. Shelley, nursing a radical disgust with the triumph of the Holy Alliance, was constitutionally "averse from a catastrophe so feeble as that of reconciling the Champion with the Oppressor of mankind" (Preface to *Prometheus Unbound*). Schlegel's stark depiction of Prometheus as Romantic emblem greeted a poet who, it would appear from his reading and from the allusions of his poetry, had long contemplated revising the mythic vision of Aeschylus. It greeted him, too, as he traveled a landscape that still bore vivid testimony to the failure of France's Promethean aspirations. The imperative thus posed to Shelley was nothing less than to transform Schlegel's quintessential tragedy into a comic vision true to both the human urge for perfection and the manifest betrayals documented throughout history. Six months after the difficult crossing of France, settled in Byron's summer estate, he began that transformation. At the same time, his fellow poet was starting his long engagement with *Don Juan*, turning a modern myth of selfish appetite and depravity into a universal comedy that faced —and resolved in perfect irresolution—the same fundamental problems of human life.

In the passage through the Alps from France to Savoy Shelley discovered a setting perfectly suited to the tragedy so powerfully evoked by Schlegel.[4] Two years before, he had been prompted by the awesome pinnacle of Mont Blanc, only slightly to the north, to rededicate his early Necessitarianism: "a faith so mild, / So solemn, so serene, that man may be, / But for such faith, with nature reconciled" (*Mont Blanc*, ll. 77-79). To introduce Prometheus to that mountain scene, however, is to open chasms of incertitude. If nature is the expression of the god of this world, it "teaches awful doubt" (*Mont Blanc*, l. 77), rather than assurance. It is Jupiter's domain—savage, rude, unimbued with spirit, inimical to human strivings—where, as Shelley noted in his journal, tyranny abounds.[5] To free Prometheus from such crags demands more than good political intentions: it demands a release of the mind from easy formulae and comfortable dependencies. Confronting the essential image of his own strivings and his own defeats throughout the sixteen months that saw his lyrical drama grow to fruition amid a panoply of other poems, Shelley was not willing, nor perhaps was he able, to retreat from either the complexity or the urgency of his vision.

For this reason his dramatic conception of Prometheus attains a maturity lacking from his earlier depictions of the Titan. In the notes to *Queen Mab*, influenced by John Frank Newton's *Return to Nature* and a curious passage in Horace, Shelley had represented Prometheus as a cosmic villain, whose introduction of fire had resulted in the cooking and eating of flesh and had driven man from the golden age of a vegetable diet into the manifold distempers of his present constitution.[6] So perverse a rendering of the myth might justify Shelley's vision of himself as *enfant terrible*, were it not so two-dimensional. Scarcely more considered, however, is the Promethean milieu that supplies emotional appeal to the third canto of *The Revolt of Islam*. Disarmed and arrested, Laon is carried to a hilltop cavern at whose entrance is a massive column, there to be chained as a display piece honoring heroic virtue and indicting society's customary treatment of redeemers. Already, Shelley can be seen imaging Prometheus as a revolutionary figure and equating the divine right of Jupiter with the arbitrary injustices of monarchs. The myth has also begun to accrete the associations that make Shelley's later drama so densely suggestive. Rescued from the Promethean cave by the Hermit, Laon finds himself transported to the earthly counterpart of the imagined paradise of Cantos I and XII. On the Hermit's island Laon is laid underground in "a small chamber, which with mosses rare / Was tapestried" (IV. 1429-30), the antithesis of the cavern of his torture and the predecessor of the moss-walled cave in which the liberated Prometheus retires with Asia.

The Promethean allusions of *The Revolt of Islam* amount to little more than heroic ornamentation, but that Shelley strains for such allusive support suggests a principal weakness in both of his early epic ventures. Unconcerned with accruing intellectual debts, he is determined to maintain a narrative independence. Echoes and influences his epics may manifest, but in plot Shelley is staunchly on his own. Such independence allows for structural experimentation, but on the other hand it places extreme demands upon a barely developed mythopoeic capacity, especially in the ambitious narrative of *The Revolt of Islam*. As the entire Romantic period attests, Satanic heroes are rather simple to execute. A strutting Napoleon modeled for twenty years, and, if he seemed to the English too unpatriotic an emblem, Lord Byron would do as well: certainly Byron himself thought so. But Shelley's endeavor in *The Revolt of Islam* to create from scratch not one, but two, perfectly heroic figures leads him toward the excessive piety of evangelical tracts. In fairness, such unnatural heroism, lacking in recognizably human features, proceeds from a severe ideological handicap. In the shadow of Milton, Shelley firmly rejects action as the customary mode of heroism, restricting Laon and Cythna to embodying intellectual and oratorical powers. Except when danger threatens, the two are physically passive. Similar problems of characterization arose earlier with the poet of *Alastor*, and with Prince Athanase who seems intended as his obverse, deluded into mistaking an earthly Venus for the heavenly perfection. A promising poem in many ways, *Prince Athanase* survives in inchoate fragments probably not because the subject was insufficiently compelling, but because once again, with few external supports, Shelley set himself to create a protagonist whose principal dynamics are intellectual and emotional. And yet, to scan Shelley's career is to realize that one of his major contributions, not only to English literature but to Romantic psychology, is his continuing analysis of passivity. As he arrived in Italy, he wrote to Peacock to report his plan for a tragedy on Tasso's madness and imprisonment, a subject with many similarities to the story of Job, which he also considered setting in dramatic form. In Beatrice Cenci Shelley found his emblem for passivity in the face of intense evil. In *Prometheus Unbound* he went to the essential mythic source. In each instance denying the need to create his basic literary materials from nothingness, Shelley at last liberates his own genius as a re-creator of myths.

Shelley's Promethean allusions contribute very little to the depiction of Laon's sufferings and endurance, for the mythic prototype embodies an intensity, a purity honed through cen-

turies, that Shelley could hardly hope to reproduce while pluck-
ing Spenserian stanzas in a six-month idyll. In confronting the
essential myth in 1818, however, he faces an opposite problem,
how to mold lines firmly drawn by tradition to his own vision of
a modern revolutionary struggle. That Shelley was conscious of
the problem—and at last confident in his solution—is clear
from the opening paragraphs of his preface, as well as from
the arrogant epigraph by which he calls upon the shade of
Aeschylus to sit up and take notice of how he has rewritten his
drama.[7] Unconstrained by necessities of invention, the poet can
devote his energies to elaborating a scheme already at his dis-
posal. But more than that, he frees himself for labors uniquely
suited to his own temperament and to the poet's education he
had needlessly claimed for himself in the *Revolt of Islam* preface. To enlarge the Aeschylean framework he inherited demanded that it be invested with contexts accumulated from
foreign cultures and later times, with a religious, philosophical,
and scientific learning unknown to the progenitor of the drama.
The variety and extent of those contexts is breathtaking, but
no more so than the essential unity Shelley molds from their
diversity. The result is a poem of concentrated intensity, opening into diffused but related meanings, a vision of epic scope
compressed into a dramatic framework that suppresses mere
action to reveal the subtler theatrics of the mind.

I

If most epics begin *in medias res*, their encompassing vision
tends to be articulated *ad centrum*. As the sixth book of *Paradise Lost* contains that heavenly field on which Christ's presence
routs the Satanic angels, and as at the same point in Virgil's
epic Aeneas descends to Tartarus to wed past and future, so the
center of *Prometheus Unbound* occurs in Demogorgon's chthonic realm where Asia confronts the ultimate force of the drama's
universe. But Demogorgon is even more tight lipped than
oracles are wont to be. Perplexed by his enigmatic evasions, she
strives to achieve final answers by summarizing her knowledge

of the universe. That long and moving account occurs at the precise center of *Prometheus Unbound.*[8]

The cosmology Asia propounds is taken directly from Peacock's abortive epic, *Ahrimanes*, which conflates a number of Greek accounts to substantiate a Zoroastrian myth. The primal source for the myth of the golden age she enunciates is, of course, Hesiod's *Theogony*, whose ontology, like those of the Orphic *Hymns* and of Aristophanes' *Birds*, postulates Love as an original power in the universe. But among major mythological systems there is no exact precedent for Asia's initial division of the universal forces into four—Heaven, Earth, Light, and Love—unless one were to include Blake's contemporary, literary mythology that groups roughly equivalent powers: Urizen, Tharmas, Los, and Luvah. Asia's quaternity, like Shelley's act structure, reflects Pythagorean numerology, as well as the balance of primary elements in early Greek philosophy: earth, air (heaven), fire (light), and water (love). Shelley, much like Blake, contents himself with a cosmos thus balanced from the beginning: even here he represses any urge to depict a primal, creative deity forming universal order from nothingness. This universe is firmly, if quietly, without point of origin. And it requires little consideration to discern that Prometheus, identified with light throughout the poem, and Asia, the child of Ocean, who is in the next scene (Act II, Scene iv) to be recognized as Venus, represent that primal light and love whose reintegration with the powers of heaven and earth we witness in Acts III and IV.

Although the central lines of Asia's cosmology are Greek, her account deliberately accentuates its parallels with the Judaic genesis. Superseding the equipoise of balanced primal powers, Saturn denies man access to them and thus builds his tranquil golden age around the vacuum of disinheritance:

> he refused
> The birthright of their being—knowledge, power,
> The skill which wields the elements, the thought
> Which pierces this dim universe like light,
> Self-empire, and the majesty of love;
> For thirst of which they fainted.   (II. iv. 38-43)

In the golden age, as in Eden, freedom is subordinated to man's innocence. And it is for the sake of that freedom that Prometheus himself instigates the revolt against Saturn, surrendering his ancient allegiances to the claims of universal justice.[9] Instead, the caretaker he supports becomes a tyrant, and after a heroic attempt to revoke Jupiter's betrayal and liberate man with fire, Prometheus is chained as an emblem of defeat. Prometheus is thus equivalent to the serpent condemned by God to ignominious exile for having gratified man's desire for knowledge and unconditional power. Like Keats writing *Hyperion* at the same time in England, Shelley enters Eden by a Greek road, preserving his vision and reportorial integrity independent of official Christian positions. Yet his intention to rewrite Milton's epic theodicy is everywhere manifest.

Asia's relation of a progressive fall is not, however, the only such history of human life and civilization in *Prometheus Unbound*. Indeed, it is one of four. The fourth act constitutes a new Genesis, as symbolized in the changing of the horological guard with which it begins: the ancient history of human depravity is at last sealed and a new volume begun. Finished it may be, but the record is not consistent. Shelley's drama begins with two successive interpretations of history that are related and radically divergent from Asia's. The outline is first suggested by the chorus of earth's energies—mountains, springs, air, whirlwinds—and then expanded in the remembrance of the ancient mother Earth. In her version there never was a golden age, but only the continuous tyranny of Jupiter. Prometheus arose in the world as a liberating principle of fertility, extending his influence from his simultaneous birth and impregnation of the Earth:

> she within whose stony veins,
> To the last fibre of the loftiest tree
> Whose thin leaves trembled in the frozen air,
> Joy ran, as blood within a living frame,
> When thou didst from her bosom, like a cloud
> Of glory, arise—a spirit of keen joy!
> And at thy voice her pining sons uplifted
> Their prostrate brows from the polluting dust,

And our almighty Tyrant with fierce dread
Grew pale, until his thunder chained thee here.
(I. 153-62)

The result of Prometheus' vain revolution is an intensification of Jupiter's despotism, with natural disasters, plague, and famine devastating the earth. The recollections of Earth's energies are even more explicit in testifying that the ensuing terror differed only in degree from what preceded it. Their Indian chronology, vastly expanding the Christian history of 6000 years, declares that for 300,000 years before the revolt of Prometheus Jupiter had reigned amid "shrieks of slaughter" (I. 80) committed by "men convulsed with fears" (I. 76). This is consistent with the Earth's later recital, but as this chorus of energies continues, it signally contradicts the Earth's explanation of Jupiter's increase in tyranny. To the Earth, it was man's insurrection that produced Jupiter's anger and revenge; but the energies, oblivious to the impact of their testimony, lay the blame directly upon Prometheus. Suicides result from men hearing "the voice of [his] unrest" (I. 92), the malediction the Titan pronounces upon Jupiter. The Spirit of the Air recalls:

By such dread words from earth to Heaven
My still realm was never riven:
When its wound was closed, there stood
Darkness o'er the day like blood.
(I. 99-102)

Borrowing the language of Ahasuerus from *Queen Mab*, this remarkable passage inverts the covenant by which God guaranteed man freedom from arbitrary punishment.[10] Between heaven and earth there now stands an anti-covenant, a seal of blood sanctioning human brutality and divine revenge. And Prometheus has written it.

In Asia's remembrance, then, Prometheus is a mediator between the Saturnian and modern worlds; the Earth conceives him as leading a doomed revolution against Jupiter's despotism; the Earth's energies portray a hatred of his oppressor so intense as to further ruin on earth. Clearly, these accounts are contradictory: Prometheus should not represent simultaneously both Christ and Ahasuerus. One is tempted to give credence to Asia's account, because of the centrality of its position and of her character. But there are no certain grounds for choice. If Asia's recollection were true, that of the Earth would appear a gratuitous confusion of the drama's cosmological foundation. To put the issue in that light, however, is itself to confuse the basic structure of the work. *Prometheus Unbound* is not merely a poem, it is a drama. Ritualistic as the action may appear, it is constructed around essentially dramatic perspectives. The Earth's limited perspective, materiality, explains her mistaking Prometheus' revocation of the curse for surrender and enforces her abdication in the third act. The absent-minded dowager surrenders her throne to the Spirit of the Earth, the adopted child of Prometheus and Asia, who are themselves children of the primordial Earth and Ocean. Asia's remembrance issues from a different level of awareness, that of the spiritual, the intuitive. If she sees larger concerns than those emphasized by the Earth, the latter cannot be dismissed simply because of their limitations. Awareness is, after all, an index of condition, and all conditions must be honored in a truly revolutionary struggle.

In his prefatory remarks Shelley emphasizes that *Prometheus Unbound* is not a didactic poem. The nonreductive energies of the drama are central to the work's ideological position. Histories are produced by individuals, each reflecting unique tastes, experiences, commitments. If those of the Earth and Asia represent—in the largest sense—religious frameworks for experience, the imperative is not to choose the right religion, but to discover the underlying commonalty of all religion. Newman Ivey White, dissatisfied with picayune quarrels, once entitled an essay, "Shelley's *Prometheus Unbound*; or Every Man His Own Allegorist."[11] Ironically, White's subtitle expresses a central truth of Shelley's skepticism and of his drama. The dogmatisms of interpreters, like the perspectives of dramatic characters, testify to human difference, but the unified reality of human desire and need underlies all attempts to codify the history of the race. Not in dogma are all religions one, but in their assertion of coherence, significance, human faith. And the principles of art are analogous to those of religion. *Prometheus Unbound*, with its irreducible dramatic perspectives and its complex and intricately learned associations, may support a multitude of critical interpretations, but its underlying vision is ultimately so simple as to enforce a powerful immediacy. Shelley transforms Schlegel's essential tragedy into an archetypal mythic drama, in which the more allegorical associations its consolidated texture unfolds, the surer are its fundamental structural, symbolic, and ideological lines.

Romantic Prometheanism may well have given Shelley impetus to pursue the myth as a profound statement of human limitations and potentialities. Byron, absorbing the myth into the projection of his own Titanic personality, had already written a *Prometheus* when Shelley began his. But the Romantic obsession with the Prometheus myth, built upon traditions of mythological commentary, draws upon the accumulation of centuries. Those traditions Shelley knows, and yet the largeness of his conception of Prometheus does not depend solely on integrating more facets of the myth than Byron chose to. Indeed, Shelley's deliberate aim is to transcend the legendary limits of the simple myth or of the Greek pantheon that contains it, gathering reverberations from remote times and diverse cultures. The learning is provided and the authority assured by the massive thrust of contemporary scholarship in syncretic mythology.

In modern civilization myth is most commonly seen as an adjunct to highly specialized social sciences, but, as a recent student of myth has remarked, "from the Enlightenment down to the mid-nineteenth century myth was thought of by many not only as *a* subject but in some sense *the* subject."[12] The fervor with which syncretic mythographers pursued the origins of civilization in the myths of disparate peoples was a hallmark of Shelley's age. In *Prometheus Unbound* the poet demonstrates that he is a willing and most capable student. Writing to Peacock early in 1819, he links his lyrical drama to the goal of syncretic scholarship:

> My 1st Act of Prometheus is complete, & I think you wd. like it.
> —I consider Poetry very subordinate to moral & political science,
> & if I were well, certainly I should aspire to the latter; for I can con-
> ceive a great work, embodying the discoveries of all ages, & har-
> monizing the contending creeds by which mankind have been ruled.
> Far from me is such an attempt & I shall be content by exercising my
> fancy to amuse myself & perhaps some others, & cast what weight
> I can into the right scale of that balance which the Giant (of Arthe-
> gall) holds.[13]

By the end of 1819 the weight would be far heavier than it was in January, for virtually every poem and prose work of the year shares the principle implicit in *Prometheus Unbound,* the "har-monizing [of] contending creeds" within a humanistic frame-work. That Shelley never wrote such a great expository work as he projected does not mean that the assumptions he voiced do not pervade his poetry. On the contrary, he adopts the story of Prometheus as an ur-myth, distinct from any of the world's practicing religions but capable of subsuming their major sym-bols, and adorns it with a learning as deep as it is extensive.

If most writers on mythology confine their subject to what, following Jacob Bryant, might be called a "new system," what distinguishes Shelley is his endeavor to enlarge his mythic con-ception to include a catholicity of interpretations. The dramatic individuality of the characters is insistent, but accompanied by mythic reveberations that insure their status as commanding symbols of human life and consciousness. Shelley's rendering of Prometheus is exemplary of his dual purpose. At the center of the drama is Asia's historical summary in Demogorgon's cave, which concentrates on the gifts Prometheus brought to earth—science, technology, medicine, art, music, and philoso-phy—and extends the similar catalog in Aeschylus to compre-hend all the fruits of the intellect. Her portrayal of Prometheus as the principle of civilization is traditional, extensively docu-mented as a historical allegory in Boccaccio's *Genealogie*

Deorum Gentilium, for instance, or in the Abbé Banier's *Mythology and Fables of the Ancients, Explain'd from History*.[14] Although the adherents of a mythography reducing its subjects to historical actuality—euhemerism—range from Diodorus Siculus to the scholars of the rational new order under Napoleon, Prometheus is more commonly identified either with natural principles, with parallels in the Judaeo-Christian tradition, or with human faculties. As the giver of fire, he is easily conflated with the sun, and, as a pagan sun god whose name means foreknowledge and who is said to have created men, he appears as one of many manifestations of Jehovah created through the dispersal of the human family.[15] The father of Deucalion, who with Pyrrha repopulated an earth laid waste by floods, he is easily equated with his son and thus with the new parent of the human race, Noah.[16] To Christian allegorical commentators Prometheus stands for intellect, *Nous*; to Neoplatonists he is construed as the daemonic mediator between heaven and earth; to the medieval intellectual his story symbolizes the mental sufferings incumbent upon contemplation; to the Renaissance humanist he represents good will and right reason in man; and to the Regency Whig gentleman, he is a lover of liberty and a martyr to the external forces of despotism.[17] Every representative of a distinct culture may be his own allegorist, but Shelley's conception is capable of subsuming them all. Prometheus is both part and whole. As he presides over "arts, though unimagined, yet to be" (III. iii. 56), he is all that man has conceived of him—and more.

Shelley's sources for Asia have been much debated but are unlikely to be easily settled, since again he means to multiply allusions rather than restrict them. In most genealogies of the Titans, Asia is not Prometheus' wife but his mother, the wife of Iapetus: Shelley's only source among ancient commentators is Herodotus. That the poet ignored the more authoritative and venerable choices of Hesiod (Pandora) and Aeschylus (Hesione) suggests an interest in associations of Asia's name. An Asia, for instance, is claimed—in Sale's commentary on the Koran, a work Shelley cites in *Queen Mab*—as one of the four perfect women in Mohammedan legend. Other affinities abound in eastern religions. *Isha* is the term for woman when she is first mentioned in Genesis (2. 23), and *Aish* is Hebrew for man: both terms derive appropriately from *Aesh*, meaning fire. *Asa-devi* was remarked to be the Indian goddess granting man's *asa*, or desire; *Hasya* to be the Indian muse of love, and *Isi* to be the great mother of Indian religion, who became hermaphroditic through union with *Isa*. In Persian *Asha* means the true, the right, and in Zoroastrianism it is associated with the purity of light. Moreover, there is an Indian legend that a world renovation will emanate from the east, accomplished through the efforts of the race of *Asae*.[18] To note such etymological similarities is not to countenance their purity, nor to maintain Shelley's knowledge of them all. Some he would have known, and certainly, he would have been saturated in the etymological virtuosity of late eighteenth-century mythologists. But at the most, such recondite cognates would have provided merely incidental authority for the major associations of Asia's name.

Shelley sets the last act of *Prometheus Unbound* in Greece, but the first three are situated in the Indian Caucasus. As man's original benefactor in Greek mythology, Prometheus stands at the fountainhead of western civilization. His consort rules over the east, for—in the opinion of Varro cited by many commentators—Asia, the wife of Iapetus, gave her name to the continent. To unite Prometheus and Asia in a symbolic drama is to join numerous contraries, including those associated with the principal cultures of the ancient world: the intellect, objectivity, productivity of the west and the emotional subtlety, intuitiveness, and meditative retirement of the east. In Varro's conceptual geography Asia lies toward the noonday sun and the south wind, whereas Europe is situated toward the dipper and north wind: such an opinion might have no basis in fact for Shelley, but in principle it was indubitable.[19]

Further associations of Prometheus and Asia in Greek mythology substantiate their union as a marriage of contraries. Prometheus, thief of fire, contrasts with the symbol of water, Asia, who is the daughter of Ocean and the counterpart of Venus rising from the sea. It is this context that motivates Shelley's careful choices of Apollo, the god who bears the sun, and Ocean, the Titan who rules the primal waters, to exchange the brief dialogue of Act III, Scene ii. And the context is carried over into the ensuing scene where Hercules arrives to liberate Prometheus. Francis Bacon interpreted his appearance in the light of Renaissance allegory: Hercules traverses the waters of human life, mutability, bringing fortitude from the wisdom represented by the sun. Fire is, of course, a venerable masculine symbol, as water is its feminine contrary. And again the two are principal symbols in eastern religions. The famous Indian reverence for the waters of sacred rivers and for fire was said by a contemporary scholar to have derived from the even more celebrated Persian worship of these elements. Ormusd (Ahura Mazda), the benevolent deity of the Zoroastrian faith, was supposed to have been created from primeval fire and water, which to the Magi are true images of the deity. The third such image is that of earth, and when the Spirit of the Earth joins Prometheus and Asia in their regeneration, the Magian elemental trinity in brought to completion. Here Greek myth is in perfect accord with its oriental counterparts: it was, one must recall, Prometheus' application of fire to earth and water that, in the first place, created man.[20]

Panthea and Ione, as graduated reflections of Asia and the "beauty unbeheld" (III. iii. 7) she herself reflects, have been variously interpreted as proof of Shelley's basic Christian sympathies (faith, hope, charity) or of his Platonic allegiances. As symbolic characters in a syncretic drama, however, they clearly comprehend both such glosses. Neither is originally one of the Oceanides, although Hesiod mentions a nymph named Panope, meaning 'giving every assistance' or 'seeing everything,' who is invoked by sailors during storms, and he lists among the Nereids an Eione, whose name Apollodorus alters to Ione.[21] The only Panthea who preserved her fame into Shelley's time was the fictive wife of Abradates, king of Susa during the reign of Cyrus. She is the title character in a heroic drama with occasional Shelleyan overtones by Thomas Maurice, assistant

47

THE ISIS OMNIA OF EGYPT,

THE INDIAN ISA, AND GRECIAN CERES.

To the Right Honourable Earl Spencer, a patron of Eastern Science, this plate is respectfully inscribed by T. M.

3. The triple goddess of India. Thomas Maurice, *The History of Hindostan* (London, 1795-98), frontispiece

keeper of manuscripts of the British Museum, scholar of Indian antiquities, and sometime poet whom Byron dismissed with Popean disdain in *English Bards and Scotch Reviewers* (ll.411-17). It is Maurice, too, who in his Indian researches provides the only relevant eastern cognate: Pandaea, the daughter of the Indian Hercules, related to the Pandu race, which is the most celebrated in Sanscrit history, and to the kingdom of Pandion in southern India.[22] Panthea's significance lies mostly in the connotations of the name itself, but with Ione Shelley relies upon abundant mythological resources. She enters *Prometheus Unbound* transformed from the Io of the Aeschylean tragedy, who in Latin and Italian is rendered as Ione. According to Natalis Comes, all commentators agree that Io is the daughter of a water god, and there even existed a group of nymphs known as Ionides, to whom a river with the suggestive name of Cytheron was consecrated. That the name is a homonym for the yoni, the celebrated female fertility symbol of Indian rites, and that in Bacchic rituals 'Io' assumes sexual connotations only accentuate the characteristics associated with the original Io of Greek myth.[23] She is, after all, identical with Isis, the Egyptian fertility goddess and in Boccaccio's account the daughter of Prometheus and consort of Osiris or Dionysus. Isis, in name as in function, recalls Isi, the primeval white goddess of India, born like Venus from the ocean, to whom Asia is related. Isis is, as well, transfigured into a moon goddess: it is Ione, fittingly, who describes the newly awakened moon in Act IV of Shelley's drama.[24]

Diverse as are the associations of Panthea and Ione, common bonds illuminate their function in *Prometheus Unbound*. Insofar as they recall geographical entities, southern India and the Ionic peninsula of western Turkey, they are appendages of the Asiatic main. As mythic personalities they are extensions of the primal goddess who is Asia. Panthea is all feminine deities, as her name suggests: Ione is a fertility goddess, the next remove on the graduated scale from the celestial to the earthly Venus. The relationship of Asia, Panthea, and Ione as reflections of one essential symbolic power is characteristically Shelleyan, but it was characteristic, too, of a common theme of scholarship in his time, and an educated reader would not have found it recondite. The triple goddess exists in many forms in Greek mythology and was being increasingly identified in eastern religions by tendentious mythologists stalking the Christian trinity with sometimes pious abandon. In *Indian Antiquities* Thomas Maurice devotes a long section, later published independently, to his "Dissertation on the Pagan Triads of Deity"; and George Stanley Faber, who was born late enough to syncretize not only mythologies but other mythologists as well, flatly states that the great goddess of all gentile myths is triplicate.[25] Shelley places three distinct but closely related extensions of one principle at the center of his drama, not to allude to an individual manifestation of the triple goddess, but to gather together, both for serious and ironic purposes, all forms. In function Asia, Panthea, and Ione are nymphs, who in the Orphic *Hymns* are depicted as mediators between heaven and earth, and who clearly embody generative forces. In principle they are the three Graces, the daughters of Venus, who attend to the well-being of man: Pasythea, who attracts; Egyales, who allures; and Euphrosyne, who allows man to retain what he deeply desires. Of the same race as the Graces are the Hours, termed by one commentator "the amiable Guides and Guardians of Life," who are likewise representative of fertility and linked with Venus: Eunomie, law; Dice, justice; and Irene, peace. Allied as well are the three Hesperides— daughters of Hesperus, the brother of Prometheus—and the triple Hecate and triple Diana, representative both of the earth and the moon, the underworld goddess and the queen of the heavens.[26] Shelley structures Act IV of *Prometheus Unbound* so that Panthea and Ione introduce us to their extensions through these two forms, the earth and the moon, amorously reunited. On the opposite extreme, in the Christian contexts of Act I, Shelley's nymphs assume the postures of the mourning women surrounding the cross on which Christ suffers.

Shelley's three nymphs also function ironically. As assuagers of Prometheus' sufferings, they contrast with the Furies who come at dawn as Shelley's psychological equivalent for the eagle

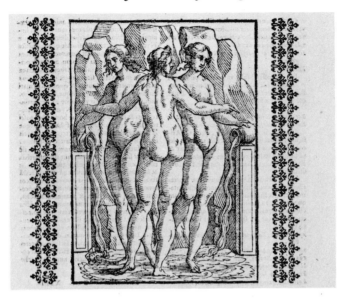

4. Three nymphs as the Graces. Natalis Comes,
Mythologiae (Patavii, 1616)

who daily gnaws the Titan's liver. Initially, the Furies were
three in number, and according to Jacob Bryant's euhemerist
reduction they were originally priestesses on Mount Caucasus.[27]
Asia, Panthea, and Ione also contrast with the shadowy three
Fates, born with Pan as the progeny of Demogorgon and Liti-
gium and shapers of man's fallen state under the rule of Jupiter.
A remarkably similar alternative is posed by Francis Wilford,
a triform goddess the Indians call the *Parcoe*. They are not fear-
some, but benevolent, representing the energy through which
their male counterpart brings conception into being. The principal goddess is that white goddess already linked with Asia, the
wife of Neptune and daughter of Nereus, whom Wilford sees
as a type of Minerva.[28]

Shelley's most obscure borrowing from the traditions of
syncretic mythology is Demogorgon, an enigma often facilely
resolved into Necessity, or, on the strength of his own partial
identification in confronting Jupiter, Eternity. He is the primal
god in Boccaccio's *Genealogie Deorum Gentilium*, which Pea-

cock owned, and, if later commentators have been less successful than Asia in penetrating this "mighty darkness / Filling the
seat of power" (II. iv. 2-3), Demogorgon was sufficiently familiar to the Marlow circle to serve as a sobriquet for one of them
in the Peacock-Hogg correspondence of 1817-18.[29] Peacock,
in his notes to *Rhododaphne*, terms Demogorgon "the philosophical emblem of the principle of vegetative life," and both
Bell's *Pantheon* and Banier's *Mythology*, acknowledging Boccaccio's authority, provide a similar gloss. Contemporary
French mythological handbooks prefer simplicity and identify
Demogorgon as Nature.[30] Boccaccio clearly provided Shelley
with more than authority, for, as Wasserman notes, Boccaccio's
own fiction of descending into Demogorgon's cave is a prototype for Asia's descent, and Shelley similarly exploits Demogorgon's association with volcanic activity. But there are subtler
recommendations to Shelley's attention as well. That Demogorgon is said to have once punished the Furies makes his overwhelming of their master Jupiter a logical extension, just as his
contrasting championship of Prometheus is supported by the
legend that he created the sun atop Caucasus. As Boccaccio
renders the gnarled branches of the ancient family tree it would
even appear that Demogorgon was Prometheus' direct ancestor, indeed, his great-grandfather.[31]

Demogorgon's identification of himself with Eternity is a
natural consequence of their ancient association: Boccaccio en-
thrones Eternity as his feminine counterpart, dwelling in cav-
ernous gloom, an association even stronger in Boccaccio's classical sources. Claudian, a principal authority, describes the cave
of Eternity as surrounded by the great tail-eating serpent, the
Ouroboros, whom Shelley depicts coiled beneath Demogorgon's
throne (II. iii. 94-98). To the Egyptians, as Shelley acknowledges
in the fragmentary "On the Devil, and Devils," the great serpent Cneph was a symbol of eternity, and, similarly enthroned
in a profound darkness, was conceived to be both preserver of
the earth and the demiurgic Mind from which the cosmos issued. Lucan, in the *Pharsalia*, likewise terms Demogorgon the
soul of the world, whose seed has produced the sun, moon, and

stars. He is the type of the great Demiurge: Plato's world soul, Moses' divine breath, Hermes' supreme intelligence, and Orpheus' divine love. Descending into the cave of the great Demiurge is the ritual process of the Orphic and Mithraic mysteries, preserved in altered form for Shelley's time in the initiation rites of Masonry. That Shelley has based much of Asia's movement in the second act upon Aeneas' descent from Avernus to the underworld, as Wasserman has carefully shown, is probably true enough, but not the final truth. For, as any intellectual of Shelley's time was aware, that descent had been strenuously argued, in Bishop Warburton's famous dissertation on the sixth book of the *Aeneid*, to be the only extensive depiction of the secret mystery rituals to have survived the ruins of pagan civilization.[32] Asia's descent into the chthonic realm has no single source. Like all the major events of the drama, it is a syncretic ritual designed to draw together its many allusions into a conceptualized human framework.

II

A glancing recognition of the means by which Shelley enlarges the symbolic import of his major characters cannot suggest the true scope of the associative relations in *Prometheus Unbound*, and in one respect it distorts Shelley's achievement. The educated nineteenth-century reader in his celebrated closet may be expected to muse over the connotations or the associations of names abstracted from the text, an experience common enough in reading lyric poetry, but *Prometheus Unbound* is a "lyrical drama," whose enduring values arise from a genuinely dramatic immediacy and compel the reader to balance a momentary context against developing structural patterns. Only on the smallest scale do Shelley's mythological referents function as static, singular allusions. Larger syncretic configurations are continuously present, framing the central action with multiple backdrops so that not even in his mountain fastness is Prometheus isolated from the consequences of human history. As the issues are cosmic, so the backdrops are woven from the universal designs of man's oldest religions. Rather than pitting them against one another for reductive purposes—as Volney, for instance, does in *Les Ruines*—Shelley labors within his syncretic vision to render them harmonious and congruent.

Aside from the obvious heritage of Greece, the Judaeo-Christian mythology forms the most immediately striking context for the values of *Prometheus Unbound*. Protected by a pagan framework, Shelley largely resists his earlier inclination to lash out at the follies of the Christian church. As in the *Essay on Christianity*, he concentrates on its religious truths, cleansed of the distortions of dogma and formalism, restored to a pristine mythic integrity. In this undertaking he is drawn as much by the emulation of Milton all the Romantics felt, as by his desire to distinguish essential from inessential conceptions of Christianity. Both impulses coalesce in the mythic comparison that immediately strikes the drama's reader—Shelley's defence of his Prometheus as "a more poetical character than Satan" (Preface, *Prometheus Unbound*). From the deification of Lucifer that occurs in the opening canto of *The Revolt of Islam*, one might have expected Shelley to invert normal Christian symbols in *Prometheus Unbound*, rather like Blake in *The Marriage of Heaven and Hell*. But the dissociation of Prometheus from Satan that Shelley attempts in his prefatory statement suggests a far subtler ethical and literary motive. Shelley there invokes *Paradise Lost* (and, by extension, *Paradise Regained*) less for purposes of argument than as works universally esteemed, preeminent among modern expositions of Christian values. If he intends to reinterpret Milton's vision, he nonetheless assumes it to be a structural constant, hovering for reference in the dim recesses of a reader's imagination. Milton's Satan, his God, even his Christ, are not recostumed to make their appearance on Shelley's cosmic stage. They retain their Miltonic integrity, functioning as standards of value behind the shifting contexts of the drama.

"A more poetical character than Satan," Prometheus is, indeed, implicitly identified in the first act with his opposite, Christ. Such a correspondence, as Wasserman notes, is author-

54

ized by Alexander Ross, though the seventeenth-century commentator, it should also be observed, buttresses this identification with thirteen others that precede it, including the more traditional explication of Prometheus as God's providence.[33] A Christian mythographer is naturally loath to equate Prometheus with Christ, since the correlative is to cast God as the vindictive Jupiter, torturing his victim on the cross. In the drama's only blatant return to the strategies of *Queen Mab*, Shelley absolves God from this responsibility, only to indict the Christian church for betraying Christ's vision and for perpetuating his crucifixion throughout modern history (I. 546-49; 603-06). Contemporary reviewers seized upon these passages as evidence of Shelley's continuing infidelity.[34] But that is incidental, perhaps even unintentional. Less prejudiced readers, sensitive to Shelley's dramatic contexts, would have understood the passages, irrespective of their claims to truth, as revelatory of the Titan's self-pity during his own passion. Truly like Christ in his agony, he is assailed by unanswerable doubts.

Prometheus, having assumed his destiny as "The saviour and the strength of suffering man" (I. 817), finds "the present . . . spread / Like a pillow of thorns for [his] slumberless head" (I. 562-63). His crucifixion is a continuing symbol of man's unregenerate condition. But the irony of Christ's body, the Church, turning upon the vital spirit that animates it, extends into the very substance of Shelley's drama. Prometheus, too, gave form to a conception: his martyrdom, originally a refusal to countenance an objective tyranny over man, has instead sanctioned it. It is this that the energies of the Earth imply in the opening chorus of *Prometheus Unbound*, and their charges are reinforced in the first dramatic encounter, that between Prometheus and the Phantasm of Jupiter.

Here, roles shift radically. Prometheus, chained to his mountain, forsaken by all but Panthea and Ione, and repeatedly accusing his mother and her sons—the Earth and its various manifestations—of scorning him (I. 113-15; 124-25), is a fit emblem of Christ. But the Prometheus of the curse has cast himself in an opposite context, representing that inscrutable and

PROMOTHEVS IN CRVCEM SVSPENSVS. 7

In requie mortui requiescere fac memoriam ejus,& consolare illum in exitu spiritus sui. Ecclesiast. 38. c.

5. Prometheus as the crucified Christ. Μικροκοσμος (Arnheim, [1609?])

ultimately unjust providence of Jehovah that the Titan himself had execrated. The imagery of the curse exposes the extraordinary role reversal of this confrontation:

> Fiend, I defy thee! with a calm, fixed mind,
> All that thou canst inflict I bid thee do.
>
> (I. 262-63)

The curse assumes a world irrevocably fallen. It deliberately reflects Jehovah's self-righteous proclamation relinquishing his fallen dominions to Satan, allowing Satanic power to be instituted over all beings but him who issued the proclamation, but at the very same moment of ceding empire ensnaring its holder in a victimizing irony: with all his power Jupiter is doomed by providence never to achieve either success or succor. To convey his meaning with clarity and dramatic thrust, Prometheus aptly quotes *Paradise Lost*:

> Heap on thy soul, by virtue of this curse,
> Ill deeds; then be thou damned, beholding good.
>
> (I. 292-93)

In the Christian myth Satanic evil is ultimately a means to Jehovah's victory. Prometheus, anticipating his own moment of victory as he ends his curse, foresees that the "lagging fall through boundless space and time" (I. 301) of the Satanic prototype, Jupiter, will be tracked only by "Scorn." The word echoes not only Prometheus' condition as a martyr reviled by the earth, but his opening self-portrait in which he conceives of his empire as solely composed of "torture and solitude, / Scorn and despair" (I. 14-15), which in turn has elicited Jupiter's scorn (I. 10). And yet, as Prometheus in that soliloquy revealed his affinities with Christ, so at this point the figure his curse anthematizes with scorn is not merely Satanic, but also bears attributes of Christ:

> . . . thine Infinity shall be
> A robe of envenomed agony;
> And thine Omnipotence a crown of pain
> To cling like burning gold round thy dissolving brain.
>
> (I. 288-91)

The imagery recalls the robe given by Medea to Creusa, the robe of Hercules, even the "Numidian seps" (III. i. 40) whose burning poison Thetis compares with Jupiter's semen. But the robe is also that of Christ on Golgotha, as the crown of pain resembles that of thorns which in the visions later in this act Christ continues to wear. In casting the execrated Jupiter as Christ, Shelley's Titan in his curse speaks with Jehovah's words, but employing the voice of another prototype. Locked into a world of ice—where "crawling glaciers pierce [him] with the spears / Of their moon-freezing crystals; the bright chains / Eat with their burning cold into [his] bones" (I. 31-33)—he reveals his ironic affinity with that Satan whom Dante discovered in the moral frigidity of deepest hell.

With the relationship between God and Satan in *Paradise Lost* assumed as context, Shelley superimposes upon it the standards of an extreme Gnosticism less sure of its identifications than of its principles. That is to say, the Gnostics commonly associated the God of the Jews with the Devil whose purpose was to crucify the Christ who entered into the mortal state of Jesus to redeem humanity. An equally valid perspective, however, is that Satan, expelled from heaven for opposing Jehovah's tyranny, is a precursor of Christ, who came into the world to overthrow it wholly. Intricately involved as are the associations Shelley creates, they emphasize a single truth: in his curse Prometheus gave birth to a human condition at once revengeful and masochistic, a veritable model for the psychological malaise perpetuated, from the Gnostics' viewpoint, in the Judaic testament.[35] The resistance Prometheus has ostentatiously undertaken for the liberation of man has, like that of Milton's Satan, simply insured man's damnation.

In relinquishing his curse, however, Prometheus transforms his mythic prototype, identifying himself with the absolute passivity and benevolence of Christ. His vision of the reviled martyr surrounded by "thick shapes of human death" (I. 587) is re-created by Asia, in the final lines of Act II, to form a paradise where all men assume Christ-like powers:

A paradise of vaulted bowers . . .
Peopled by shapes too bright to see . . .
Which walk upon the sea and chant melodiously!
(II. v. 104, 108, 110)

In the very next scene—the first of the third act—Demogorgon, reanimated with the powers of Christ, confronts Jupiter. As *Paradise Lost* provided mythic context for the dramatic confrontation of the first act, in Act III Shelley appropriately shifts to *Paradise Regained*. Here, Jupiter has the Satanic role all to himself, combining it with the overweening hubris of a Greek tragic protagonist. He relies on an assumed omnipotence, like Milton's second Satanic figure designing Christ's fall from the pinnacle, but instead precipitates his own:

The elements obey me not. I sink
Dizzily down—ever, forever, down.
(III. i. 80-81)

His echo of Prometheus' tragic refrain from the first act—"Ah me, alas, pain, pain ever, forever!" (I. 23, 30, 635)—is no more accidental than the symphonic elaborations upon it, suggesting an eternity of love, that counterpoint the rapturous duet at the end of Act II (II. v. 65, 71, 78). The self-contradicting principles that kept Prometheus chained to the Caucasus have been separated. The Satan who is Jehovah's agent is at last unified with his creator and cast forth, as the Satan who is the prototype of Christ is resurrected. The brief dialogue of Apollo and Ocean that follows Jupiter's fall not only symbolically resolves the feud between Titan and god, but at last explicates the significance of the morning star that has quietly dominated the dawning heavens of the first two acts. The "pale stars of the morn" (I. 539) in the Furies' view had shed scant light on the night of earth's misery; to Mercury they were silent monitors "That measure and divide the weary years / From which there is no refuge" (I. 363-64). Almost unnoticed, they give way to the single eastern star that is Panthea's signal, as Prometheus voices his last line of the act: "I said all hope was vain but love: thou lovest" (I. 824). This confluence receives immediate punctuation in Asia's ravishing description of "The point of one white star . . . quivering still / Deep in the orange light of widening morn" (II. i. 17-18). So it is that, as Ocean marks the alteration of his realm, the white star will pilot future mariners through the night (III. ii. 23-34), and Apollo is called to his morning duties by "The small, clear, silver lute of the young spirit / That sits in the morning star" (III. ii. 38-39). Now that Lucifer has regained his rightful seat in the day star, he becomes indistinguishable from the great goddess who is the evening star, Venus, even as at last Prometheus and Asia are joined in eternal love.[36]

Ocean's "unpastured sea hungering for calm" (III. ii. 49) under the benign influence of Lucifer and Venus suggests a further Judaic context for *Prometheus Unbound*. Having conflated the dramas of genesis and of Christ's passion and resurrection, Shelley in addition follows Milton's example, in Books XI and XII of *Paradise Lost*, adumbrating his themes within a postdiluvian history. As is true of so many aspects of *Prometheus Unbound*, the scholarship of the late eighteenth century is of more moment than the accumulation of knowledge we derive from Victorian biblical researches. At the turn of the century a paucity of accurate data supported rife and sometimes wild speculation on the metamorphoses of Noah, by which the patriarch of the postdiluvian world was elevated into the paternal deity of gentile cults.[37] Among his many manifestations is that of Prometheus, who shaped man and gave him the tools by which he, in turn, might shape his society. But the means by which Prometheus became assimilated to Noah is almost more important than the identification itself, for it is this that allows Shelley naturally to surround his Titan with associations unknown to Aeschylus and to Milton, and to create a universality for his drama that is more than imaginary.

In his effort to extend the religious contexts of *Prometheus Unbound* beyond those assumed from Milton, Shelley's most significant means is his knowledge of geography, which he announces in the very first line—not of the poem, but of the drama: "A Ravine of Icy Rocks in the Indian Caucasus." It was not until 1963 that a commentator thought to question so curiously pointed a stage direction, and even then the associations of the setting were barely sketched.[38] The Indian Caucasus, the Hindu Kush (or ancient Paropamisus) mountains, extend westward of the Himalaya chain into the forbidding tract where today the borders of India, Pakistan, Afghanistan, the Soviet Union, and the People's Republic of China nearly touch. An ancient geographical crux as well, it was for centuries conceived as the eastern extremity of Persia, the northern boundary of India, and the southern extension of Scythia or Tartary. For all these nations its realms were legendary, a focus of history and myth. As a landscape of fertile suggestiveness, the Indian Caucasus was unsurpassed until the present century, when its evocative nature was shifted somewhat to the east: there, in even greater inaccessibility, Abominable Snowmen walk in the insubstantial tracks of the Devas of eastern mythology and James Hilton has rebuilt Shangri-la from the exploded legends of Cashmir.

Shelley's choice of the Indian rather than Georgian Caucasus rests on a complicated mythic rationale: it also has a historical one. The late eighteenth century witnessed a running, brutal battle in the Georgian Caucasus between the forces of Catherine the Great, the Turkish sultan, and the Persian shah. To place Prometheus as tutelary deity above the armies of contentious imperialism would scarcely testify to the perfectability of man. That Czar Alexander, the least benevolent of the despots who joined the Holy Alliance, ruled the Georgian Caucasus in Shelley's time, must have whetted his search for a location less contaminated by modern associations. It is true enough that British imperialism had moved into the Indian Caucasus in a search for allies and citadels from which to withstand any thrust of the modern Alexander, Napoleon, into southern Asia. But Napoleon was on St. Helena, Victoria not yet born, and England in control of a relatively minor portion of the Indian subcontinent as Shelley wrote his drama: the Afghan wars, in territory

6. Syncretic mythology. Charles François Dupuis. *Origine de tous les Cultes* (Paris, [1795]), frontispiece. *Courtesy the Newberry Library, Chicago*

still largely unmapped, would have seemed inconceivable.[39]

Whatever its romantic values geographically, the mythic associations of the Indian Caucasus were extraordinary, distributed among all Asian cultures, even—with some stretching—the Judaic. The first English writer to identify Ararat with the Indian Caucasus was Sir Walter Raleigh, who in the *History of the World* cited Gropius Becanus to the effect that the ark had been built there and summoned the authority of Marcus Porcius Cato to affirm that the human race was reborn "in Scythia Saga." Scythia Saga Raleigh glosses as Sacae, which he locates "undoubtedly under the mountains of Paropanisus."[40] Numerous commentators repeat and expand Raleigh's contention. Thomas Maurice introduces it into his Indian researches, muttering cautious reservations about disputing scripture. The less constricted Francis Wilford makes it central to his essay, "On Mount Caucasus." And George Stanley Faber, judging it "universally agreed" that the ark landed in the Indian Caucasus, speculates on whether its site was the peak of Chaisa-gar (Cashgar)—venerated as the throne of Solomon by the Moslems and as the home of Shama (Shem), builder of the sacred town of Bamiyan, by the Buddhists—or of Nau-banda in Cashmir, where the Puranas, at least as Faber reads them, declare Satyavrata to have anchored the ark.[41] The testimony of these contemporaries of Shelley is especially significant: they support their assertions not merely by scripture, but by legends of the major eastern religions, whose boundaries touch and whose texts conflate in the Caucasus. All variants of the one true religion came about in the dispersal of Noah's family: Mount Caucasus, the origin of all the great rivers of Asia, is no less the source of its myths.[42] It is the source, too, of classical European mythology, according to Faber, who reinforces Jean Sylvain Bailly's general conclusion—in *Letters upon the Atlantis of Plato*—that the Atlantides descended originally from Mount Caucasus, bringing with them the basic formulations of ancient religion. The migration extended in all directions, even across the ancient land link to North America. Maurice, elaborating Samuel Shuckford's speculation, concentrates on the similarities between the American and Asiatic Indians. Faber—a dedicated follower of Jacob Bryant, the acknowledged patriarch of the Noachian mythographers, who had designated Caucasus as the mountains of the postdiluvian original race of Cush—draws the self-evident links with Cusco in the Peruvian Andes.[43] Though many of the scholarly legions that succeeded Bryant disagreed with his etymologies, his blurring of historical chronologies, and his pronounced tendency to bluff his way to conclusions reached before he began his research, nonetheless almost all supported and elaborated his underlying thesis.

Among these, at least for poetical purposes, was the young Shelley. In *Alastor* the poet's grand tour of the orient reaches its eastern terminus in the vale of Cashmir beneath Mount Caucasus, whence he turns back to cross the Caspian Sea in his boat and pass into a cavern on its western shore. The remainder of the poem depicts the slow attainment of the summit of a second mountain chain from whose height the poet contemplates the realm of death—the Georgian Caucasus overlooking the Black Sea and, beyond its expanse, Europe. Among the multiplying ironies of *Alastor*, none is more striking than that the poet traces the origin of man to Caucasus, then again on Caucasus finds his death. The confusion of two geographical entities under a name comprehending opposites is an exact counterpart to the visionary maiden of the poet's imagination who promises perfect life and in the end grants only death.[44] Prometheus is wiser. The journey he undertakes between Acts III and IV begins by reproducing the poet's itinerary westward, but, bypassing the second Caucasus, ends in Greece, where the Promethean entourage presides over the second awakening of the human imagination.

The Noachian context of *Prometheus Unbound* is, like the Satanic, both serious and ironic. Noah, repeopling the earth, became its source for inventions and arts. Through him man was granted a second opportunity to create a perfect society according to God's plan. But even before the dispersal the bickerings of his sons presage the failure attendant upon the dissipation of the one race and one language. Thus, Noah is an essentially tragic figure, remaining on Mount Caucasus as his good intentions slowly revert into palpable defeats. In this sense he is a prototype of Prometheus chained to the Caucasus, protesting his righteousness, impotent to alter the degeneration surrounding him. But the covenant Prometheus represents is, as the Spirit of the Air suggests, one of blood rather than peace: the deluge will not end until Prometheus reforms. And at this point a true covenant, symbolized by Lucifer-Venus shedding the balm of light upon calm waters, prepares the way for a journey undertaken to reconcile the fragments of the race:

> Man, oh, not men! a chain of linkèd thought,
> Of love and might to be divided not.
> (IV. 394-95)

In this ironic retracing of the dispersal, the integrated race recovers even the purity of its original language:

> . . . a perpetual Orphic song,
> Ruling with dædal harmony a throng
> Of thoughts and forms, which else senseless and shapeless were.
> (IV. 415-17)

The movement of *Prometheus Unbound* is not to regain paradise, at least as that term is customarily employed in Christian commentary. Chance, mutability, death—qualities which God excludes from Eden and which Shelley attempts imaginatively to deny in *Queen Mab* and *The Revolt of Islam*—retain their integrity in this regenerate world. But what man has regained is exactly the limited perfection of his postdiluvian state, where, as the *Quarterly Review* represented it early in 1820, "all mankind spake one tongue and were gathered together as one family . . . in the plans of Shinar, or in the mythic regions of the snow-clad Caucasus."[45]

If Mount Caucasus became identified with Ararat by Biblical historians, antiquarians of the East discovered other parallels hardly less significant to the conceptions of *Prometheus Unbound*. Mount Meru, the Indian paradise and home of Dionysus to which Shelley seems to allude in the final canto of *The Revolt*

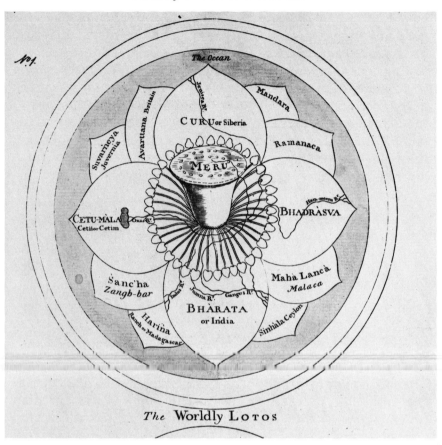

7. Mount Meru as lotus and polar paradise. *Asiatic Researches*, Vol. 8 (London, 1805). *Courtesy the Newberry Library, Chicago*

of Islam, was designated as the Caucasus and located with admirable, if unfounded, precision by Francis Wilford somewhat north of Cabul, the modern capital of Afghanistan, in the ancient kingdom of Little Bokhara. If one could believe European interpreters, the Indians flocked to it on pilgrimage. Those who remained at home to travel in the imagination invested the mountain with an erotic symbolism like that Shelley attaches to Acts I and II of *Prometheus Unbound*: "*Méru* is the sacred and primeval *Linga* [phallus]: and the Earth beneath is the mysterious *Yóni* expanded, and open like the *Padma* or *Lotos.*" The Abbé Lambert found nothing so remarkably impious in his travels through the Caucasus, but he discovered another terminus for pilgrims in Mount Pir-pangial. Claiming it to be the loftiest of all the Caucasus mountains, he specifically denominated it the habitation of Prometheus on the strength of legends of an ancient man worshipped there by pilgrims.[46] Yet another venerable mountain, this with extensive ramifications in both Indian and Persian mythologies, is likewise converted into Caucasus—Mount Caf. Asia, in Keats's catalog of the Titans in *Hyperion*, is described as "born of most enormous Caf" (II. 53). In some accounts Caf is designated as the home of the griffin Simorg, who with his great eagle-head approximates the legendary tormenter of Prometheus. More significantly linked with Shelley's conception is Caf's reputation as the home and battleground of the fabulous demons of eastern myth, the Peris and Devas. Their ethical conflicts are transposed into the machinery of Act I of *Prometheus Unbound*, which pits the malevolent Devas, as Furies, against the alternative Spirits of Love.[47]

A further legendary mountain, prominently associated with Caucasus, provides Shelley with much more than incidental poetic machinery for his drama—indeed, offers him the richest vein of ancient myth he draws upon in his syncretic quest. Distinguished as Ararat, as Meru, as Pir-pangial, and as Caf, Caucasus was also thought to be Mount Albordj, the mountain of life in Zoroastrian traditions. There Mithra dwells, and there the great legislator of ancient Persia, Zoroaster, conversed with the supreme being, descending after ten years with the sacred books of the Persian religion. In 1771, after centuries of European ignorance and neglect, the *Zend-Avesta*, a considerable portion of the sacred text pieced together from fragments still retained by the Indian Parsees, was published in a French translation by a dedicated scholar named Abraham Hyacinth Anquetil du Perron. Although the fame of both the man and the sacred texts he painstakingly collected has receded once more into obscurity, it was a major event in the history of European civilization.[48]

The *Zend-Avesta* was the first in a succession of eastern sacred texts whose publication opened entirely new cultural vistas to the late European Enlightenment. Its immediate, wide fame clearly precipitated Charles Wilkins' translations of the *Bhagvat-Geeta* in 1785 and the *Heetopades* in 1787.[49] Unlike the Hindu sacred books, however, the *Zend-Avesta* was the property of a mere sect, the Parsees, who, distanced in time and place from their ancestors and constantly persecuted, had lost much of the substance of the Zoroastrian faith while pursuing its rituals. Consequently, there were no authorities to confirm the accuracy of Anquetil du Perron's rendition, the fame of which was only increased by its tenure as the subject of learned controversy. Both John Richardson, who was also Jacob Bryant's major disputant, and Sir William Jones, England's leading orientalist, seriously questioned its authenticity. And well they might, for in significant ways it overturned generally accepted notions of Zoroastrianism derived from its heretical Christian offshoot, Manicheanism. Later historical researches, having validated Anquetil du Perron's conclusions, incidentally support the complex uses to which Shelley puts them in *Prometheus Unbound*. The controversy might well explain his silence concerning the Zoroastrian elements in his drama. But that he had to have known the *Zend-Avesta* is clear from the contexts of the drama, and the source of that knowledge is equally clear from the contexts of his life. Thomas Love Peacock cites the *"Vie de Zoroastre"* that prefaced Anquetil du Perron's translation in *The Philosophy of Melancholy*; and in the fragmentary annotations to *Ahrimanes* twice refers to the *Zend-Avesta*. Moreover, numerous other references to Zoroaster in his writings suggest a detailed and continuing interest in the Persian mythology.[50]

The basic ritual of Zoroastrianism, the worship of fire and, by extension, of the sun, establishes an immediate correspondence with the myth of Prometheus. The Hellenistic Stoic Dio Chrysostom was the first to relate that when Zoroaster ascended Mount Albordj he dwelt there in flames. By ancient tradition the summit of Mount Caucasus, the highest point in Asia, touched the sun, which, in the passage already cited from Boccaccio, Demogorgon himself is said to have created. Zoroaster, enveloped by that essential energy, translated it into its earthly manifestation, the sacred laws of the ancient Persians.[51] As representative lawgiver, Zoroaster clearly has affinities with Moses, though, perhaps because such a supposition verges on heresy, mythologists concentrate on other parallels: Buddha, Belus, Nimrod, Vishnu, Noah, and Christ.[52] The historical Zoroaster lived in the sixth century, b.c., but the mythic Zoroaster, separated into as many as six incarnations, ranged in time from the Christian era to 5000 years before the fall of Troy. As might be expected, the Moslem destruction of Persian records was a considerable impetus to the creative propensities of mythographers.[53]

When Zoroaster returned from Mount Albordj, he settled in Balkh, situated in the plains just northwest of the Caucasus chain and reputed to be the oldest city in the world. In Balkh he established his school for the Magi and built the principal fire temple of his religion, consolidating this early seat of science and poetry into a center famous throughout the ancient world. There, according to venerable traditions, Pythagoras came to study, and from Balkh the two sages journeyed together across the Caucasus to educate and be educated by the learned Gymnosophists of northern India. From these associations the basic formulations of Zoroastrianism penetrated southern Asia and all of Europe. Threatened Christian apologists might lamely argue that Zoroaster was a slave in Daniel's Babylonian house;

but it was obvious to the free spirits of Shelley's time (as it is to religious scholars today) that Judaism borrowed heavily from Magian sources. In short, Zoroaster could be regarded as the greatest lawgiver and most venerated sage of the ancient world: like Prometheus, a reformer, a deliverer, the inventor of arts and sciences—the first humanist.[54]

The Zoroastrian machinery of the first act of *Prometheus Unbound* has appeared to have little purpose beyond the befuddlement of readers. Involved and esoteric as it is on the surface, however, it is organically related to the deepest insights both of Shelley's vision and of the religious system on which he draws. Shelley's deliberate complexity insists on a contextual awareness far removed from a modern sphere of knowledge but common to contemporary intellectuals: he carefully announces the context in the Earth's mysterious account of the Magus Zoroaster meeting his double and bids us become Magians ourselves if we are to relate this scene to the entirety of the drama. Literally from first to last, *Prometheus Unbound* is a Zoroastrian drama.

Prometheus' opening enumeration of the "Gods and Dæmons, and all Spirits / . . . who throng those bright and rolling worlds" (I. 1-2), the stars and planets, stands in perfect symmetrical balance with Demogorgon's majestic calling of the celestial roll at the end:

> Ye kings of suns and stars, Dæmons and Gods,
> Ætherial Dominations, who possess
> Elysian, windless, fortunate abodes
> Beyond heaven's constellated wilderness.
> (IV. 529-32)

As the drama opens, the sidereal spirits—all but Prometheus—are under the tyrannical dominion of Jupiter; at its end, Demogorgon summons them to their freedom: "Our great Republic hears: we are blest, and bless" (IV. 534). Such an animated universe derives from ancient Sabian star worship, which, degenerating into astrology and necromancy, was restored to a spiritual integrity in the Magian reforms. Zoroastrianism conceived of the stars as composing the realm of the saintly blessed, whose beneficent influence sheds light through the darkness. On that influence Demogorgon calls in his ritual benediction, much as Zoroaster is instructed by Ormusd, the deity of light, to pray to the heavenly powers for deliverance from the evil of Ahriman.[55] A similar context informs Prometheus' opening monologue. Although by the standards of Zoroastrian rites the frustrated and unregenerate Titan is initially an ironic figure, his invocation of the four elements and of the energies of the Earth reproduces the basic Zoroastrian formula for prayer. Herodotus, who offered Shelley his sole classical authority for Asia as Prometheus' wife, was the first western writer to document the essential Magian ceremony:

> ... they call the whole circle of heaven Zeus, and to him they offer sacrifice on the highest peaks of the mountains; they sacrifice also to the sun and moon and earth and fire and water and winds. These are the only gods to whom they have ever sacrificed from the beginning; they have learnt later, to sacrifice to the "heavenly" Aphrodite, ... called ... by the Persians Mitra.[56]

In comparison with such a prayer that of Prometheus is heavily ironic. He, too, sees the whole of the heavens under the power of Jupiter and has sacrificed himself in a vain martyrdom without ever establishing a satisfactory communication with the elements or with the earth he prays to. And like the Persians he has learned late to sacrifice to the Mithraic principle, since it is only in the scene we witness that Prometheus surrenders his self-righteous anger to the love that, in Asia, secures his release. Until then, he, like the human race, is wracked by the demonic legions of the evil principle, Ahriman's "Earthquake-fiends" and "genii of the storm" (I. 38, 42), against whom his ritual prayers are ineffectual. Only after thirty centuries has the Magus become a sage.

Although the revocation of the curse that suddenly erupts from Prometheus' prayer is one of several striking events in *Prometheus Unbound* that deliberately lack a sufficient cause,

8. Zoroastrian emblem: a magus and his double or Fravashi. Jacob Bryant, *A New System; or, An Analysis of Ancient Mythology* (London, 1774)

the subsequent and explicitly Zoroastrian exposition, which summons the Phantasm of Jupiter, by anatomizing the Titan's mental condition justifies his act. Shelley's doctrinal base for this scene could only have come from Anquetil du Perron, and his accuracy in manipulating what is one of the least explicated or comprehensible sections of the *Zend-Avesta* is remarkable. The Phantasm of Jupiter is a Fravashi (Feroüer in Anquetil du Perron), a daemonic force resembling that which Socrates claimed to possess and, in the aggregate, bearing affinities with the pantheon of Christian saints. The Fravashis are active, guardian spirits who "if [men] are in distress relieve them, coming to their aid with the pure productions of Ormusd"; they are "the pre-existent souls of men," "the spiritual powers that are indissolubly linked with each and every human being and with humanity as a whole."[57] Many of the Fravashis invoked in the *Zend-Avesta* are conceptual: some are illustrious men. Shelley's version enlarges on the implications of his model, making the underworld on which Prometheus calls a repository of the potential, as well as actual, history of the earth. In these Elysian Fields eternal properties are defined by the human intellect. Nothing that has been thought is denied existence. Nothing that is beyond the human imagination exists.

The Earth's mysterious account of Zoroaster's encounter with his doppelgänger has generated an understandable search for Shelley's source, which has been as industrious as it has been unsuccessful. Scholars of Zoroastrianism, no less than of English Romanticism, generally concede Shelley's originality.[58] Still, numerous documents were available from which to extrapolate such a meeting: the many legends of Zoroaster's remarkable powers; his reputation for spiritual flight above the earth (in which Ianthe is very much in his tradition, if not his debt); the contemplative nature of his life; and widely reproduced religious icons showing a heavenly duplication of the magi's earthly offices. There is, too, an exact source for the double itself. In the Iescht (Yasht) Farvardin Zoroaster, after praying to an extensive catalog of Fravashis, turns at length to his own: "I worship the pure and holy Fravashi of the Sapetman Zoroaster, whom Ormusd conceived from the very beginning, whose ear he has instructed, and whom he formed to greatness in the midst of the provinces of Iran." The prayer concludes with a summary: "I worship the holy Fravashis of all these beings, and my own."[59]

The Earth's recollection of Zoroaster's encounter with his double is meant to spur Prometheus to summon his own Fravashi: instead, refusing to allow the curse to pass his lips, he calls upon the Phantasm of Jupiter. But Prometheus' sense of surface niceties conceals a Jungian slip. The being he raises— with "gestures proud and cold, / And looks of firm defiance, and calm hate, / And such despair as mocks itself with smiles" (I. 258-60)—is a just spiritual representative of the figure who began his curse, "Fiend, I defy thee." Gaining access to another world where potentiality is as sharply delineated as actuality, the Titan is allowed to observe the inextricable relationship between himself and Jupiter, between self-regarding good and self-serving evil. Ultimately, they are the same. The Phantasm of Jupiter reads back Prometheus' curse, in effect cursing that being who, by first uttering the imprecation, ironically cursed himself and all those who sought his protection. "I gave all / He has" (I. 381-82), Prometheus accurately acknowledges of Jupiter. Comrades in rebellion against Saturn, they have remained in linked manacles underneath the cloak of their antagonism. As Zoroastrian doctrine informs the appearance of the Phantasm, those echoes continue as the enlightened Prometheus reaffirms his disavowal of this silent partnership. In rejecting his curse and the mental kinship with his oppressor, the Titan speaks with a moving formulaic selflessness—"It doth repent me" (I. 303)—strongly recalling the standard. Zoroastrian prayer of repentence for evil thoughts, words, or actions: "I renounce them by these three words: I repent them (*je m'en repens*)."[60]

The Zoroastrian echoes of the first act, however, seldom have so direct a link with the true forms of the religion. From the invocation of the primary elements and the prayer to the Fravashi, to the irresolute battle between the good and evil spirits,

Shelley emphasizes ironic dimensions. In subsequent acts those ironies dissolve as he draws on further Zoroastrian rituals to epitomize the reunion of the now liberated Prometheus and Asia. Whereas the drama began with a prayer to external nature from the mountainous altar of the Titan's sacrifice, its counter-movement is to an alternate site for worship, the Promethean cave of interior symbols. Mountaintops and caves are the two sacred locations of Persian worship, reported by countless students of myth. Jacob Bryant, for example, gives the following account, which Shelley would have seen, inasmuch as it comprises the initial note to Peacock's ode personifying the object of Zoroastrian worship, "The Spirit of Fire":

> Men repaired in the first ages either to the lonely summits of mountains, or else to caverns in the rocks, and hollows in the bosom of the earth; which they thought were the residence of their gods. At the entrance of these they raised their altars, and performed their vows. . . . When in process of time they began to erect temples, they were still determined in their situation by the vicinity of these objects, which they comprehended within the limits of the sacred enclosure. . . . Amongst the Persians most of the temples were caverns in rocks, either formed by nature, or artificially produced.[61]

Ubiquitous as Zoroastrian cave worship is, the actual cave Prometheus describes at length in Act III, Scene iii, directly reflects a commonly cited passage from Porphyry's commentary on Homer's cave of the nymphs, *De antro nympharum*. Among the easily accessible sources for Shelley was Thomas Taylor's translation:

> . . . The Persians, mystically signifying the descent of the soul into an inferior nature and its ascent into the intelligible world, initiate the priest or mystic in a place which they denominate a cave. For according to Eubulus, Zoroaster first of all among the neighboring mountains of Persia, consecrated a natural cave, florid and watered with fountains, in honour of Mithras the father of all things: a cave in the opinion of Zoroaster bearing a resemblance of the world fabricated by Mithras. But the things contained in the cavern, being disposed by certain intervals, according to symmetry and order, were symbols of the elements and climates of the world.[62]

9. Zoroastrian cave temple. Jacob Bryant, *A New System; or, An Analysis of Ancient Mythology*

Shelley's refinement of the legend is to transpose its terms from religion into art. Zoroaster's religious grotto, from which subsequent eastern, Mithraic, and Greek cave worship emanates, becomes itself a symbol—of the creative mind, of the gestating womb of art. The symbols Zoroaster ordered within the cave are the same as those Prometheus continually interweaves in new artistic combinations. Art, rather than religious doctrine, is the mediating power linking the eternal and mortal: the human symbols that form the material for its creation are, as Prometheus says, "the mediators / Of that best worship, Love, by him and us / Given and returned" (III. iii. 58-60). As the diction implies, the same principle—worship—underlies Zoroaster's long labors to create the *Zend-Avesta* within a cave on Mount Albordj and the artist's effort to create harmonious order from the tumultuous experiences of his life.[63] But more than this, the balanced Zoroastrian contexts of mountain and cave sharpen our awareness of the extent of the revolution Prometheus has undergone. The altar of the drama's beginning, erected to the principle of self, allows only one worship, which is hate. In exchanging mountain for cave, an external and unresponsive nature for a world of intellectual symbols, Prometheus commits himself to the destiny of man, to a human fellowship and the love that renders it possible.

This generative cave has further reverberations in eastern legend. Both Diodorus Siculus and Arrian report that the Macedonian army discovered a great cave, which they took to be the cave of Prometheus, in crossing the Indian Caucasus. Faber remarks several sacred caverns in this area: one on Mount Parnassus above Nusa, where there were said to be caves sacred to Atlas and to the Earth; another on the Indian Ararat, containing the bodies of the two great patriarchs of the human race, Adam and Noah. The most celebrated cave in this region, however, is that at Bamiyan, on the trail crossing the Caucasus from Persia to India. There, massive images of a man, woman, and child had been raised within niches carved into the mountain face, and between the man's legs was cut an entrance into a cave used, according to Shelley's contemporaries, as a Mithraic fire temple. The volume of commentary on this phenomenon, as well as the associations erected around it, suggest that Shelley is drawing upon it for his depiction of the cave inhabited by Prometheus, Asia, and the Spirit of the Earth.[64]

In particular, it seems likely that Shelley had access to the dissertation "On Mount Caucasus" by the enterprising orientalist Francis Wilford, either as originally published in the *Asiatic Researches* or as condensed by Faber in his *Origin of Pagan Idolatry*. This remarkable essay portrays Bamiyan as the Thebes of the east, the source of holiness and purity in the world, its name identical with one of the pseudonyms of Vishnu and of Shem, the patriarch who built it. A later patriarch, Abraham, was also said to have resided there. Near the city is a small lake from which four rivers run, identified by Wilford as the fabled Lake Manasarovara and the four rivers of Paradise. Since both Persian and Indian legends also place the progenitors of the human race in this region, to Wilford it is clearly the true site of Eden. But it is also the location of the cave of Prometheus, who is actually Pramathesa, a servant of the god Mahadeva (Siva), who was set upon through error by the eagle-headed Garuda and released by Haraja (Hercules). Following his Indian pundits, Wilford discovers a second cave near Bamiyan, "the oracle of UMA or UMASA, which is a name of the EARTH, considered as the *Magna-Mater*, and perhaps from it, is derived the *Latin* word *Humus*."[65] These two caves bear unmistakable similarities to the two caves described by Prometheus and the Earth in the third scene of Act III, which, though judged from different perspectives, are one and the same.

Shelley's derivation of his Promethean cave from a Zoroastrian model is supported by the symbolic revision of the cave that the Spirit of the Hour intends to create in the sun. There the entire assemblage will be sculpted in "Phidian forms" (III. iv. 112) in the center of a temple:

> Beneath a dome fretted with graven flowers,
> Poised on twelve columns of resplendent stone,
> And open to the bright and liquid sky.
>
> (III. iv. 116-18)

Not only was the eastern fondness for domes said to derive from the Mithraic cavern, whose dome symbolically represented the heavens, but the particular domed temple Shelley here delineates has a precise architectual history:

> The Monoptere was a circular edifice without walls, having a dome supported by columns, and was, doubtless, the invention of Zoroaster, or some ancient zealous fire-worshipper of Persia, to preserve the consecrated flames that glowed on their altars from being extinguished by the violence of rain and tempests.[66]

Thus, the Spirit of the Hour's fire temple is the symbolic equivalent of the Promethean cave. Each is appropriate to its own element, the fire temple being organic to the sun as the Zoroastrian cave is to the earth. Once again, Shelley's symbols of congruence reflect the harmony of a regenerate universe.

But if the caves and their symbolic manifestations in the third act are reminiscent of the primal cave in which Zoroaster cast the elements of the universe in symbolic form, the abyss of the second act is no less directly drawn from Zoroastrian ritual. As Boccaccio notes in describing the birth of religious worship: "the rustics . . . entered caves in the deepest and most secret recesses of the earth, where in darkness and the grand silence caused by the absence of light, there arose religion and natural fear; and to the ignorant was born the suspicion of a divine presence, a divinity whom they imagined to exist beneath the earth, Demogorgon."[67] The significance of caves in ancient rites was considerably sophisticated by Shelley's time. Mythologists like Charles François Dupuis and Thomas Maurice devote marked attention to it, and Faber—in both his *Dissertation on the Mysteries of The Cabiri* and *Origin of Pagan Idolatry*—views the cave as an essential symbol of all religion. Such mythologists provide ample authority not merely for the cave symbolism of Shelley's drama, but for his symbolic elaboration of it as well. The principal cave ritual to which Bishop Warburton traces the descent of Aeneas is the Mithraic initiation cult. Arising in the east, it influenced Greek mysteries like the

Eleusinian and finally became a major force on late Roman religious practices. Though the ritual details largely retained the mystery with which the priesthood enveloped them, the underlying purposes were well understood. Dupuis, for instance, suggests that the candidate was led into a symbolic realm returning him to the perfect condition of his soul as it "descended by generation into the visible and material world created by the great Demiurge."[68] Asia's journey is just as clearly to the essential Power sustaining the phenomenal world, and in the final lyric of the second act she explicitly characterizes her journey as moving back through time for rebirth "to a diviner day" (II. v. 103). The spirits accompanying Asia and Panthea in their descent resemble closely the priests of a mystery cult, guiding the soul to its confrontation with the symbolic forms of the world:

> To the deep, to the deep,
>   Down, down!
> Through the shade of sleep,
> Through the cloudy strife
> Of Death and of Life;
> Through the veil and the bar
> Of things which seem and are,
> Even to the steps of the remotest throne,
>   Down, down!
>   (II. iii. 54-62)

In the powerful confrontation between Asia and Demogorgon, she struggles—much like Keats's poet undergoing initiation in *The Fall of Hyperion*—to ascend those steps and achieve total comprehension. Shelley may well have fashioned the dialogue from a Zoroastrian catechism, the forty-third of the prayers collected by Anquetil du Perron under the rubric, Vendidad Sadé. The prayer reproduces Zoroaster's demand for ultimate knowledge, to which Ormusd responds shortly and obliquely. Both the driving intensity of the questions and the oracular vagueness of the reply approximate Shelley's dramatic scene.[69]

To summarize to this point the Zoroastrian contexts is to be struck by the range of Shelley's knowledge of the religion and the extent to which it informs the ritualistic patterns of *Prometheus Unbound*. The lyrical drama begins and ends with prayers to the elements, arching over the world from an immense height. The second episode, Prometheus' summoning of the Phantasm of Jupiter, derives from the doctrine of the Fravashi. The agony Prometheus endures at the hands of the Furies, and its opposing movement with the Spirits of Love, have their source in the antagonism of the Devas and Peris, the genii of Persian and Indian antiquity who inhabit Mount Caf. The French mythologist Antoine Fabre d'Olivet records that Prometheus was a leader of the Peris, a sophisticated and pacific tribe, who were driven from Mount Caf by the warlike Devas, a Scythian tribe, settled in Tartary and were later reorganized under the leadership of their greatest legislator, Zoroaster.[70] So convenient a historical coincidence is far from Shelley's purpose, but the materials so easily conflated by fanciful mythography are symbolically linked in the spiritual bifurcation Prometheus suffers in Act I. Act II, with Asia as protagonist, is throughout a Mithraic initiation into the deep mysteries of the world. Her own cosmology, though not accurately Persian in detail, derives from Peacock's pseudo-Zoroastrian account in *Ahrimanes*. And in the third act, Prometheus and Asia join in a humanist priesthood to preside over the Zoroastrian cave containing the symbolic forms—the basis of all art—through which man recreates the essential order of his universe. As pronounced as is Shelley's debt to this religious system, obviously he molds the basic Zoroastrian patterns continuously into his own distinctive forms. Yet, even so, one must contemplate why, in the first place, Shelley informed the structure of his drama with so many Zoroastrian contexts that no educated reader of his time could miss them.

Prometheus Unbound, of course, is not unique among Shelley's writing in its reflection of the Zoroastrian and Manichean ethical duality. Certainly, *The Revolt of Islam* elaborates the precisely Manichean ontology of its first canto. Attacks on Shelley's views, no less in this century than in the Regency,

frequently anathematize his besetting sin as a pervasive, adolescent Manicheanism, separating black from white universally,
and ignoring the subtle shades in which they merge. The charge
carries a weight of truth when applied to the poet's English
period—both early epics are flawed by their simplistic assign-
ment of good and evil into camps so completely irreconcilable
as to preclude by any means attaining the envisioned paradise
—but it wholly distorts the unique achievement of the later
poetry. What distinguishes Shelley's Italian period is the ambiguity, moral and otherwise, that he discovers in all conditions
of life. A brave and unostentatious skepticism informs every
major poem.

Indeed, the Zoroastrian context of *Prometheus Unbound*
quietly rejects the Manichean principles around which Shelley
organized *The Revolt of Islam*, even as it retains their
semblance; and again, his educated public was familiar with
distinctions likely to escape a modern reader. What Anquetil
du Perron's translation made quite apparent was that Manicheanism, far from being simply a reformulation of Zoroastrian
principles within a Christian framework, constituted a marked
alteration of the parent religion. In returning to the tenets of
the pristine faith, Shelley had compelling historical reasons.
The venerable station of the Caucasus as the original seat of
man establishes corollaries that contemporary antiquarians—
especially those refusing to engage in Christian apologetics
—were quick to pursue. Dupuis's *Origine de Tous les Cultes*,
for instance, develops the thesis that all Near-Eastern and European religions evolve from a Zoroastrian original. His lengthy
treatment of Christianity begins with a sentence thrust from
the intellectual center of the French Revolution: "Understanding the mysteries of the believers in that Mithraic cult known
under the name of the Christian religion depends everywhere
on explicating the sacred allegories of the Zoroastrian religion
adopted by the Jews in their cosmogony."[71] Dupuis's country-
man Paul-Henri Mallet, in his influential *Northern Antiquities*
traced the Scandinavians back to Persia, suggesting that cor-
respondences between northern and eastern mythologies were

the result of their migration. Jean Sylvain Bailly extended their similarity to encompass all the Celtic nations, and with charming pertinacity he was seconded by Charles Vallancey, who insisted that the Irish were originally Persian and that the Druid priests were actually Magi. Thomas Maurice, convinced by Vallancey, added that the Brahmans also derived from the Magi, a thesis elaborated by Faber. Asia thus repeats accepted theory in Demogorgon's cave when she asserts that, as civilization developed, "the Celt knew the Indian" (II. iv. 94). Furthermore, as Zoroaster educated the Greek sages, his doctrines pervaded their theology and philosophy, and, as George Sale observed, a similar imprint was manifested in Mohammedan practice and doctrine. If one adds to this catalog the generally accepted notion that—in the words of Sir William Drummond—"the ancient Indians, Persians, Tartars, and Chinese, had at one period a common system of law, religion, and science," the Persian derivation of every major religion of Asia and Europe can be assumed. Dupuis lists twenty-four cultures in both hemispheres believing in the two antithetical principles that distinguish Zoroastrianism.[72]

Thus, Zoroastrianism was, in the dominant scholarly view of the early nineteenth century, the first religion whose doctrines confronted and attempted to resolve the most serious of ethical questions, the origin of evil; and its formulations profoundly influenced others. Because of that, whether Shelley agreed with the Persian resolution is beside the point. Like the contents of the shadow world Prometheus invokes in Act I, the Zoroastrian formulation, reiterated throughout the ancient world, is an intellectual reality of the human experience. Later religions may have refined it, but the essential antitheses remain. As Plutarch suggested in writing the major classical account of Zoroastrianism, *De Iside et Osiris*, "the great majority and wisest of men" have believed in the two principles.[73]

In representing the Zoroastrian dichotomy, Shelley takes pains to force his reader to recognize that these are two principles, not two beings. The drama turns upon our realization that Prometheus' curse has maintained Jupiter's power, and in the face-off between Prometheus and Jupiter we are shown similitude, not difference. In his renunciation of hatred, Prometheus at last succeeds in identifying himself with the good, thereby defining and extirpating evil. In the Zoroastrian formulation 12,000 years must transpire between the creation and destruction of Ahriman: 3,000 years for the separation and definition of the two principles, 3,000 years in which Ormusd holds his strength followed by an equal period in which Ahriman appears victorious, and a final 3,000 years, beginning with the birth of Zoroaster, in which the forces of good slowly conquer those of evil. Accordingly, Shelley's drama immediately reveals that Jupiter has chained Prometheus to Caucasus for "Three thousand years of sleep-unsheltered hours" (I. 12), at the end of which time Prometheus is released and Jupiter overwhelmed.[74] Jupiter, diligently earning his identification with Ahriman, is responsible for the active evil plaguing the earth, but he is only its servant: the Earth reminds the Titan that numerous gods "Have sprung . . . / From all-prolific Evil since [his] ruin" (I. 213-14). In similar terms Prometheus describes the fiends of his torment as emanating "From the all-miscreative brain of Jove" (I. 448). As the evil genii who administer Ahriman's evil will, they are active forces of the "mis-creative" power, subtler versions of the armies of Othman, who in *The Revolt of Islam* carry out the perverse parody of the seven-day creation in blood. Mercury execrates the Sphinx, "subtlest of fiends, / Who ministered to Thebes Heaven's poisoned wine— / Unnatural love and more unnatural hate" (I. 347-49). The Furies whom Mercury thus drives back ask for mercy, exclaiming, "We die with our desire" (I. 351). The phrase is not loose vernacular, but a precise rendering of the inner dynamic of a life force turned back destructively upon itself. In a cancelled draft for the third act, Shelley described Jupiter as "A sunless power, a dark yet mighty faith" (III. iv. 174), which is an exact representation of the Persian Ahriman.

But Shelley found in Anquetil du Perron a third principle, and it was the French scholar's insistence that the Zoroastrian religion contained a subsuming power that provoked learned orientalists into disputation. That power, Zurvan (Zervan in Anquetil du Perron), is now recognized as a fairly late addition to Zoroastrian doctrine, superimposing a monotheistic structure upon the original dualism. But Anquetil du Perron accepted the fusion as central, attempting in his commentary to justify the Zurvanite principle as essential to the intellectual structure of the faith. He called the principle *le Tems sans bornes*, time without end, responsible both for bringing into being the antithetical principles and for at last resolving Ormusd within himself and rejecting Ahriman. The part of *le Tems sans bornes* in Shelley's syncretic drama is assumed by the "mighty Power," Demogorgon, who, when asked by Jupiter to define himself, responds, "Eternity. Demand no direr name" (III. i. 52). Despite the injunction numerous critics have demanded that Demogorgon be named Necessity, a rubric he obligingly adopted when he appeared as the Zurvanite first principle in Peacock's *Ahrimanes*.[75]

But that semantic quarrel, which has tested the patience of generations of scholars, is of considerably less moment than the traditions surrounding Zurvan and their import for Shelley's conception. According to some commentators both Ormusd and Ahriman sprang into being simultaneously, the result of Zurvan's brooding, "How shall my power appear if there be nothing to oppose me?" Other interpreters refine this notion, probing the mental state responsible for Zurvan's sudden question. To them Ahriman came into being because Zurvan doubted his own power and his purpose. And in a profound sense Doubt is the fundamental motive force of *Prometheus Unbound*, the reason that Jupiter derives his power from Prometheus.[76]

The Zoroastrian conceptions, influencing the structure, machinery, and ideas of *Prometheus Unbound*, reinforce the ethical problems and antitheses at the drama's core. The central metaphor issues from the same source. Prometheus, the benefactor who gave fire to man, is the mythical servant of the power that the Persians worshiped as the purest symbol of divine attributes. Prometheus' identification with Zoroaster through geography and legend enforces this fundamental affinity. For, if Prometheus gave man the power by which to create civilization, Zoroaster was motivated by a similar humanistic goal. Shelley's respect for the Persian religion is one of the few serious affirmations he voices in the witty fragment, "On the Devil, and Devils," which he probably wrote in 1819:

> The Magian worship of the Sun as the creator and preserver of the world . . . is a poetical exposition of the matter of fact, before modern science had so greatly inlarged the boundaries of the sensible world, and was, next to pure Deism or a personification of all the powers whose agency we know or can conjecture, the religion of the fewest evil consequences. (*Prose*, 7:100)

Shelley is not alone in conceiving of Zoroastrianism as an early, uncontaminated natural religion. As the Wanderer in Wordsworth's *Excursion* surveys the world's faiths, he first fixes his attention and praise on the Zoroastrian. But if the mature Wordsworth, having conflated the temple of nature with an Anglican cathedral, valued Zoroastrianism chiefly as a non-idolatrous predecessor of Christianity, Shelley was free of such tendentious motives. That the religion refused images or altars and was practiced in nature without temples, except to protect the sacred fire, was widely known. Equally admirable to Shelley would have been the vegetarianism practiced by the Persians; and one even supposes him pleased to countenance what others roundly condemned, the Persian approval of incest. Zoroaster's reforms were social as well as religious, enjoining love and benevolence, concentrating on making the fabric of human society accord with the ethical purity of the divine plan. A French handbook on eastern religions thus summarizes the values of the Magian religion:

> Purity of thought, purity of speech, purity of action: such is the express recommendation of Ormusd; such will be the basis of conduct for Zoroaster's disciples. One easily senses that these principles would be fundamental in a religion all of whose efforts are directed at turning back the empire of Ahriman and the evil genii it has produced. A long life, saintly power, numerous children, great wealth,

joy, pleasure, good will: these are proclaimed for all those who submit to the faith. Abundance in all things is promised as the certain reward of regularity and virtue. This is a most common refrain in the prayers addressed to the divinity. Abundance, it is said, will come to the just man who is pure.[77]

The modern mythologist Joseph Campbell succinctly frames the appeal such a religious conception would have for a thinker like Shelley. Noting that early oriental mythologies are metaphysical, rather than ethical, in organization, Campbell emphasizes that for the Persians, "the crucial line of decision between ultimate being and non-being was ethical. In Zoroaster's new mythic view . . . the world, as it was, was corrupt—not by nature but by accident—and to be reformed by human action."[78] Central to such a humanist ethic is an emphatic belief in an individual's free will. Nothing could be farther from the inner nature of Zoroastrianism than the fatalistic astrology it replaced. R. C. Zaehner remarks the extent to which the Zoroastrian reforms concentrated on liberty of mind:

> Zoroastrianism is the religion of free will *par excellence*. Each man is faced sooner or later with making his choice between Truth and the Lie. . . . on all levels were the two principles opposed, and so [Zoroaster] came to see that the whole cosmos, both material and spiritual, was shot through with this elemental tension: over against a transcendental Good Mind stood the Evil Mind, over against the Bounteous Spirit the Evil or Destructive Spirit, over against Right-Mindedness Pride and so on; and on every level a choice had to be made, Ahura Mazdah, the Wise Lord, himself not being excepted.[79]

Prometheus, the benefactor of man, is not excepted either: he, too, must confront his ethical choice on all levels.

Shelley's description of Magism, defining "the Sun as the creator and preserver of the world," quietly assimilates Zoroastrian and Indian mythologies, as was the common practice of his time. The researches of Bryant, Maurice, and Faber among others authorize it, and Francis Wilford feels no need to discriminate between Persian and Indian traditions as he surveys Mount Caucasus.[80] Even closer to Shelley is the example of

87

Peacock, whose *Ahrimanes* is constructed on a systematic conflation of the two traditions. Ormusd is seen as combining the
qualities of Brahma and Vishnu, the creator and preserver of
the world, and Ahriman as a simple translation of the destructive power of Siva. Peacock, ignoring differences between the
religions in view of the important strengths they share, almost
certainly derived his hybrid mythology from Shelley's friend
John Frank Newton, whose vegetarianism was both radical in
its political implications and extraordinarily learned in its
sources. Newton was obviously aware that both Zoroastrian
and Indian religion enjoined a vegetable diet, but he grafted to
his amalgamation a primitive zodiacal astrology similar to those
advanced in the natural mythography flourishing among the
French revolutionary intelligentsia: the school of Bailly, Volney,
and Dupuis. Years after putting off such childish things, but
with a sustained relish for the recondite, Peacock described
Newton's curious mythology in these terms:

> He held that all diseases and all aberrations, moral and physical, had
> their origin in the use of animal foods and of fermented and spir-
> ituous liquors; that the universal adoption of a diet of roots, fruits,
> and distilled water, would restore the golden age of universal health,
> purity, and peace; that this most ancient and sublime morality was
> mystically inculcated in the most ancient Zodiac, which was that of
> Dendera; that this Zodiac was divided into two hemispheres, the
> upper hemisphere being the realm of Oromazes or the principle of
> good, the lower that of Ahrimanes or the principle of evil; that each
> of these hemispheres was again divided into two compartments, and
> that the four lines of division radiating from the centre were the
> prototype of the Christian cross. The two compartments of Oromazes
> were those of Uranus or Brahma the Creator, and of Saturn or
> Veishnu the Preserver. The two compartments of Ahrimanes were
> those of Jupiter or Seva the Destroyer, and of Apollo or Krishna
> the Restorer.

Newton's conflation of Jupiter with the destructive Ahriman
and Apollo with the restorer finds a distinctive echo in *Prometheus Unbound*. In the opening scene of Act III we witness the
overthrow of Jupiter's "all-miscreative" power, followed in the

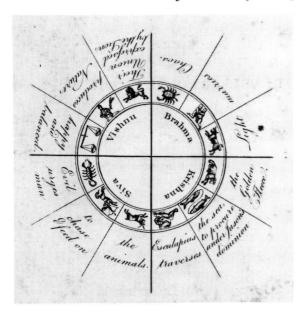

10. The zodiac. John Frank Newton, *Three Enigmas Attempted to be Explained* (London, 1821), frontispiece. *Courtesy the Library of Congress*

11. The zodiac of Dendera. Dominique Denon, *Voyage dans la Basse et la Haute Égypte* (Paris, 1802)

next scene by Apollo, who describes the fall and the subsequent restoration of peace.[81]

Still, that Shelley borrows Newton's conceptions to buttress his own structure might suggest a greater influence than in fact exists. The kind of syncretic mythology that moved Newton is esoteric and idiosyncratic. Shelley, on the other hand, engages —with an undeniably massive learning—in drawing together the central mythologies of Asiatic and European culture. His employment of Zoroastrianism as the central religious structure testifies to commonly accepted notions of both its antiquity and purity. Doubtless there were those who, because of the extent of its ancient civilization, would claim the primacy of Indian mythology. But that religion, rather than suffering rigorous persecution, had flourished, even proliferated, accompanied by excesses that were infamous. The procession at Jagger-naut, depicted with abhorrence in *Queen Mab* and imaginatively recast into the metaphorical substance of *The Triumph of Life*, was a refined model for every hideous perversion resulting from superstition, and the same ignorant spirit upheld the cruel rigidities of the caste system. In all aspects of life the intimate association of Indian state and church produced spiritual and physical tryrannies as inimical to human happiness as any vili-fied in *Queen Mab*. Shelley would not have considered himself hyperbolic in *A Philosophical View of Reform* when he asserted that "The Indians have been enslaved and cramped in the most severe and paralysing forms which were ever devised by man" (*Prose*, 7:17-18). But for him, even broader philosophical issues would have justified a Persian over an Indian model. If the Zoroastrian religion directed its energies toward the manifesta-tion of divine virtues within temporal structures, exactly the opposite was the case with Hinduism. British travelers were obsessed with the gruesome ascetism of the Indian Brahmans, detailing minutely the physical deformities they perpetrated upon themselves in tempering their souls to heavenly demands. Moreover, the Indian mythological history, which covers an immense span of time, is generally cyclical, repeating the basic creative and destructive pattern consequent upon the working relationship of Brahma and Siva. In contrast, the struggle between Ormusd and Ahriman, though couched in dire and often histrionic terms, is conceived upon a progressive model. Gradually and despite momentary setbacks, the committed adherents of virtue and benevolence win their struggle over the empire of Ahriman.[82]

But though, generally speaking, Shelley deliberately subordinates the Indian mythology to a Zoroastrian model, there is a further ancient religion that he carefully assimilates to his syncretic accretion. After the reunion of Prometheus and Asia the Earth enjoins them to journey from the Caucasus across Asia to a new home that they will find in the grove of Colonus, near the site of Plato's Academy. Their first landmark will be "Bacchic Nysa, Mænad-haunted mountain" (III. iii. 154). Nysa, another mountain in the Caucasus chain, was renowned as the birthplace of Dionysus, who with his followers traversed Asia to enter Greece by the exact route Prometheus follows. Faber depicts Dionysus as another of the many incarnations of Noah, the first to bring men into communities, to codify laws and agricultural knowledge: thus conceived, he is also the type of Prometheus. Shelley knew the extravagant history of the Bacchic journey from Nonnus's *Dionysiaca*, which he ordered shortly before leaving England.

The carefully placed allusions to Dionysus in Prometheus' journey and in Asia's descent to Demogorgon's realm invoke something more than a fertility figure to complement the regenerate earth. Beyond those traditional associations, Dionysus was also the principal deity of the Orphic theology, which, marred only by puritanical austerity, enjoined the human race to rebirth and brotherhood. Also arising in the east, it furnished Greek culture with many proto-Christian traits. Bailly and Volney both considered the Orphic cult to be imbued with Magian conceptions, Volney even going so far as to claim that all of Zoroastrianism was contained in its tenets. Both Pythagorean and Platonic systems were likewise considered compatible with the Orphic theology: Thomas Taylor, as one of his early contributions to the befuddlement of classical philosophy, translated the Orphic *Hymns*, adding a commentary that treated them as Neoplatonic documents.

There is little doubt as to the affinities of the Orphic and Mithraic mysteries. Both Dionysus and Mithra are life forces, mediating between heaven and earth, motivated by love of man and serving human society. Taylor styled the Orphic *Hymns* "the initiations of Orpheus": as the celebrant penetrated their enigmatic invocations of divine power, he was to come ever closer to realizing the oneness and harmony of the universe. An epitome of this process is exalted as a Mithraic ritual in the famous thirty-sixth discourse of Dio Chrysostom, the fable of the cosmos as a chariot drawn by four horses. The soul that attains perfect harmony is empowered by the loving Jupiter, and, undergoing a mystical marriage—the *hieros gamos* of the Orphic initiation—expands its mastery to divine proportions. *Prometheus Unbound*, as a drama of liberation and harmonious regeneration, repeats this parabolic pattern within an emphatically humane perspective.[83]

The famous Orphic *Hymn to Jupiter*, from which Peacock quotes in his notes to *The Philosophy of Melancholy*, is, in his words, a "sublime enunciation of the system of the EN TO ΠAN," of universal oneness or the One Mind.[84] The Dionysus who is the principle of fecundity energizing this universe in the *Hymns* is, like Orpheus their author, an emblem for imaginative inspiration. Shelley implicitly defines Dionysus in this role as Asia stands before the portals to Demogorgon's realm:

> Whence the oracular vapour is hurled up
> Which lonely men drink wandering in their youth,
> And call truth, virtue, love, genius, or joy;
> That maddening wine of life, whose dregs they drain
> To deep intoxication, and uplift,
> Like Mænads who cry loud, Evoe! Evoe!
> The voice which is contagion to the world.
> (II. iii. 4-10)

Such inspiration does not stand by itself in aesthetic splendor, but is based in a fundamental human capacity. Demogorgon, in one of his few affirmative statements, reads Orphic doctrine to Asia: to "Fate, Time, Occasion, Chance, and Change," he asserts, "All things are subject but eternal Love" (II. iv. 119-20). So the Orphic *Hymn to Love* affirms, in Thomas Taylor's weak translation: "thee, all Nature's various realms obey, / Who rulest alone with universal sway."[85] Asia, whose initiation in the mysteries is already far advanced, replies to Demogorgon's statement: "my heart gave / The response thou hast given" (II. iv. 121-22).

Shelley comprehends within his fourth act both this Orphic principle and the majestic confluence of earthly and heavenly harmonies that the *Hymns* inculcate. And as the Orphic doctrine discovered by Asia in the depths of the earth is seen to govern the motions of the stars, a like transposition accompanies the fulfillment of Prometheus' long-frustrated aspirations. Within the Greek pantheon Orphic thought practiced much the same sort of syncretic formulation that Shelley applies to all major religions. The Orphic Jupiter, whom Peacock characterizes as the One Mind, is identical, in the elaboration of Proclus upon Plato, with Cronus or Saturn, and both are symbolized by that Sun venerated by the Zoroastrians and served by Prometheus. Faber, after rehearsing these mythic figures as identifications of the One Mind or *Nous*, goes on to recall that Cronus and Prometheus are themselves assimilated in the twelfth *Orphic Hymn*. His associational logic may seem stretched for the sake of argument, but his implicit conclusion, derived from mythological syncretism, is in accord with those Earl Wasserman distilled from the study of Shelley's idealist philosophy: Prometheus represents the One Mind, beyond time and comprehending the finite mental faculties of individual men.[86] To contemplate the mythological analogies, however, is to discern an extraordinary, apparently intentional irony that remains hidden from a precise metaphysical analysis. If Prometheus is the One Mind, he is also the Orphic Jupiter who, in claiming his rightful station, casts out the cruel and reductive usurper who has ruled human destinies for thirty centuries.

Disarming fears that are self-created, Prometheus quells a

universal discord to reunite with his consort and with her to preside as symbolic extensions of a fully realized golden age of humanity. His goal has been an exact complement to that of his creator, who, sifting through the strife of "contending creeds," traces their common harmonies in human life. Shelley, too, if only in the imagination, bestows an elemental flame upon the single family of man.

3

SKEPTICAL IDEALISM AND THE PHYSICS
OF PARADISE

For the paternal mind sowed Symbols in Souls;
Replenishing the Soul with profound Love.

He who knows himself, knows all things in himself.
—Chaldean Oracles of Zoroaster

Shelley's learned fusion of occidental and oriental mythic structures in *Prometheus Unbound* constitutes a complex extrapolation of the marriage of west and east symbolized by Prometheus and Asia. To the extent that they attain an archetypal stature, they contain multitudes, who are revealed in the receding vortices of mythic allusion. Yet, however much a universality composed solely of such traditional elaborations might satisfy a Peacock, to Shelley it would appear inadequate to the charge he had set himself. The strength of his own philosophical inclinations, not to mention the pressure of his irreligion, contributes to his gathering further ramifications to his drama. If all religions are essentially a single faith, it is necessary, in order to avoid mere ceremony on the one hand or mere superstition on the other, to distill from the myth its relevance to an actual human condition. Shelley refuses the alternate options his generation posed: either the English tendency to subordinate foreign mythic structures to a single Christian orthodoxy, or that of the French to see them as imaginative flights unfortunately divorced from the natural laws they once preserved

95

mnemonically. Both efforts deny the spiritual realities of human life, the first by limiting them to a single dogmatic standard, the second by reducing them to materiality. Once again, Shelley's endeavor is to unite rather than fragment: in its philosophical and psychological dimensions *Prometheus Unbound* does not deny the integrity of the mind nor of the world, but asserts that only in their balanced interaction can there be either mental health or truth. The skeptical model from which these attitudes take form is enunciated by Prometheus in describing the cave in which he and Asia will be united:

> And hither come, sped on the charméd winds,
> . . . .
> The echoes of the human world . . .
> . . . .
> And lovely apparitions, dim at first,
> Then radiant—as the mind, arising bright
> From the embrace of beauty (whence the forms
> Of which these are the phantoms) casts on them
> The gathered rays which are reality—
> Shall visit us. . . .
>
> (III. iii. 40, 44, 49-54)

That the phenomenal world assumes meaning through the organizational structures of the mind has a corollary: by changing the mental structures, one can alter the world. On Prometheus' shift of attitude, not only the drama, but the entire cosmos turns.

Shelley's insistence on the power of mind to define reality conditions his intense preoccupation with what the preface terms "imagery . . . drawn from the operations of the human mind." For all the learned contexts assumed by *Prometheus Unbound*, on the simplest and most profound level it constitutes the anatomy of a single mind whose faculties are projected into separate characters and whose subtle intercombinations form the substance of dramatic conflict and resolution. Prometheus has held a three-thousand year empire over not the snows and bleak crags of Caucasus, but the psychological landscape of "torture and solitude, / Scorn and despair" (I. 14-15). He claims that throughout this period he has preserved a throne visited not by emissaries, but by "The ghastly people of the realm of dream" (I. 37). And as he attempts to communicate with the comforting Earth, he strains to comprehend his links with an internal rather than external phenomenon: "Obscurely through my brain, like shadows dim, / Sweep awful thoughts, rapid and thick" (I. 146-47). The shadow world he at last invokes is a mental universe, containing both those things that have physically existed as well as "Dreams and the light imaginings of men, / And all that faith creates, or love desires—/ Terrible, strange, sublime and beauteous shapes" (I. 200-02). In other words, he has attained a world of intellectual symbols, reflecting the nuances with which the human mind endeavors to establish coherence and dominion in the fluid consonance of time and space.

Prometheus' encounter with the Phantasm of Jupiter is actually only an elaboration of the instantaneous mental encounter at the beginning of the drama, which, producing so sudden a revocation of the long-treasured curse, must surprise even its author. As if by chance, in contemplating the moment when destiny will give him victory, he voices a simile epitomizing the conceptual framework that has bound his thought. He celebrates the

> . . . wingless, crawling hours, one among whom—
> As some dark priest hales the reluctant victim—
> Shall drag thee, cruel King, to kiss the blood
> From these pale feet, which then might trample thee
> If they disdained not such a prostrate slave.
> Disdain? Ah no! I pity thee.
>
> (I. 48-53)

Vindictive, self-righteous, gaining encouragement from the dramatization of his own martyrdom, Prometheus summons to his aid the very idolatry and superstition that in the figure of Jupiter he has so long withstood. The word "disdain"— implying pride, elitism, sanctimoniousness, moral rigidity, denial of community—tolls Prometheus back from his fantasies

to his sole self. Disdain is the easy mask of self-delusion, asserting moral superiority and creating scapegoats, martyrs, pros-
trate slaves. Prometheus' intuitive stumble over the roughness
of his ethical ground ends the stalemate cherished for centuries
as a service to man, propelling the suddenly awakened hero
into self-analysis.

The result of that inner probing is the series of projected
conflicts that comprise the first act. To set the curse within an
objective framework is to discern not only its ethical inadequacies but its affinity to the set of mental attitudes that constitute Jupiter. Such a revelation tempts one to succumb to the
newly ascertained and distrusted affinity, to define a suscepti-
bility to moral weakness as a propensity, to negate the passion
for justice in the recognition that the motives supporting it are
flawed. Mercury represents Prometheus' immediate impulse,
upon revoking his curse, to surrender as well the entire rationale
for his resistance.[1] Instead, the Titan enforces his resolve by
subordinating the question of imperfect means to his vision of
a perfect end. So limited, if firm, a resolution can quiet his urge
to capitulate, but offers no grounds by which to dispel his
doubts about its achievement. The Furies who arise to plague
Prometheus once he has defeated the Mercury within "are the
ministers of pain, and fear, / And disappointment, and mis-
trust, and hate, / And clinging crime" (I. 452-54), the personifications of his doubt, preying on his vulnerable honesty
(I. 456-57), insinuating that evil is beyond human control, that
corruption is intrinsic to the nature of the universe:

> The good want power, but to weep barren tears;
> The powerful goodness want: worse need for them;
> The wise want love, and those who love want wisdom;
> And all best things are thus confused to ill.
>   (I. 625-28)

Mental projections, the Furies depict a frightening universe of
oxymorons, self-negating and amoral, which Prometheus cannot deny but only compassionate. Not realizing that the assertion of pity is itself a contradiction of the Furies' vision, that it

alone is sufficient to force their retirement, Prometheus repeats the despairing refrain of his imprisonment, then proceeds to explicate his condition.

> Ah woe! Alas! pain, pain ever, forever!
> I close my tearless eyes, but see more clear
> Thy works within my woe-illumèd mind,
> Thou subtle Tyrant!
>
> (I. 635-38)

Against the specter of good intentions confounded to hellish ends, Prometheus can pit only the constancy of such intentions in the human mind. The spirits that arise with the Furies' departure confirm the human urge to love in its many guises. Unconsciously, Prometheus has come to a resolution his intellect cannot articulate. Surveying the mental journey he has traversed during the act and the mental landscape yet lying before him, he finds his only satisfaction in the resolute honesty with which he has confronted the terms of his world. A tenuous stability accompanies his achievement of this limbo of honest intellect:

> There is no agony and no solace left;
> Earth can console, Heaven can torment no more.
>
> (I. 819-20)

The titanic figure who has thus dominated the stage of an irresolute first act is an embodied intellect divorced from its natural supports and turned within to seek rational truths. It finds instead paradoxes, oxymorons, enigmas, which resist its utmost energies. Because the isolated intellect can separate and analyze, it distinguishes the parts of a universal perspective without being able to resolve them into a whole. Prometheus in his self-analysis boldly misses the point. The revocation of the curse has established new conditions, but he is still fettered to the terms of the old. Yet, while intellect troubles itself into an impasse, intuition and feeling are quietly revitalized. In the second act we repeat the basic movement of the first with a new mental framework as focus. Asia represents the emotive faculties of the mind, its sensibility long divorced from that sense—the intellectual faculties—which Prometheus embodies.

Asia's progress, if basically equivalent to Prometheus', is different in kind. Where Prometheus moves by quick logical syllogisms, intensely preoccupied with rational premises and implications, Asia follows her intuitions: "I feel, I see . . ." (II. i. 27), "I feel, I know it" (II. iv. 31).[2] Consequently, the second act, though in no way as rich as the first in subtle ironies and balances—their appeal, after all, is to intellectual analysis —is far more difficult to comprehend. The journey of Asia and Panthea results from the same compelling echoes issuing from three different dreams: the first, narrated by Panthea, is reinterpreted by Asia, then interrupted by Panthea's account of a second dream, the interpretation of which prompts Asia's remembrance of her own corroborative dream. So involved and interwoven a progression leads the characters farther and farther into the unconscious, with the reverberations intensifying in the process. The dream world is like Panthea's eyes into which Asia searches: "dark, far, measureless; / Orb within orb, and line through line inwoven" (II. i. 116-17). The echoes draw Asia and Panthea down into the voluptuous natural world of fauns, contrasting with the bleak physical properties of the earth the intellect invokes in Act I. And beyond that close, dark fecundity of Pan's dominion they force themselves to continue: down into the volcanic earth that embodies the life force in greater concentration and finally to the seat of Power itself, Demogorgon. The great confrontation scene that ensues is essentially one of self-communion, in which Asia is forced beyond personalities to identify the principles motivating them. The constituent parts of "the living world" (II. iv. 9) she has passed through are not natural objects, nor even their mythic extensions—fauns, satyrs, Pan—but "thought, passion, reason, will, / Imagination" (II. iv. 10-11). Separating good from evil, she defines the ethical duality in mental terms: intellectual beauty (II. iv. 12-18) and self-torture (II. iv. 19-28). The latter she would hope to eradicate by localizing it in a transcendent power: "a world pining in pain / Asks but his name: curses

shall drag him down" (II. iv. 29-30). But like her male counterpart, Asia is in ironic error: curses have only given power to
Jupiter. Demogorgon, refusing to identify an "other" for Asia
to vilify, forces her back on the self, and the culmination of her
great monologue is to absolve Jupiter from absolute responsibility. He, too, has been ruled: "All spirits are enslaved which
serve things evil" (II. iv. 110). In this comprehension Asia has
achieved the resolution to her questions. Not rationally articulated, it is nonetheless responsible for the sudden clarity in
which her catechism progresses. When Demogorgon expresses
his one deep truth, more striking from its singularity, that to
mutability "All things are subject but eternal Love" (II. iv. 120),
Asia's response is internalized:

> So much I asked before, and my heart gave
> The response thou hast given; and of such truths
> Each to himself must be the oracle.
> One more demand; and do thou answer me
> As my own soul would answer, did it know
> That which I ask.
>
> (II. iv. 121-26)

She asks, of course, when the hour of Prometheus' release will
arrive, thus producing it. Demogorgon is motivating force: he
answers "As [Asia's] own soul would answer," because he is
the oracular inspiration of her soul, with which Asia has established a perfect communication. Her interior journey has been
to the source, and she returns reborn "to a diviner day" (II. v.
103) as a resplendent Venus.

From the heights of an intellectual Caucasus to the profound
darkness of an intuitive Cashmir, from essential fire—Lucifer—
to elemental water—Venus—commonalty reigns. The visionary marriage of Prometheus and Asia at the end of Act II fulfills
the dream union of the act's beginning, which has led Asia into
the fecund womb of earth to be reborn. From this visionary
intercourse and conception Demogorgon comes to life, not as
the child confidently expected by Jupiter and Thetis, but as the
issue of Prometheus and Asia: a potential now informed and
empowered. In other words, the motive force Asia has tapped

stirs the Promethean intellect from its passive limbo into willed reformation. Through his imagery Shelley returns us to the tensions of the opening act. Jupiter establishes his similitude with the unregenerate Prometheus just as early in the first act the Titan's soliloquy was uttered in Jupiter's voice. The soul of man remains unrepressed, to Jupiter's anger,

> . . . though my curses through the pendulous air,
> Like snow on herbless peaks, fall flake by flake,
> And cling to it; though under my wrath's night
> It climbs the crags of life, step after step,
> Which wound it, as ice wounds unsandalled feet.
>
> (III. i. 11-15)

The images are not merely those of Prometheus' imprisonment. The five lines incidentally mix what were conceived as disparate at the beginning of the drama but which continuing discovery has shown to be mutually implicated: Prometheus' curse and Jupiter's torture. Apollo, in the traditional Greek role of messenger reporting Jupiter's fall, opens the second scene with a similar emphasis of imagery. He compares Jupiter's fall to that of an eagle on Caucasus overwhelmed by a raging storm. The eagle is, of course, Jupiter's emblem, but the Caucasus is Prometheus' domain. The eagle is assimilated to the storm that was its element, and Prometheus unchained. Thus have "All things . . . put their evil nature off" (III. iv. 77), defined in the catalog of the Spirit of the Hour as creations of the self: "hate, disdain, or fear, / Self-love or self-contempt" (III. iv. 133-34). No longer are souls "self-consumed" (III. iv. 146); no longer does "the heart deny the *yes* it breathes" (III. iv. 150). The reformed mind has created a new heaven and new earth.

The rational emphasis of Acts I and III centers on the relationship of Prometheus, the Earth, and Jupiter. As humanity's mythic representative Prometheus, in cursing Jupiter, has ironically instituted Jupiter's power and has cursed the earth on which man lives. Acts II and IV center on Asia (or her reflections) and Demogorgon, suggesting that the wisdom of the

102

heart, once impassioned, subsumes intellectual analysis within a harmonious and progressive vision. As Prometheus has identified the Jupiter within himself, so Asia must discover that Demogorgon abides within in order to empower the Titan to purge the god. Shelley has set in a linear, dramatic framework what is, in fact, an instantaneous moment of inspiration, irradiating the mind and energizing the will. One must, of course, acknowledge that something else occurs in this instant of mental revelation, the regeneration of the entire earth.

That the magnificent cosmic celebration of the fourth act is the logical and necessary result of the psychological readjustments of the preceding scenes is the inductive leap Shelley's strategy forces his readers to contemplate. So sudden a shift from psychological microcosm to universal macrocosm demands that we return to the early acts to discover a substantial justification for this radical enlargement of perspective. The justification relies on a further extensive context of the drama, which initially might seem contradictory to the philosophical idealism that slowly gathers from the psychic anatomy, that of scientific law. But Shelley's genius in this drama is to resolve apparent oppositions into congruence, even on the most basic level. This is no ploy of sophistry, but a deeply held commitment to the oneness of human experience. It is what allowed Shelley, to some minds far removed from the world of common sense, to be the last poet in English to pervade his writing with the solidity of scientific truth.

I

At no time, either in his multiplication of religious contexts or in his concern with psychological nuance, does Shelley deny that man inhabits a world bounded by natural law. Indeed, far from concealing the operations of nature within the trappings of ancient mythology, he demands emphatically that we recognize the integrity of both. But insofar as natural law appears in conflict with mental reality, a reader is forced to question his own ways of perceiving. Fact is merely fact, a bedrock not an edifice. The errors of the play—and of the world—arise from mistaken notions of fact. Jupiter, it is clear enough, is not a fact, but a woefully misconceived interpretation. As Blake expresses the fundamental truth of Romantic philosophical idealism, "The Eye altering alters all" (*The Mental Traveller*, l. 62). The revolution that reunites Prometheus and Asia transforms their vision, and ours.

Among the "foul shapes . . . / Which, under many a name and many a form, / . . . Were Jupiter, the tyrant of the world" (III. iv. 180, 181, 183), was a conception of natural law as a prison. The Earth refuses to repeat Prometheus' curse, "lest Heaven's fell King / Should hear, and link me to some wheel of pain / More torturing than the one whereon I roll" (I. 140-42). The Earth conceives of her cosmic orbit as tyrannically ordained by a deterministic natural principle; caught in the same cosmic prison are "those million worlds which burn and roll / Around us" (I. 163-64), with no freedom and no peace. Mercury shares essentially the same astigmatism: the stars can only "measure and divide the weary years / From which there is no refuge" (I. 363-64). The world is thus conceived to be cyclical, its repetitions as inevitable as the tyrannical principle that enforces them. In such cycles there must be impulses to fertility as well as to destructiveness: Prometheus is, in the Earth's view of history, a fertility figure whose sacrifice is the logical corollary of his generative birth. Prometheus conceives himself in slightly different guise: he is imprisoned; one day he will be released. His verbal patterns are passive, which is why he hangs upon his destiny for thirty centuries, numbering the "sleep-unsheltered hours" (I. 12), the "wingless, crawling hours" (I. 48). In the second act, Asia similarly waits for the destined hour of promise, and the third act opens upon Jupiter's expectations for total mastery. In such a suspension the Earth stands upon her hopeless natural religion, and Prometheus, Asia, and Jupiter upon their transcendental and deterministic one: life is conceived as durance, Jupiter's "faithless faith" (III. iii. 130). All of nature is manacled by "the links of the great chain of things" (II. iv. 20), Shelley's ironic epitome of the *ancien régime*.

Jupiter, like many critics, conceives of Demogorgon as Necessity: he gets his just and logical deserts. His bluster conceals his passive subservience to a deterministic conception, and he is overwhelmed and destroyed by his own mind. Prometheus' curse has similarly activated a determinism that gives Jupiter wholesale power over human life. Determinism, however, exists only if it is conceived to exist. Shelley makes this emphatic in the propelling metaphorical structure of the second act. From the dreams of Panthea and Asia arise echoes, which command that they follow. The two are said to be drawn "By Demogorgon's mighty law" (II. ii. 43), which

> . . . wakes the destined: soft emotion
> Attracts, impels them. Those who saw
> Say from the breathing earth behind
> There steams a plume-uplifting wind
> Which drives them on their path, while they
> Believe their own swift wings and feet
> The sweet desires within obey;
> And so they float upon their way,
> Until, still sweet but loud and strong,
> The storm of sound is driven along. . .
> (II. ii. 50-59)

This chorus is remarkably, even wonderfully ambiguous, in time values (the "saw" of l. 51) as in motive force. Asia and Panthea are attracted and impelled, drawn and pushed. From one perspective a cloud is driving them, but in the ensuing scene, as they reach the cave to which "the sound has borne" (II. iii. 1) them, Panthea and Asia discover "the oracular vapour" (II. iii. 4) before them. By the end of the act the stream of sound has become a great river on which Asia's soul floats "Without a course, without a star, / But by the instinct of sweet music driven" (II. v. 89-90). And as she moves into her visionary paradise, all around her violate the apparent absoluteness of natural law to "walk upon the sea and chant melodiously" (II. v. 110). The act thus ends by returning us to the music of its beginning, as the love duet replicates the dream. The echoes of love conveyed by dreams have become reality through the intensity of Asia's desire. The metaphor for that desire, a stream of sound, cannot be localized. It is neither wholly external, nor wholly internal. It derives from Prometheus, from Demogorgon, from Asia herself. The complexity of this image pattern is meant to transcend logic by confounding the fragmenting discriminations that support it. "Demogorgon's mighty law" is desire, a quickening force within, which in the musical flood of the fourth act drives the stars as well.[3]

Corresponding to the conceptual leap from mental microcosm to universal macrocosm, the stream of sound compelling the second act is in the fourth transformed metaphorically into an electromagnetic field. In the final scene of Act III Asia is identified as its source. The "delicate spirit / That guides the earth through heaven" (III. iv. 6-7) enters in the form of atmospheric electricity, and Panthea recalls that before Jupiter assumed power the spirit had attended Asia in order "to drink the liquid light / Out of her eyes" (III. iv. 17-18). Similarly, at the beginning of the second act Panthea had interpreted the radiant light of her dream as Prometheus' love which "Steamed forth like vaporous fire" (II. i. 75). These terms—"liquid light," "vaporous fire,"—are synonyms, as Shelley recasts the myth, for the substance Prometheus gave to man—that ether which was considered the basic fluid of the universe by Shelley's most ancient as well as most contemporary sources of philosophy. The Stoics defined ether as intellectual fire; to the Platonists it was the vehicle for soul; in ancient Indian science it was a fifth element called *akass*, "the great principle of vitality and bond of all existence."[4]

Bishop Berkeley observes that the "pure invisible fire or æther doth permeate all bodies, even the hardest and most solid, as the diamond."[5] Thus the "spirit . . . darted like a beam from" the earth, "penetrates" the moon's "frozen frame" (IV. 327-28) and is, in turn, restored to the earth: "It interpenetrates my granite mass" (IV. 370). Berkeley's summary definition of ether helps to clarify its role in Shelley's drama:

This æther or pure invisible fire, the most subtle and elastic of all bodies, seems to pervade and expand itself throughout the whole universe. If air be the immediate agent or instrument in natural things, it is the pure invisible fire that is the first natural mover or spring from whence the air derives its power. This mighty agent is everywhere at hand, ready to break forth into action, if not restrained and governed with the greatest wisdom. Being always restless and in motion, it actuates and enlivens the whole visible mass, is equally fitted to produce and to destroy, distinguishes the various stages of nature, and keeps up the perpetual round of generations and corruptions, pregnant with forms which it constantly sends forth and resorbs. So quick in its motions, so subtle and penetrating in its nature, so extensive in its effects, it seemeth no other than the vegetative soul or vital spirit of the world.[6]

The love duet of the earth and moon—in mythological terms celebrating the incestuous union of Prometheus' children, Deucalion and Isis—hymns a bursting forth of the "mighty agent" in volcanic sexuality:

> Ha! ha! the caverns of my hollow mountains,
> My cloven fire-crags, sound-exulting fountains,
> Laugh with a vast and inextinguishable laughter.
>
> (IV. 332-34)

The earth is Danaë-like, receiving the impregnating influences of the ether emanating from all the bodies of the universe— "All suns and constellations shower / On thee a light, a life, a power" (IV. 440-41)—and passing them on to the moon.[7] This cosmic sexual union is imaged in terms of lightning. Upon the dead moon "love / Bursts in like light on caves cloven by the thunderball" (IV. 354-55). And the earth's suddenly reawakened force has arisen "like a storm, bursting its cloudy prison / With thunder" (IV. 376-77). The turbulent energy unleashed by the agent of ethereal fire is universally galvanic. The cosmos is charged with an electrical force of overwhelming power, emanating from what Berkeley calls the "vegetative soul or vital spirit of the world," what Peacock had termed "the principle of vegetative life," and what Shelley in the fourth act defines as "the Spirit of Might / Which drives round the stars in their fiery flight" (IV. 148-49), Demogorgon.

With a compressed power as remarkable as his fusion of mythologies, Shelley envelops his fourth act in a syncretic physics, which is both traditional and audaciously experimental. It was not until 1820, the year in which *Prometheus Unbound* was published, that Hans Christian Oersted proved a connection between electricity and magnetism, and the two were not actually systematically conflated until Einstein's paper on relativity in 1905. But the link between ether and electricity was well established—indeed, pursued with a religious fervor —in the eighteenth century. Experiments and treatises drawing connections followed one another with a prodigious intensity. The vital spirit was the essence alike of the galvanism by which Victor Frankenstein—"the modern Prometheus"—infused the Adam of his miscreation with life, and of planetary motion. So universal a force had political implications as well—radical, secular, democratic—and Shelley was not the first to seize them. Ether is another tool that the antiestablishmentarian Volney wields in toppling monarchs and priests from the eminences of power.

> The more I consider what the ancients understood by *ether*, and *spirit*, and what the Indians call *akache*, the stronger do I find the analogy between it and electrical fluid. A luminous fluid, principle of warmth and motion, pervading the universe, forming the matter of the stars, having small round particles, which insinuate themselves in bodies, and fill them by dilating itself, be their extent what it will, what can more strongly resemble electricity?[8]

The poet who rewrote Volney in his two early epics might be expected to know this passage. But it is also likely that he knew another, which adds several elements missing from Volney's rhapsody, establishes the ethereal power in that "molten magma, the obscure and terrible volcanic agent in the depths of the earth" (G. M. Matthews' description of Demogorgon), and relates the power to the operations of the mind.[9] It appears in an essay by George Dyer, who elsewhere shows himself to be a shrewd follower of Humean skepticism, and was published by Leigh Hunt in his short-lived *Reflector*.

> . . . I see nothing absurd in supposing that Genius is the effect of some electrical principle. The electric matter, that great fifth element, affects all nature; it glitters in the meteor, flashes in the lightning, rolls in the thunder, and in the bowels of the earth excites all those mighty commotions which shake and overturn vast districts: it is well known, too, that it resides in the different parts of the human body, and has a mighty influence over it. Mr. Brydone, in the first volume of his Travels, gives several remarkable instances of the power of electricity on the human body; and it might, perhaps, be employed in accounting for some of the phœnomena of the human mind. Mirabeau, in that chapter of his Système de la Nature in which he endeavors to show that our intellectual faculties are ultimately to be traced to sensation, excepts no mental operation from this role.[10]

Dyer's synoptic argument, impressive though it may be for its unity, at the same time in its glance at French materialism frames the imperative question that underlies both Shelley's summoning of physical law to buttress his dramatic structure and the heritage of commentary that has accrued as a result. If one conflates ether, electricity, magnetism, universal gravitation, linking them all to the operations of the mind, do they constitute Necessity? The answer depends on how one defines the term. Indeed, the entire vision of *Prometheus Unbound* turns on the question of definition. Demogorgon has not created a rudimentary nuclear reactor by which he generates a super-abundance of energy. The imaginative structure of Act IV is predicated not on a new force in the universe, but on a new vision of universal forces. The stars of Act IV are unchanged from those Mercury saw measuring and dividing the weary years in Act I, yet now they dance in a universal gala. The earth holds the same course through the heavens execrated as "a wheel of pain" in Act I, yet now it is conceived as a circle of perfection. And the humanity that was burdened with hatreds in Act I now composes the "intertranspicuous" spheres (IV. 246) all in perfect harmony within the Earth's larger sphere.

What is absent is Jupiter, and Jupiter is a mode of perception.

The universe of the first act is a tyranny; that of the last act is a creative anarchy. The difference is psychological, both initially in viewpoint and ultimately in how such a viewpoint determines the fruits of life. If Necessity is an external force, impelling all things to fulfill its behest, the universe is deterministic. If Necessity is internal desire—motive force—compelling all things to fulfill themselves, then free will is everywhere evidenced. The specific change that occurs in *Prometheus Unbound* is to substitute for a universe of domineering objective law a universe ubiquitous in love. The universal attractive force we know as gravitation is only the magnified power of the love we feel as persons. The perfect balance of the cosmos, resulting from millions of magnetic fields harmoniously interacting, is a model for a society compelled by its myriad individual attractions to an intensity at once perfectly free and harmonious. Demogorgon is a power always present: he alters the universe only if the mind alters. In discovering him at the center of consciousness, Asia discovers him throughout the universe. The tyranny that is at the center of Prometheus' consciousness as the drama begins is Jupiter, the opposite of the principle of attraction represented by Demogorgon. He is the principle of alienation, defining the world as composed of otherness, granting the sense of individual identity on the condition that it be assumed in the bleak and bitter isolation of a psychic Caucasus. Like Demogorgon, he is an impulse in all men, a kind of Necessity. As Magians, we have a choice.

II

Among the many artistic achievements of *Prometheus Unbound* is one of enduring, fascinating paradox: though nearly free of topical allusions and even of an ideological structure derived from political and economic theory, it is consistently a more radical document than *Queen Mab*. Not only does it plumb further into the indebtedness of social organizations to mental attitudes, but it honestly resolves difficult questions that

Shelley attempted to avoid in the first poem. No sops are tossed to lull the disquiet of timid readers. Still less is Shelley willing to imply what intellectually he would refuse to countenance. Beyond death there are no answers: to depend on blandishments of a heavenly pantheon spun from wish fulfillment is to delude oneself into contentment with worldly injustice, to play into Jupiter's hands. The poise achieved in the triumphant conclusion is qualified by its delicacy. Jupiter remains a latent potential in the rule of love even as Demogorgon threatened the rule of fear. Though humanity has willed its transcendence of mutability, it has not denied the integrity of change. The conditions of the universal order are unalterable. Man can will the end of a competitive system, but cannot dispel the contraries necessary for the achievement of harmony. The fourth act opens on the pale stars fleeing the rising sun, "As fawns flee the leopard" (IV. 7). This is no pallid and peaceable kingdom: the "tiger joy" (IV. 501) sports in the jungle. In *Prometheus Unbound* Shelley, like Margaret Fuller, has determined to accept the universe and does so triumphantly. He trades his worn juvenile fantasies for an imaginative vision that is capacious, mature, and wholly true to its own commitments.

The structure and genre of *Prometheus Unbound* complement its intellectual forces with remarkable sensitivity. The poles of this imaginative field are the spiritual history of the human race, reflected in a syncretic mythology, and the order of natural law, which human strivings must accommodate but not slavishly enshrine, the former casting on the latter "The gathered rays which are reality" (III. iii. 53) and creating the "work . . . called the Promethean" (IV. 158) through the quasi-divine infusion of spirit into materiality. Demogorgon is the life force linking the individual to the universal, that "personification of all the powers whose agency we know or can conjecture" that Shelley, in his remarks on Magians (*Prose*, 7:100), considered the goal of a pure natural religion. To abstract the poetic structure is to discover a movement of Blakean simplicity, a revolution substituting for the negation of human effort a true system of contraries in which Prometheus and

Asia unite and then commit themselves to the familial happiness of a reborn spirit of the earth.

In form *Prometheus Unbound* transcends the conventions it assumes. Its first act is an austere, ironic tragedy, broken by the protagonist's refusal to bear the tragic burden, to participate in the agony that is his destiny. The mellow, pastoral warmth of the second act is similarly overwhelmed by the intense intellection that transpires in Demogorgon's cave. The anticipated reintegration of the third act, conventional as it is to tragicomedy, is subordinated to a political anatomy twice emphasized. But the last act then daringly reinvests this realistic plateau with the mythological machinery of the first two acts, elevating it to an ecstatic intensity in which the "lyrical drama" becomes the libretto to a supramundane opera, extending the earlier "stream of sound" toward the music of the spheres. As an entity *Prometheus Unbound*, encompassing one dramatic type after another, re-creates that "lawless" form, the masque, on a sublimely ritualistic plane scarcely foreshadowed by its pompous, frivolous predecessors, a plane supported by disciplined formal balances and a synthesis of disparate traditions and cultures even as it transcends them.[11]

Prometheus Unbound, indeed, is the epitome of that literary phenomenon Angus Fletcher terms transcendental form: "any poetic structure that by design includes more than its traditionally accepted generic limits—the classical limits of the genre —would allow it to include."[12] In an important sense Shelley goes beyond the Renaissance models of composite art from which Fletcher derives his conception. *Prometheus Unbound*, by assimilating one genre after another to its expanding structure, reflects countless and even contradictory literary conventions, suspending them within its ambience as it forges a unique form no longer dependent on the generic conventions it contains. The structure dazzles less by its virtuosity than by its perfect congruence with the modes and themes of the work. Cosmologies are like genres, explanations of the foundations of a form, which a mythological system extends, amplifies, and encloses. Scientific systems manifest a similar organization. To conceive of one's purpose as subsuming the world's major mythologies and as gathering to that syncretic vision an equivalent unification of scientific knowledge demands a literary form as diverse in its energies as it is one in its genius. *Prometheus Unbound* is not merely concerned with regeneration: it embodies regeneration. Its theme is its mode. For organizational structures Shelley looks to the past—to religion, to science, to art—but his purpose is to organize the future. As Fletcher emphasizes, "both Spenser and Milton in their major works move toward the ultimate perfection of transcendental form; that is, they utter a prophetic poetry."[13] Shelley's synoptic structure, with its many disparities unified through imaginative vision, portends a politics in kind, based on the organizational structures wrought by the human mind, but liberated from the rigidities of convention into the exuberance of imaginative form.

Encyclopedic in knowledge and in structure, *Prometheus Unbound* derives its ethos from the Miltonic epic, both from *Paradise Lost*, an epic diffuse in generic reflections as in subject, and from *Paradise Regained*, which centers a single expanding consciousness within a cosmic theater, distilling from the mind's journey into its dark interior a revolutionary enlargement of vision.[14] Wordsworth epitomizes this process within the third book of *The Prelude*, offering as he does so a comparably non-Christian conception of that central power of the mind Shelley called Demogorgon:

> As if awakened, summoned, roused, constrained,
> I looked for universal things; perused
> The common countenance of earth and sky:
> Earth, nowhere unembellished by some trace
> Of that first Paradise whence man was driven;
> And sky, whose beauty and bounty are expressed
> By the proud name she bears—the name of Heaven.
> I called on both to teach me what they might;
> Or turning the mind in upon herself
> Pored, watched, expected, listened, spread my thoughts
> And spread them with a wider creeping; felt
> Incumbencies more awful, visitings

Of the Upholder of the tranquil soul,
That tolerates the indignities of Time,
And, from the centre of Eternity
All finite motions overruling, lives
In glory immutable.

(III. 108-24: 1850)

Comparable as is Wordsworth's effort, in an important sense Shelley intends to surpass such a view. If only rhetorically, Wordsworth distinguishes between external and internal planes of reality, whereas Shelley attempts on all levels to make them interpenetrating. *Prometheus Unbound* is at its most abstract level wholly a psychodrama whose achievement of formal balances mirrors a finely discriminated mental balance. And it is on this count that he could claim, in writing to Peacock, that "It is a drama, with characters & mechanism of a kind yet unattempted."[15] Had Shelley the opportunity to have known his contemporary, William Blake, who in a more traditional epic form realized the same radical ends, he might have diminished his claims. But in the context of the literature he knew—and it was a vast enough knowledge—his claim to originality is just.

The claim could be pressed on other, larger grounds. After Milton a theodicy must almost necessarily return to the question of knowledge as its locus. In *Hyperion*, for example, Keats shifts his model to a Greek myth whose resemblance to the fall of the angels had been frequently remarked by commentators. Dissociating himself from Milton's religious orthodoxy, Keats makes little effort to alter the master's interpretation. The fall is one into moral knowledge, a realization that good and evil, or pleasure and pain in Keats's customary terminology, are inextricably mixed. Thus Apollo's access of "Knowledge enormous" (III. 113) makes him not only a god, but because he inhabits a pagan universe, a tragic poet as well. His sole consolation for forced removal from the Huntian Eden he longs to retain (III. 100-03) is breadth of vision. The earth is a vale of soul-making whose principal yield is perspective. Wordsworth, who retreats from Keats's capacity to suffer, nonetheless accommodates his comic vision to an orthodox model, faithfully dismissing evil as a misunderstanding of ultimate good, finding redemption in the natural rhythms of the earth, in natural piety. Shelley is clearly much closer to Wordsworth than he is to Keats despite the superficial resemblance of his classical model. Probably much of this stems from his likeness of aim: a comic vision must predicate a congruence and harmony between human and natural realms. But the differences are more significant than the similarities in aim. To Shelley the natural order is amoral and apolitical: in a word, it is inhuman. And since reality is an imaginative construct, only the mind can determine if reality is to be harmonious or not. The problem of knowledge has no necessary connection with the cosmos: it is purely and profoundly a psychological problem, and the fall is a psychological event.[16]

Prometheus gave fire to man conceiving that it would engender both power and liberty. It provided neither. Instead, Jupiter assumed nearly total dominion and deprived man of his freedom. That is to say, man has in his hands the capacity to build a wholly fulfilling culture, but has turned the tools to contrary ends, perversely limiting himself wherever possible, choosing to be impotent. Initially, the urge is understandable as a simple reaction to mortality, to the "chance, and death, and mutability" (III. iv. 201) that are inescapable concomitants of existence. One of Jupiter's "foul shapes" is Jehovah, stern upholder of law, and, though Shelley's philosophical antinomianism is nowhere near as intensely or as extensively portrayed as is Blake's, his drama strongly implies that man has taken refuge from the responsibilities of existential freedom in the rigidities of law.

As with Blake, Shelley believes the underlying problem with knowledge to be the ease with which it can be divorced from human relevance and assume an objective integrity. Knowledge accumulates faster than it can be assimilated to humane ends: it becomes itself an end, gathering independence and the appearance of total integrity.[17] The primitive urge, documented with ideological intensity by the radical mythologists of France, to explain natural phenomena in mythic terms is a characteristic imaginative propensity, but when the myths are elevated into a separate, divine realm, Jupiter takes his throne. Shelley represents Jupiter imagistically as the fount of idolatry (III. iv. 164-76, 180-89), which is exactly that impulse to deify the objective world. He is all transcendental deities, and his principal threat is posed by a humanized divinity whom he will always crucify.

But having elevated the external natural order to a transcendental position, man finds that his conception betrays its author, driving him to curse the monster of his own creation. That curse is a seal ratifying a perpetual state of seige, in which humanity loses its fraternity and retreats into the locked prison of the self. The process is suicidal, as the Earth intimates in imaging her hatred of Jupiter as a contagion spread throughout the atmosphere. The order breaks down progressively, for individuals, surrounded by the tensions of a murderous society, respond neurotically, their mental faculties dividing, their will to act rendered impotent. Prometheus, in chains and separated from Asia, is a dramatic emblem of schizophrenia.

Ironically, the assertion of self results in the destruction of self. That is Shelley's shrewd reduction of the Zoroastrian cosmology to human proportions. Ahriman and Ormusd come into being by Zurvan's preoccupation with his glory, which is expressed as doubt. Multiplying bifurcations "measure and divide the weary years," as one's sense of the fragmented nature of one's own identity issues in a fragmenting conceptual framework. The "Tems sans bornes" is engulfed by the finite motions of time. Again and again, Prometheus invokes the "retributive hour" (I. 406): he is obsessed with "the wingless, crawling hours" (I. 48) that document his existence. Shelley's psychological acumen is remarkably modern. Jupiter is a sense of identity achieved negatively, that is to say, by continually distinguishing otherness. Time is the mental framework in which such an ego sustains its independence. All things are subject to time "but eternal Love," which is not only the assertion of community, but the tearing down of the barriers by which the ego has preserved its identity. The Hours "bear Time

116

to his tomb in eternity" (IV. 14) as the last of the relics of Jupiter's reign. Henceforth there will be not everlasting life, but life absolved from the threats of time, which is, in conceptual terms, eternity. Shelley has transformed the Zoroastrian duality into an exact model of the Freudian. Jupiter is Thanatos: the ego's fears of solitude, of destruction, result in its reliance on law, on large social units defacing the individual through conformity. The reunited Prometheus and Asia are Eros, holding what Peacock represented as "love's Promethean lamp," a fire confident in its own energies and in its capacity to be self-fulfilling in the absence of external structures.[18] Freud conceived of the duality as basic both to the psyche and society and therefore irresolvable. But Shelley sees such an argument to be only the last and slyest of Jupiter's mental forms, created by self-doubt to perpetuate self-doubt. His reliance on the sufficiency of Eros is the most radical assertion of *Prometheus Unbound*.[19]

The erotic eternity Shelley imaginatively renders in Act IV is a communitarian anarchy that trusts in the natural capacity of energy to create a fluid stability: both the framework of molecules and the course of the stars testify to this natural order of unceasing motion. The chariot of the reborn earth with its intertranspicuous spheres is the emblem for the universal process invoked on both a cosmic and microcosmic level in the duet of earth and moon and again in Demogorgon's summoning of the universal principles at the end. Imaging the dissolution of time in the harmonies of eternity, it is most fittingly, too, an emblem for the structure of the drama itself, for its creative superfluity of lyrical forms that discover congruence within the large design, for its synthesis of religious forms and myths within the sublime ritual of Prometheus' release from agony. And finally, as an emblem of man's liberation into the perspective of eternity, the changeless change of the exuberant young earth perfectly reflects the arching structure of Shelley's unsequestered form. Drama progresses on a linear plane: lyric plumbs a moment extracted from time. *Prometheus Unbound* is a drama probing causality, the difficult adjustment of minds, their subtle interactions. But it is as well a sustained lyric that celebrates the single moment in which dawn comes to the human race. It begins with Prometheus looking forward into eternity and closes with Demogorgon looking back to time, essentially the same moment.[20] This intense poise, balancing time and the timeless, is at once so assured and so delicate as to strain the bounds of credibility and of literature.

4

THE RULE OF AHRIMAN

But when retired in my cell I have studied & contemplated the various motions and actions in the world the weight of evil has confounded me—If I thought of the creation I saw an eternal chain of evil linked one to the other—from the great whale who in the sea swallows & destroys multitudes & the smaller fish that live on him also & torment him to madness—to the cat whose pleasure it is to torment her prey I saw the whole creation filled with pain—each creature seems to exist through the misery of another & death & havoc is the watchword of the animated world—And Man also—even in Athens the most civilized spot on the earth what a multitude of mean passions— envy, malice—a restless desire to depreciate all that was great and good did I see—And in the dominions of the great being I saw man [reduced?] far below the animals of the field preying on one anothers hearts; happy in the downfall of others— themselves holding on with bent necks and cruel eyes to a wretch more a slave if possible than they to his miserable pas- sions—And if I said these are the consequences of civilization & turned to the savage world I saw only ignorance unrepaid by any noble feeling—a mere animal, love of life joined to a low love of power & a fiendish love of destruction—I saw a creature drawn on by his senses & his selfish passions but untouched by aught noble or even Human—
. . . To whom then should I ascribe the creation? To two principles? Which was the uppermost?
—Mary Shelley, Discourse of Diotima from "The Fields of Fancy" (1819)

The legends associated with Prometheus and the Judaic genesis myth are remarkably similar, not only in conceiving man as molded from clay and animated with the divine spark, but also in the patriarchal prejudices that dominate both major cultures of the ancient world. Had God not created Eve from

Adam's rib, continuing umbilical fragmentations might have been avoided. By the same token, had Prometheus not created Pandora, angering the chauvinistic elders of the divine pantheon, the human race might have been spared the dowry of evils manifolded within the chest entrusted to her care. Her curiosity, like Eve's, got the better of the human race, leaving the merest thread from which to spin the future—hope. Small consolation it may be, yet Demogorgon insists that it is fully sufficient: "to hope, till Hope creates / From its own wreck the thing it contemplates" (IV. 573-74) is to create the essential structure for freedom. Demogorgon's optimistic benediction may compel us with its authentically Mozartean tonalities, but, needless to say, Shelley was familiar with dramatic models who viewed enlightenment with different eyes. The sharpest contrast is offered by Beatrice Cenci, who in a comparable final scene contemplates hope as the last and most devastating irony in the cabinet of the gods' secrets:

> Worse than despair,
> Worse than the bitterness of death, is hope:
> It is the only ill which can find place
> Upon the giddy, sharp and narrow hour
> Tottering beneath us.
> (*The Cenci*: V. iv. 97-101)

Pointedly invoked by Demogorgon and by Beatrice, hope is a key term in both *Prometheus Unbound* and *The Cenci*. It is repeatedly emphasized near the end of each act of Shelley's lyrical drama, where it is commonly wedded to the potentiality of love. Demogorgon's concluding testament is thus a coda gathering these reverberations into a final statement. In *The Cenci*, on the other hand, a similar emphasis on hope produces a markedly divergent impact. There, hope is generally ironic, as in Cenci's hopes for his sons Rocco and Cristofano in the banquet scene or in Orsino's shrewd manipulation of the illusive expectations that enforce Giacomo's impotence. Where irony recedes, hope retains its negative connotations, testifying to the uncertainties of human existence. So Beatrice wearily equivocates her Christian commitment: "You do well telling me to trust in God, / I hope I do trust in Him. In whom else / Can any trust? And yet my heart is cold" (V. iv. 87-89). The invocation of hope is concentrated in the final scenes of the tragedy, and Beatrice's stern rejection of it is as true an epitome of the term's meaning in this dramatic world as is Demogorgon's affirmation to *Prometheus Unbound*. In *The Cenci* hope is simply one of the many delusions men practice upon themselves to keep from confronting the essentially destructive nature of the world.[1]

Shelley wrote *The Cenci* between the composition of the third and fourth acts of *Prometheus Unbound,* and it would be natural enough for an echo from one work to infiltrate the other. But to end both dramas with precisely opposed injunctions suggests not unconscious transference, but deliberate transvaluation. Nor is this a singular instance. On all levels of execution—the conflicts of character, thematic preoccupations, dramatic devices, even poetic imagery—*Prometheus Unbound* and *The Cenci* continually reflect one another. And yet neither in ethics, in metaphysics, nor, indeed, in temperament do the dramas seem to accord. In brief, the universal corruption of *The Cenci* appears flatly to contradict the universal benevolence of *Prometheus Unbound.*

The subject of both dramas written by Shelley in 1819 is liberation, and they are accordingly dominated by images of imprisonment. Both depict what Shelley repeatedly describes as "the oppressor and the oppressed" locked in unrelenting enmity: Prometheus and Jupiter, Beatrice and Count Cenci. Thirty centuries have passed since Prometheus began his sentence, bound by "the links of the great chain of things" (II. iv. 20). Beatrice Cenci is likewise a Promethean victim, whom her father "pens up naked in damp cells / Where scaly reptiles crawl, and starves . . . there, / Till she will eat strange flesh" (III. i. 46-48). She has been forced to look upon her "beloved Bernardo, when the rust / Of heavy chains has gangrened his sweet limbs" (II. i. 70-71). The Palazzo Cenci is a prison almost as isolated from the commonalty of human life as the Caucasus: even its garden, the ironic *hortus conclusus* where Beatrice meets Orsino in the second scene, traps her into reliance on animal shrewdness to outwit the "sly, equivocating" (I. ii. 28) priest. To Cenci the world beyond his gates is "Loud, light, suspicious, full of eyes and ears" (II. i. 178), and he retreats with his family to his mountain stronghold, the Castle of Petrella, in the Appenines: "'Tis safely walled, and moated round about: / Its dungeons underground, and its thick towers / Never told tales" (II. i. 169-71). Again, even when Beatrice emerges from the thick towers of the castle, she remains within its battlements; and, ironically, their being opened to Savella, the Papal Legate who comes to arrest the murdered Count, introduces only a new threat. From Cenci's prison-castle, the family is removed to that of the Pope, the Castel Sant'Angelo, to await execution for the crime—thence, as Beatrice perceives in the final scene, "To be nailed down into a narrow place; / To see no more sweet sunshine; hear no more / Blithe voice of living thing" (V. iv. 51-53). In the extremity of her vision Beatrice apprehends the ultimate extension of these images: that her grave, the final prison, will be indistinguishable from her father's bed, where she will be confined and violated forever. The incessant rhythms of sexual attack are in a human realm equivalent to the daily tortures Jupiter's eagle inflicts upon Prometheus.

Both Titan and popular heroine suffer imprisonment for refusing to concede their will to another's tyranny. The "unextinguished fire" (III. i. 5) of the free soul in *Prometheus Unbound* is responsible for "hurling up insurrection" (III. i. 8) against Jupiter. Cenci's tirade in the first scene of the second act similarly focuses on conspiracy and revolution (II. i. 130-55), and his silent ally, Pope Clement VIII, "holds it of most dangerous example / In aught to weaken the paternal power, / Being, as 'twere, the shadow of his own" (II. ii. 54-56). Cenci, like Jupiter, attacks Beatrice in order to "extort concession" (IV. i. 171), to subjugate her "stubborn will . . . by its own consent" (IV. i. 10-11). Others save themselves by temporizing like Mercury, but Beatrice, as Lucretia testifies, has endured with Promethean fortitude:

Until this hour thus you have ever stood
Between us and your father's moody wrath
Like a protecting presence: your firm mind
Has been our only refuge and defence.

(II. i. 46-49)

The Promethean intellect conserves its strength until it triumphs, but Beatrice's mind is assaulted and overwhelmed.
Every objective referent is cast in doubt, and at last only by a
superhuman—some would say existential—effort of the will
does Beatrice escape her father's prediction that she would "Die
in despair, blaspheming" (IV. i. 50). Assuredly, Cenci is over-
thrown as decisively as Jupiter, and with the same megaloma-
niacal expectation of plunging the world into ruin with him,
but Beatrice is no triumphant Prometheus.[2] Indeed, as she well
realizes, her death symbolizes her father's victory, the triumph
of the spirit of Jupiter. In place of the ecstatic fulfillment of
human promise that ends *Prometheus Unbound*, Beatrice foresees a wholesale reversal of potentiality, a "wide, gray, lampless, deep, unpeopled world" where "all things then should be
. . . my father's spirit" (V. iv. 59-60). Bernardo envisions her
death as shattering the "perfect mirror of pure innocence"
(IV. iv. 130): "To see thee, Beatrice, / Who made all lovely
thou didst look upon. . . / Thee, light of life . . . dead, dark!"
(V. iv. 132-34). Similar images celebrate the climactic assertion
of harmony in *Prometheus Unbound*: "Asia, thou light of life,
/ Shadow of beauty unbeheld. . . / Henceforth we will not part"
(III. iii. 6-7, 10).

The dramatic enlargement of focus that occurs in the fifth
act of *The Cenci* implicates the Papacy, judiciary, and Roman
nobility as being among "those foul shapes. . . / Which, under
many a name and many a form, / . . . [Are] Jupiter, the tyrant
of the world" (*PU*, III. iv. 180-81, 183). The activities of Orsino
extend the parallels further. For throughout this tragedy he
performs a role equivalent to that of Mercury, the sycophantic
servant of evil: a priest of the Christian God, Orsino is a minor
bureaucrat in the clerical hierarchy, currying favor, securing

his opportunities through treachery and betrayal. Seemingly closer in dramatic function is the parallel between Savella and Demogorgon. Both appear without warning upon the stage to force dramatic catastrophes to a head; both represent a larger scale of justice than that informing the limited familial perspective of the other characters. But to pursue the parallel is to realize that below surface affinities lie the incongruities of parody. The system of justice Savella represents is arbitrary and, like all tyrannies, whimsical in its cruelties. Had Beatrice waited, after again being raped, she would have had the satisfaction of witnessing her father arrested and executed without cause. Instead, she is herself arrested and executed for doing without authority what the Pope designed. Of the manifold tragic ironies in *The Cenci* none is starker.

The relationship of Savella to Demogorgon is microcosmic of the form in which the same issues pervade these dramas. The first two acts of *Prometheus Unbound* project symbolically a rigorous self-analysis in which the Titan sifts his motives and adjusts his psychic framework to accommodate a new ethical premise. Asia's journey to the epicenter of the feeling mind similarly entails a progress in readjustment. But in the world of *The Cenci* those who preserve their integrity longest are precisely those who do not probe motives, values, implications, or assumptions, but like Camillo inhabit their small sphere of impotence with kindly self-deception. All others of any importance dominate the stage by introspective soliloquy, of which no scene before the murder of Count Cenci is free. In the midst of one of these, Orsino summarizes the course of introspection in this drama:

> . . . 'tis a trick of this same family
> To analyze their own and other minds.
> Such self-anatomy shall teach the will
> Dangerous secrets: for it tempts our powers,
> Knowing what must be thought, and may be done,
> Into the depth of darkest purposes:
> So Cenci fell into the pit.
> (II. ii. 108-14)

Here is the obverse of the anarchy celebrated in Act IV of *Prometheus Unbound*, as just an argument for the urgency of dictatorial order as Hobbes might have designed. To delve into the mind is to cast off social restraints, to retreat into onanistic gratification of the senses and into the solipsism of the isolated ego. The resulting existential void, lacking either external order or internal restraint, breeds the monomaniacal craving for power that motivates Cenci, as well as the authoritarian assertion of it by the Pope, who becomes, in Camillo's words, "A rite, a law, a custom: not a man" (V. iv. 5). The deeper that Beatrice penetrates her own values and faiths, the less firm she discovers their foundation to be; thrown upon the welter of experience, ideals of justice, benevolence, and fraternity, are swamped. Asia can accept the maxim that "The deep truth is imageless" (II. iv. 116), yet float freely on the swell of music, trusting her intuitions and the supremacy of love. But Beatrice through three acts of the tragedy likewise cannot articulate the "firm, enduring truth" (III. i. 61) she knows to be expressed in her violation: "I . . . can feign no image in my mind / Of that which has transformed me" (III. i. 108-09). Her brief seizure of madness issues from a loss of stable referents, expressible truths:

> The pavement sinks under my feet! The walls
> Spin around! I see a woman weeping there,
> And standing calm and motionless, whilst I
> Slide giddily as the world reels.
> (III. i. 9-12)

Self-analysis produces not assurances and adjustments, but abrogations: distrust of the world continually impinging on one's consciousness, a fear of persecution and its corollary, a defensive will to persecute. Orsino submits that, were he to allow Beatrice to escape his designs upon her, he would be a fool, "not less than if a panther / Were panic-stricken by the antelope's eye" (I. ii. 89-90). Ironically, the priest exactly applies Prometheus' figure for the priesthood that has perverted Christ's vision and persecuted its true adherents "As hooded ounces cling to the driven hind" (I. 609).

The furthest extension of this human nature, red in tooth and claw, Shelley elaborates in Cenci's curse of Beatrice, the utterance not of "a man, / But [of] a fiend appointed to chastise / The offenses of some unremembered world" (IV. i. 160-62).

> Earth, in the name of God, let her food be
> Poison, until she be encrusted round
> With leprous stains! Heaven, rain upon her head
> The blistering drops of the Maremma's dew,
> Till she be speckled like a toad; parch up
> Those love-enkindled lips, warp those fine limbs
> To loathéd lameness! All-beholding sun,
> Strike in thine envy those life-darting eyes
> With thine own blinding beams!
> > (IV. i. 128-36)

Beneath the Gothic excesses of this tirade is a remarkable juxtaposition: the forces Cenci calls upon are the same "Heaven and Earth. . . / And Light and Love" Asia enumerates as primal powers (II. iv. 32-33). Moreover, in executing this scene, Shelley accumulates even more striking borrowings from *Prometheus Unbound*. For Cenci's curse is an elaboration within a human perspective of the cosmic malediction repeated to Prometheus by the Phantasm of Jupiter:

> Rain then thy plagues upon me here,
> Ghastly disease and frenzying fear;
> And let alternate frost and fire
> Eat into me, and be thine ire
> Lightning, and cutting hail, and legioned forms
> Of furies, driving by upon the wounding storms.
> > (I. 266-71)

Cenci's soliloquy preceding the curse, in which he projects the ruination of his family, the destruction of his belongings, and finally his own death when God ordains it—"He will not ask it of me till the lash / Be broken in its last and deepest wound; / Until its hate be all inflicted" (IV. i. 66-68)—likewise draws upon the substance of Prometheus' curse:

Let thy malignant spirit move
Its darkness over those I love:
On me and mine I imprecate
The utmost torture of thy hate.

(I. 276-79)

Shelley's reduction of Prometheus' noble defiance to the ugly, unnatural tonalities of Cenci reveals their underlying sameness, starkly outlining the dimensions of the Titan's unwitting alliance with Jupiter. If Beatrice is portrayed as a Promethean victim, Count Cenci just as clearly fulfills the family resemblance by assuming the other Promethean role, that of egomaniac who, to preserve his own inviolability, incidentally curses his creation and thereby himself.

As Shelley insinuated that this aspect of Prometheus' endurance was indivisible from the sovereignty of Jupiter and bore the mark as well of the fallen Demiurge of Gnostic traditions, in Count Cenci he identifies a diabolism as unmitigated as it is intense:

I bear a darker deadlier gloom
Than the earth's shade, or interlunar air,
Or constellations quenched in murkiest cloud.

(II. i. 189-91)

Cenci's retreat from the "insolent light" (II. i. 180), his jealousy of it and his attempt to extinguish it in Beatrice are all hallmarks of the Persian and Manichean Ahriman. The insistence with which his curse emphasizes the grotesque and unnatural culminates in the open assumption of Ahriman's cosmic campaign:

O, multitudinous Hell, the fiends will shake
Thine arches with the laughter of their joy!
There shall be lamentation heard in Heaven
As o'er an angel fallen; and upon Earth
All good shall droop and sicken, and all things
Shall with a spirit of unnatural life
Stir and be quickened ... even as I am now.

(IV. i. 183-89)

127

In the *Boun-dehesch*, which Anquetil du Perron subtitled "Cosmogonie des Parses," Ahriman's victories on earth are accomplished with poison and pollution through such agents as serpents, toads, and scorpions.[3] The terms are commonly diabolic, but the intensity with which they inform the imagery surrounding Count Cenci, especially on his last appearance in the fourth act, suggests an attempt on Shelley's part to portray the Count psychologically as Ahriman. In that period of the Zoroastrian time scheme in which Ahriman extends his powers throughout the universe, he corrupts the entire earth, whose regeneration is possible only because the testicles of the dying great bull are conveyed to the moon, whence the armies of Ormusd re-create terrene life in their counteroffensive.[4] When Ahriman rules unopposed over the earth, it will conform exactly to Beatrice's visionary description of it as a "wide, gray, lampless, deep, unpeopled world" where all things manifest her "father's spirit" (V. iv. 59-60)—like the moon before it is reawakened in the fourth act of *Prometheus Unbound*. It is essential to Shelley's design that Cenci's power be directed against a symbol of the pure generative forces of the world. The syphilitic imagery with which both Beatrice and Count Cenci comprehend his assault lends a measure of verisimilitude to the mythic formulations Shelley draws upon: namely, the Manichean legend that the evil legions of Ahriman saw in a blazing corona above them the nude figure of a virgin whose beauty and insubstantiality at once inflamed and frustrated their passion. As a result, they ejaculated black clouds that encompassed the earth with pestilence, from which arose the unnatural forms of life into which man is now born.[5] It is as such a cloud that Beatrice, struggling to articulate the consequences of her violation, images her father's semen.

> There creeps
> A clinging, black, contaminating mist
> About me . . . 'tis substantial, heavy, thick,
> I cannot pluck it from me, for it glues
> My fingers and my limbs to one another,
> And eats into my sinews, and dissolves

My flesh to a pollution, poisoning
The subtle, pure, and inmost spirit of life!
(III. i. 16-23)

From this union—Cenci prophesies in cursing his daughter—
will be born the symbol of his victory and of her corruption, a
monster: "A hideous likeness of herself" (IV. i. 146), who will
"from its infancy / Grow, day by day, more wicked and deformed" (IV. i. 150-51).

The Count's exultation over the progeny of his rape only
moments before his own death makes explicit the most striking
of the parallels between *Prometheus Unbound* and *The Cenci*,
for it duplicates the formulation of Jupiter's scene of triumph
and defeat with equivalent irony. Jupiter, too, looks to the birth
of a monstrous projection of himself to seal his tyranny over
the earth, a progeny likewise the result of a forcible violation
imaged in terms of poison:

> ... Thetis, bright image of eternity!
> When thou didst cry, "Insufferable might!
> God! Spare me! I sustain not the quick flames,
> The penetrating presence; all my being,
> Like him whom the Numidian seps did thaw
> Into a dew with poison, is dissolved,
> Sinking through its foundations"—even then
> Two mighty spirits, mingling, made a third
> Mightier than either ...
> (III. i. 36-44)

As the ravishing of Beatrice Cenci parallels that of Thetis, so
both parody the ecstatic visionary union between Prometheus
and Asia at the end of Act II of *Prometheus Unbound*. From
that marriage, in contrast to the sterile, violent union of Jupiter
and Thetis, is born the revolutionary force that overwhelms
Jupiter's tyranny, Demogorgon. The marriage of Prometheus
and Asia symbolizes wholeness, harmony, rebirth; the vicious
rape of Beatrice at an equivalent point in the drama—between
Acts II and III—symbolizes cacophony, rapacity, the brutal conflict of individual wills to power. In the spring of 1819, as Shel-

ley composed the third act of *Prometheus Unbound,* he began his Roman researches on the Cenci legend reported in the preface to the tragedy. In other words, as he executed the luxurious banquet scene in which Jupiter celebrates his violation of Thetis, he began to formulate a far more extensive parody of the harmonious myth of the reunion of Prometheus and Asia, in which both banquet and violation are amplified. *The Cenci* is the tragedy within *Prometheus Unbound,* rendering with tragic realism the mythic relationship of Jupiter to Thetis and to the world over which he wages his tyrannical powers. In the place of harmony is division; for the ecstasy of love are substituted the passionate contortions of hate; for hope, despair; for regeneration, unending corruption: for Heaven, Hell.

I

Beyond the reflections of *Prometheus Unbound* glimmering in the dark turbulence of *The Cenci* is a shadowy context that underlies both works and illuminates their essential affinities: the *Prometheus Bound* of Aeschylus. "Contemplate me, how unjustly I suffer" (1093), Prometheus cries to his spectators as the long night of punishment begins. This final line gathers into poised irresolution the disturbing implications that have clamored more and more insistently through Aeschylus' tragedy. The question of justice posed unremittingly in *Prometheus Bound* is the source of its profound power. "No one is free except God" (50), Kratos reminds Prometheus at the beginning of the tragedy, and its subsequent episodes are conclusive in their proof of his assertion.

Except for the trace of self-pity and condescension that marks Prometheus as he prepares himself for his destiny, his stoic endurance is almost abstract in its purity. Outcast from the realm of the gods, he is nonetheless inhuman, divided by his immortality from the experiences of men. "What comfort from ephemerals?" the Oceanides ask: "Did you not see a universal pall, the weak impotence by which the blind race of men has been fettered?" (547-50). Eleven lines later, a representative of this wretched human condition is driven upon the stage to exhibit the psychic as well as physical wounds man suffers at the hands of the gods. "What land? What race?" (561) cries the afflicted Io, her name an unadorned cry of woe, as she bursts upon the stage. Her frenized but basic questions continue: "What reason, O son of Cronus, what possible reason did you have to judge me in error and yoke me to these miseries: ah, must you so oppress a poor, frantic creature with fear of the stinging madness?" (577-81). Similarly, Io's counterpart in Shelley's tragedy "enters staggering, and speaks wildly" (III. i. s.d.), uttering equivalent, unanswerable questions about the realm she has entered, the identity suddenly thrust upon her: "O, God! What thing am I?" (III. i. 38) and, in response to her incredulous mother, "Who art thou, questioner?" (III. i. 40) . . . "Who art thou?" (III. i. 56). Doubting her identity, Beatrice Cenci likewise questions the abrogation of justice symbolized in her father's assault.

> What have I done?
> Am I not innocent? Is it my crime
> That one with white hair, and imperious brow,
> Who tortured me from my forgotten years,
> As parents only dare, should call himself
> My father, yet should be! Oh, what am I?
> What name, what place, what memory shall be mine?
> What retrospects, outliving even despair?
> (III. i. 69-76)

Both women are driven into exile from the normative values of human society: if others delight in life, they crave only its cessation. "What profit is there in life for me?" Io exclaims: "it is better once for all to die than to suffer evil all one's days" (747, 750). Beatrice echoes Io's despair: "Before worse comes of it / 'Twere wise to die: it ends in that at last" (II. i. 56-57). She, too, has been visited by a "god-sent disease that wastes [her], infecting [her] with maddening stings" (*PB*, 596-98), a mental "tempest and a blighted form" (643-44).

Io's account of Zeus's infatuation with her intensifies Aeschylus' portrayal of an irrational and amoral divine power whose whimsical grip descends upon the earth without warning. Failing to seduce her in her home, Zeus ruins her father and arranges her banishment, then is forestalled in his designs by the outraged Hera, who, unable to harm her husband, vindictively disfigures Io and plagues her long wanderings.

> Finally, the oracular pronouncement that came to Inachus was distinct, clearly enjoining, commanding, him to banish me from home and country so that I would drift without ties to the farthest extremities of the earth: and if he chose not to, a fiery thunderbolt would descend from Zeus and decimate his entire race. Prevailed upon by the Loxian oracle, he drove me forth and shut his door to me, he as unwilling as I. But the force of Zeus's stricture compelled him to do it. And then immediately my mind and body were tortured out of shape, and, as you see, horned, and pricked by the gadfly's sharp pincers, with frantic step I went forth. . . . (663-76)

The apt remark of the Oceanides—"What a vicious suitor for your hand, child, you have attracted!" (740)—is true as well of Beatrice Cenci, who, as the dehumanized object of others' lusts, must rely on a mercy they never accord her.

Both Io and Beatrice discover that escaping physical lust only implicates them more deeply in a system of justice that equally dehumanizes them. Hera persecutes Io as obdurately as the Pope pursues the execution of Beatrice. Argos, Hera's agent of justice, tracks Io with "unadulterated wrath" (678), but is himself constrained by the arbitrary, inscrutable justice he serves. His death, like that plotted for Count Cenci by Clement VIII, is only an episode in Io's continuing persecution: "But suddenly an unanticipated stroke of fate took his life; yet still, frenzied by the divine scourge, I am driven from land to land" (680-82). As Beatrice envisions that her father after death will "fix / His eyes on mine, and drag me down, down, down" (V. iv. 66-67), so Io recognizes that the injustice of which she is a victim transcends the barrier between life and death—"for with his treacherous eyes he [Argos], whom earth cannot hide, is ferried from death to stalk me as I wander, wretched, on the hungry sands by the sea" (569-73). The horrified reaction of the Oceanides to Io's history is reproduced by Shelley's Oceanides, forced with

Prometheus to contend with the furies as they trace the wastes of human history, and likewise informs the conception of tragedy as ambiguous horror that Shelley propounds in his preface to *The Cenci*:

> Ah, ah: leave off, alas! Never did I think—never—that such foreign terms would come to my ears, nor that such outrages and miseries, as hard to look on as to bear, would freeze my spirit with the two-edged sword of fear. Alas, such a fate! I have shuddered to look upon the fortune of Io.
>
> (PB, 687-94)

That "two-edged" is an adjective twice used by Beatrice before her accusers is, perhaps, the least of the Aeschylean accents that fall from her lips.[6]

And yet, as much as she resembles Io in most respects, Beatrice is even devoid of a Prometheus who can offer foretaste of a future when her suffering will end. Alone, isolated, stung repeatedly by knowledge of the evil implicating her, Beatrice can at best realize an existential liberation that frees her from dependence on either past or future. But to do so, she must surrender the one consolation Prometheus had claimed to provide mortals left by his imprisonment without an intercessor before Jupiter's absolute power: "I settled blind hopes among them" (PB, 252). If in the end Beatrice can transcend Io's passionate lamentation and adopt something of a Promethean fortitude, she gains a universal perspective without the compensation of omniscience or immortality. For her, the significance of Prometheus to human life lies in his stance. His gift of hope is illusory. His gift of knowledge, even worse, is inimical to all assurances and destructive of "The subtle, pure, and inmost spirit of life."

II

Evil multiplies in *The Cenci* with such intensity that it seems self-generating. Once Beatrice falls prey to the lusts of the Count and Orsino, to the political maneuvers of the Pope and Cardinal Camillo, she is helpless to preserve her independence.

In this sense she is the exact counterpart of Io, victimized first by Zeus's infatuation and then by Hera's revenge. As Aeschylus recounts the myth, Io's long sufferings will at last issue in her transfiguration into the fertility goddess Isis, part of the slow process through which Prometheus and Zeus are to be reconciled. Human suffering yields a constrained but balanced maturity to the race. But conditional or meliorative solutions are precisely what Beatrice rejects, in her murder of her father, in her trial, and in the final poise with which she faces execution. If divine justice and human integrity are to have value, they must be absolute. Like Shelley, she cannot subscribe to compromise by "reconciling the Champion with the Oppressor of mankind." But unlike Shelley, who views her condition not only with the "restless and anatomizing casuistry" he mentions in the preface but with compassion as well, Beatrice Cenci is already compromised by her culture and her religion.

The Cenci is a Renaissance tragedy not in the literary sense so often ascribed to it, that is, a late bloom from a Jacobean vine. It is a tragedy of Renaissance Christian humanism, of a culture that thought it possible to liberate the human mind within a Christian and largely feudal structure. For Shelley, from first to last, the two are incompatible. In *Queen Mab* he depicted how the structures of state and church enclose and vitiate the spiritual energies of man, maintaining that only by surmounting them can one be free. But that formula, if an enduring truth to Shelley, ignores the complexities of the human condition, ignores not only the process of liberation he was to examine in *The Revolt of Islam* but, more importantly, both those intellectual and emotional forces of inertia acting potently to restrain so drastic a rejection and those political pressures sanctioned to subvert it. The Beatrice Cenci who pleads with the noble guests at her father's banquet speaks for her culture, calling on the assembly to affirm its ideals, to use its traditional sources of power. Her faith in these, however, is subtly reinforced by the culture itself, for outside its bounds, outside her defined role, a woman of station simply cannot exist. To free herself Beatrice could have recourse only to the brothel or convent, prisons of the flesh and spirit. Or to prison itself, the last refuge of the outcast. And it is to this point that Beatrice, as she frees her mind from its customary dependencies, inevitably tends. A Renaissance Promethean, she is manacled to her condition by her culture and can find no way to break the chains.

There is, however, the appearance of a way. If Beatrice has a tragic flaw, it is implicitly her Christianity. Ironically, where Shelley ceases to flail at religious orthodoxy, his vision is most penetrating, most devastating. For Christianity, which survived as a corporate structure by being more flexible than its competitors, supports both Cenci's power and Beatrice's seizing of the law against it. Christianity is, as Shelley's preface asserts, "in the mind of an Italian Catholic . . . interwoven with the whole fabric of life." Enveloping the entire culture, Christianity sustains its social, as well as religious, hierarchies: it is "not a rule for moral conduct," but rather a model—for the domestic tyranny of Count Cenci, for the arbitrary strictness of the Pope, for Beatrice's demand for absolute justice. Had Beatrice not been trained from childhood to weigh the comparative gradations of sins, she would have lacked authority for the casuistry by which she justifies her father's murder.[7] Had she not been imbued with Christian demonology, she would not have conceived her rape as a Satanic violation of God's *hortus conclusus.* But for that matter, without that same conception, neither would Count Cenci have seen her defiance as like that of Lucifer and placed himself in the role of the Gnostic Jehovah crucifying Christ; nor would the introspective Orsino have talked himself into trying to "flatter the dark spirit, that makes / Its empire and its prey of other hearts. . ." (II. ii. 159-60).

The abuses to which this Christianity lends itself stem from the transcendental structure of its faith, at once beyond but supporting the power of man. As an enveloping system, Christianity justifies society, frames it with coherent order, explains evil, demands accountability. To abrogate the system is not to discharge the needs it serves. Rather it is to acknowledge that there is no subsuming order into which the pervasive savagery of this Renaissance culture can be assimilated—no order at all.

From a radical vantage point Shelley portrays the dilemma and, with it, the utter breakdown of the liberal view of society. The model of a vindictive, arbitrary deity justifies a brutal society, but the society flourishes because the brutality would be unendurable—mere chaos—without the model. The pattern is worse than self-defeating: exemplified in the careers of Count Cenci and his daughter, it is suicidal. The sole triumph in this destructive milieu is individual enlightenment. Exiled from her place in society and on the threshold of death, Beatrice attains an existential limbo, where, like that of Prometheus at the end of the first act, "There is no agony and no solace left; / Earth can console, Heaven can torment no more" (I. 819-20). Without faith but with compassion, Beatrice can in the moments left her convert hell into heaven. With faith, man has converted earth into hell.

III

The Gnostic reverberations of *The Cenci* afford Shelley traditional support for the position he had asserted in *Queen Mab* and even more strongly in the *Essay on Christianity*, that the church has not merely compromised the teachings of Christ, but has reversed them.[8] With one eye on heaven and the other on the machinations of earthly power, it has converted earth into a hell in which the good is subverted, the meek destroyed, the powerful rewarded. The rights of man are denied in the name of the might of God, an infallible monolith assaulting humanity with an endlessly reductive violation of integrity. To be passive is to be sacrificed; to act is to commit evil.[9] The legend from which Shelley derives such metaphysical consequences, however, is based in a culture two centuries past when he wrote *The Cenci*. If the Holy Alliance had temporarily reenthroned the *ancien regime*, a new world could not long sustain so reactionary a structure, as *The Revolt of Islam* suggests. The question left standing by the cultural setting of *The Cenci* is the extent to which evil exists, or how evil exists, independent of hierarchies of religious and social authority. That question

136

Shelley posed himself in the two poems he wrote before and after *The Cenci—Julian and Maddalo* and *Peter Bell the Third*.[10]

Recent commentary has emphasized that *Julian and Maddalo*, once thought to be merely an autobiographical fragment curiously disrupted by the Maniac's soliloquy, is instead a finished poem whose drafts bear evidence of careful structuring and thoughtful revision. Its three-part structure—the conversation of Julian and Maddalo, the Maniac's soliloquy, and the epilogue furnishing the oblique perspective of a later time—is characteristically Shelleyan in the way its spheres shift, at times reflecting and at other times overlapping or enveloping one another. In this way the structure accurately recapitulates the dramatic confrontation of the three main speakers of the poem —Julian, Maddalo, and the Maniac—each distinct, yet in the varying lights and atmospheres of the poem's setting each complexly related to the others. The customary but facile transposition of Julian and Maddalo into Shelley and Byron, though warranted both by the facts and by the philosophical positions the two take, obscures the fictive complexity of the poem and divorces it from the author's own strivings. Julian and Maddalo stand for tendencies within Shelley himself, as within any sensitive observer of the world. Julian voices the forceful idealism of *Prometheus Unbound*, a comic vision, whereas Maddalo counters that man is too weak to alter his circumstances, which is the tragic perspective underlying the "sad reality" of *The Cenci*. G. M. Matthews observes that *Julian and Maddalo* "forms a stylistic bridge between the idealism of *Prometheus Unbound* and the realism of [*The Cenci*]."[11] Yet the bridge is more than stylistic: *Julian and Maddalo*, planned late in 1818 and written, it would seem, the following spring as Shelley was finishing the central acts of *Prometheus Unbound* and beginning his work on *The Cenci*, seems a deliberate attempt to suspend his comic and tragic visions within a single ambience, to test them for value and wisdom against that weight of experience that breaks hearts and maddens the mind.

The poem begins in a wasteland, an expanse of sand supporting "one dwarf tree and some few stakes / Broken and unrepaired" (10-11), a setting conducive to Julian's imaginative projections, but inimical to their realization. The philosophical questions that dominate the first part of the poem arise naturally, indeed inevitably, from such a nexus of potentiality and frustration. As Julian notes, they are the same questions addressed by the fallen angels beginning to explore the ethical and ontological ramifications of hell. "Vain wisdom all, and false Philosophie," admonishes Milton, but nevertheless such questions propel the skeptical mind seeking its conditional certainties.[12] Hell is a state of perpetual irresolution: and this desert that prompts Julian and Maddalo into discussion conceals perilous dangers. Abandoned by his lover, the Maniac "wandered then / About yon lonely isles of desert sand / Till he grew wild" (247-49). Where there are no boundaries, the mind easily falters beneath the burden it must assume.

The mental sand castles of Julian's idealism, built against the sublime Italian sunset, thus give way to Maddalo's metaphor for the human sublime, a towering madhouse islanding profound suffering. There, the soul, like a bell above the roil of conflicting passions, contending thoughts, frustrated desires, exerts no direction, but tolls funereally as the sun traces its career across the sky. The sunset's glory is only ironic, mimicking the soul's unrealized potentiality as it fades into night. The madhouse over which the soul presides with perfect impotence is "A windowless, deformed and dreary pile" (101), an emblem of human limitation and isolation like the barren islands Shelley cites in *Lines Written Among the Euganean Hills*. And, as in that poem of the preceding autumn, the Maniac can never escape his agony: "I met pale Pain / My shadow, which will leave me not again" (324-25).[13]

The concluding remark of Shelley's preface to *Julian and Maddalo* shifts our focus from the urbane discriminations of the friends to the *angst* of the Maniac, which is the pressing context for all philosophy: "The unconnected exclamations of his agony will perhaps be found a sufficient comment for the text of every heart." They are, indeed, "unconnected exclamations," sensible enough in their fluid development, yet wholly resisting the reader's desire for a logical elucidation of this madness. As the Maniac cannot explain why he is mad any more than why his lover forsook him, neither can Beatrice Cenci articulate the metaphysical dimensions of her rape. The violation is itself the point, suddenly and totally altering one's past relations with the world, substituting a vacuum, the profound sense of loss, of existing within negation. Were the Maniac less demanding, less sensitive—less human—he might have escaped his condition. But as "a nerve o'er which do creep / The else unfelt oppressions of this earth" (449-50), he is as susceptible to illness as to health, to blight as to nurture. Seeking perfection within a mortal realm, he inherits the customary Shelleyan doom: but even the madness that results from insupportable tensions cannot erase or resolve them.[14] His madness is a continuing process, as, locked within his mind, he contends with elemental disorder. "The dagger heals not but may rend again" (357).

What the Maniac's deranged mind gropes toward but fears to accept is that love is as destructive a passion as hate, that to open oneself to possible spurning is in effect no different than sealing oneself into prescribed and frigid forms of conduct:

> It were
> A cruel punishment for one most cruel,
> If such can love, to make that love the fuel
> Of the mind's hell; hate, scorn, remorse, despair.
> (438-41)

The lines echo Prometheus' description of his empire during imprisonment over "torture and solitude, / Scorn and despair" (I. 14-15). The Maniac attempts, as well, to achieve the Promethean release: "Here I cast away / All human passions, all revenge, all pride; / I think, speak, act no ill. . ." (501-03). But he well understands his failure to transcend his condition by willed selflessness: no matter how chastened the mind, "I do but hide / Under these words, like embers, every spark / Of that which has consumed me" (503-05). The individual wrong can be forgiven; what the madman cannot forgive is the scheme of things that allows injustice. Try as he might, he remains in Beatrice Cenci's condition, unable to free his mind from its craving for the absolute. The opening lines of his soliloquy imply the nature of his obsession:

> "Month after month," he cried, "to bear this load
> And as a jade urged by the whip and goad
> To drag life on, which like a heavy chain
> Lengthens behind with many a link of pain!"
> (300-03)

Like Prometheus in his icy solitude, like the Earth, like Mercury, the Maniac measures out time as bondage, the victim of changeless change, conscious, as Shelley put it in the *Alastor* volume, that "Nought may endure but Mutability." The failure of his love signalized the inadequacy of all dependencies, for with the acknowledgment that time changes all things came its corollary, that he was powerless to shape his life, let alone the world he must live in. In this feeling the Maniac is surely not unique: in truth, he only transposes the metaphors of the opening of *Lines Written Among the Euganean Hills*, where the mariner finds himself "Day and night, night and day, / Drifting on his dreary way" (5-6). Nothing lasts; nothing can be predicted; nothing can be controlled. The Maniac's conclusion is ironically reinforced by the report of the epilogue: that Julian for all his good intentions to reclaim the madman after all had other obligations to which he returned, that years later he has come once again to Venice to find Maddalo who has in turn wandered off to Armenia, that the madman's lady, her pride chastened, returned but again left, that the Maniac died, that the lady died.

Heraclitean fires burn in the furnaces of hell. The Maniac bemoans "the full Hell / Within me" (351-52): even "love [is] the fuel / Of the mind's hell" (440-41). The madhouse where he is content to exist is pictured as a grotesque inferno of crossed purposes, where inchoate noises are all that testify to a human society:

The Rule of Ahriman

The clap of tortured hands,
Fierce yells and howlings and lamentings keen,
And laughter where complaint had merrier been,
Moans, shrieks, and curses, and blaspheming prayers.
(215-18)

And in the world outside a storm rages, partly emblematic of the human environment it engulfs, but testifying as well that the natural world is capable of reverting from the grand harmonies of sunset to the contentious tumult of raw energies. Confronting so catastrophic a sundering of human and natural stabilities, Julian attests that "our argument was quite forgot" (520). Abstract formulations pale before the intense reality of human suffering.

But that way madness lies, too, for to see only a world of disjointed ends, frustrations, failures, is to cast oneself into the welter of passivity in which the Maniac drifts. Madness is a potentiality for both Julian and Maddalo, for the fervent idealism of the one as for the pride and abiding consciousness of limitation in the other. The twenty years of flux that intervene between the main part of the poem and its epilogue, however, do not bring madness, but rather a continuation of friendships, of commitments, of all that counts for civilized life. It has been said that Julian, in returning to England rather than remaining to try to nurse the madman back to sanity, exhibits a moral failing.[15] Perhaps, instead, he shows his wisdom: Maddalo already is present to help the madman. Julian, urged by his friendship, the beauty and art of Venice, and compassion for the human condition, considers remaining but decides against it because he is not an "unconnected man" (547). "The following morning, urged by my affairs, / I left bright Venice" (582-83)—left Venice to take up his own commitments, to pursue his obligations to a human and humane community. Whatever philosophical differences distinguish them, both Julian and Maddalo share an abiding charity. The unanswerable speculations of the beginning are subsumed within the answerable ethics of the end.

141

It is on this affirmative, though never wholly resolved, note that *Julian and Maddalo* concludes. Maddalo's daughter sums up the career of the madman and his lover—"They met—they parted" (608)—not with cynicism, but with a stoic understanding that lives and passions are not eternal. But at the same time she manifests a determined commitment to social continuities, receiving her father's old friend "kindly . . . with a manner beyond courtesy" (592-93). This is something less than a willful delusion, a pretense of stability: it is rather the active assertion of meaning, of significance, of moral order. Shelley seems to imply that this is a natural and necessary part of life. The impulse that makes Maddalo's daughter greet Julian with such kindness is akin to that which provokes even the Maniac into music:

> And those are his sweet strains which charm the weight
> From madmen's chains, and make this Hell appear
> A heaven of sacred silence, hushed to hear.
>
> (259-61)

It is akin, too, to the impulse that prompts Shelley himself, in an existence as marked with exile and journey as the lives of Julian and Maddalo, to compose poems, even ones deliberately left unfinished.

IV

Hell is a city much like Venice, much like London. The personal questions implicit in the objective philosophical and ethical dialogues of *Julian and Maddalo* are how the poetic temperament can survive hell, how it can accommodate itself to such an environment without compromise, how it can alter rather than passively support the framework within which it is doomed to exist. The Maniac, whose music calms all who hear it and who unburdens his grief in language "Such as in measure were called poetry" (542), has been deformed by the exigencies of hell. Maddalo's summary of the madman's experience ironically ascribes to him a role he has abdicated:

142

The Rule of Ahriman

> Most wretched men
> Are cradled into poetry by wrong,
> They learn in suffering what they teach in song.
> (544-46)

The voice descending from the tower to compose the inmates may soothe its own and others' griefs, but it cannot educate. Its melody brings at best a momentary interruption in the otherwise unrelieved cacophony of the asylum.

The Maniac seems the exact embodiment of what Wordsworth saw as the tendency of an excessive sensitivity:

> We poets in our youth begin in gladness;
> But thereof come in the end despondency and madness.[16]

To Shelley, Wordsworth's foresight may have saved him from madness only to allow hell to triumph in another form. His decay was worse than a failure of vision: it was a disaster for the age. That the greatest of living poets should have succumbed to diabolic wiles was both admonishment and threat to those still struggling in his wake. Shelley's elegiac lament for the "lone star" that has fallen in "To Wordsworth," the sonnet published in the *Alastor* volume, gives way in *Peter Bell the Third* to a stern and austere satire, whose ease of composition cannot belie the urgency with which Shelley examines the poet's role in hell.

The anatomy of London as hell, which comprises the brilliant third part of the satire, transposes the madhouse community of *Julian and Maddalo* into contemporary industrial society. In this world there is no rational order, no harmony of purpose and pursuit. Society is not an incorporated body, but a concatenation of individuals each clawing to get ahead of his competitors. Goals are short lived, perhaps even undefined, but no less assiduously pursued in the scramble:

> Thrusting, toiling, wailing, moiling,
> Frowning, preaching—such a riot!
> Each with never-ceasing labour,
> Whilst he thinks he cheats his neighbour,
> Cheating his own heart of quiet.
> (197-201)

143

Present participles, dangling without specific reference, mirror the inchoate strivings of this society. No single being, however honorable or pure his motives, can stand against it, for decency is merely a further aberration among many others. Ironically, Wordsworth himself provides the only comparable urban landscape during the Romantic period, though one with which Shelley would have been unacquainted: the grotesque emblem of Bartholomew Fair in Book VII of *The Prelude*:

> All out-o'-the-way, far-fetched, perverted things,
> All freaks of nature, all Promethean thoughts
> Of man; his dulness, madness, and their feats
> All jumbled together to make up
> This Parliament of Monsters....
> ....
> Oh, blank confusion! and a type not false
> Of what the mighty City is itself....
> (VII. 687-91, 695-96: 1805-06)

Wordsworth goes on to excoriate the reductive nature of all experience in this urban hell, where men are "melted and reduced / To one identity, by differences / That have no law, no meaning, and no end" (VII. 702-04: 1805-06). Under this "Oppression . . . even highest minds / Must labour" (VII. 705-06: 1805-06), admits Wordsworth, but Shelley's metaphor is more extreme. For the mind can bear the aches of oppression, but one's constitution has little natural resistance against contagious disease that decimates whole populations:

> Thus, as in a town, plague-stricken,
> Each man be he sound or no
> Must indifferently sicken.
> (247-49)

Moral contagion is the worldly equivalent of Christian damnation: "All are damned—they breathe an air / Thick, infected, joy-dispelling" (257-58). Thus pressed, the metaphor recalls the Earth's condition under the Promethean curse: "the thin air, my breath, was stained / With the contagion of a mother's hate / Breathed on her child's destroyer" (I. 177-79). Such pestilence, once it infects the system, is self-perpetuating. And at that point, this hell is not simply, as Sartre might say, other people (217-21), but also fulfills Satan's prescription: "My self am Hell," he acknowledges in a moment of profound comprehension (*Paradise Lost*, IV. 75).

Shelley's dual, and seemingly contradictory, emphasis on the illimitable contagions of society and the individual's responsibility for his own damnation reproduces exactly the condition of Prometheus in the opening act of his drama. The mental torture Prometheus endures is a hell produced when his individual will, attempting to defy the world, but impotent to change it through defiance, finds its counterpart in a world where, as the leading Fury summarizes it, "all best things are thus confused to ill" (I. 628). The implicit truth of Prometheus' condition, that he is himself responsible for this hell, is openly, if ironically, assumed in *Peter Bell the Third*. Wordsworth has sold himself to the devil in order to save himself from the uncertainties a poet experiences in struggling to reveal truth.

The third Peter Bell is the third avatar of Wordsworth, projected upon the poet's own conception of his development in such poems as *Lines Written a Few Miles Above Tintern Abbey* and *Ode: Intimations of Immortality*. The progress from innocent identification with the natural world to a realization of human limitations and inadequacies issues in a "philosophic mind" which, for all its visionary rhetoric, has essentially, in Shelley's view, defined man as naturally depraved, requiring the fear of eternal punishment in order to effect virtue on earth. Leigh Hunt's excoriation of the poem—in *The Examiner* of May 2, 1819, p. 282—as "another didactic little horror of Mr. Wordsworth's, founded on the bewitching principles of fear, bigotry, and diseased impulse" reflects the hatred of Methodist enthusiasm that barred his sympathy even for a poet like Blake. Shelley certainly would have agreed with Hunt that Wordsworth's *Peter Bell* issues from a "philosophy of violence and hopelessness" (p. 282), but his concern is much larger than Hunt's, much larger, indeed, than the poet Wordsworth himself. Shelley did not have a copy of *Peter Bell* when he wrote his satire, nor did he write under the immediate influence of Hunt's review (or that by Keats of John Hamilton Reynolds' parody of Peter Bell, published in *The Examiner* a week earlier). That the satire was written quickly does not mean that its issues had not been meditated for some time. What Hunt condemns as Methodistical is Shelley's moral concern throughout the poetry of this year, especially in the psychological torture of the first act of *Prometheus Unbound*: "The very hope of such things as Methodism is founded in hopelessness, and that too of the very worst sort,—namely, hopelessness of others and salvation for itself" (p. 282). Wordsworth is a Promethean, gifted with the creative spark, who has chained himself in self-defeating mental formulations.

In a generation of social upheaval, destructive warfare, and profound technological change, a generation whose extraordinary instability went far toward producing the compulsion for stability that marked England's Victorian empire, it was easy to blame the turmoil on divergence from settled modes of conduct. Wordsworth's agrarian conservatism, sincerely human in its loyalties, came at last to accommodate itself to the very different conservatism of modern power politics, demanding a strong and traditional government in order to preserve the basic freedoms of Europe or England because the uneducated masses could not be depended upon. Shelley often attacks this cant in his prose tracts: in *Peter Bell the Third* he focuses on its philosophical underpinnings. To conceive of natural man as depraved is to insure his depravity, and finally to insure one's own. It produces revulsion and self-righteousness, and a corresponding movement into isolation, scorn, even disdain: the Promethean pattern. Such attitudes are basic to the hell surveyed in the third part of the poem. The power of Wordsworth's attraction to the natural world might have saved the poet from this drift toward solipsism, but, at least in Shelley's mind, the drift suggested an incongruity between Wordsworth's protestations and his true condition. That power was a rhetorical facade for the impotence of a "moral eunuch":

> He touched the hem of Nature's shift,
> Felt faint—and never dared uplift
> The closest, all-concealing tunic.
>
> (314-17)

"A solemn and unsexual man" (551), Wordsworth adopts a philosophy inimical to the fertile life of society—or of poetry.

When Peter arrives in hell, he does not know it, nor does the devil who supervises affairs recognize his servant:

> Each had an upper stream of thought
> Which made all seem as it was not;
> Fitting itself to all things well.
>
> (108-10)

The state of hell begins in myopia and swiftly extends to self-delusion. What Keats described as the "egotistical sublime," Shelley sees as that extraordinary capacity for absorbing the world into the self that marks so much of Wordsworth's great poetry.[17] But Wordsworth's vaunted balance of inner and outer realities, which is a fixed goal of Shelley's as well, is easily perverted into mere self-absorption:

> All things that Peter saw and felt
> Had a peculiar aspect to him;
> And when they came within the belt
> Of his own nature, seemed to melt,
> Like cloud to cloud, into him.
>
> (273-77)

Although in *Adonais* self-knowledge is conceived to result from the spirit's casting out of itself to unite center with circumference, Peter only draws in:

> He had a mind which was somehow
> At once circumference and centre
> Of all he might or feel or know;
> Nothing went ever out, although
> Something did ever enter.
>
> (293-97)[18]

147

Even if this poet "new created all he saw / In a new manner" (304-05), he is essentially unimaginative because the mind never goes forth, but instead draws the world to it. Self is never lost or denied, but rather is gratified, sanctified. The fourth section of Shelley's satire is entitled "Sin," and through all its diverse charges one essential trait emerges. The poet's solipsism, his lack of imagination, his puritanical frigidity: all deny the claims of the external world in the preeminence of self. Nature charges her servant with false love: unlike her, he will not "Yield love for love, frank, warm, and true" (324). And she learnedly quotes Boccaccio on natural re-creation and renewal (328-29), implying that Peter's isolation dooms him to decay.[19] Peter's failure, in the largest sense, is a failure to love. It is the sin that isolates him, that holds his imagination in check, and that makes him spurn his fellows into damnation.

The heading for the fifth part of the poem—"Grace"—continues the transposition of theological terms into their ethical and humanistic equivalents. The main figure—"a mighty poet —and / A subtle-souled psychologist" (378-79)—is Coleridge, and the grace he brings is imaginative vision, which inspires his fellow poet to his finest achievements. Coleridge, though possessed of a fire that Wordsworth lacks, shares his inability to balance his mind and the world. Learned, penetrating, enthusiastic, he knows all things but his own mind, "which was a mist" (382). Rather than use his knowledge for the benefit of the world—"This was a man who might have turned / Hell into Heaven" (383-84)—Coleridge has retreated into conceptual indulgences. And when Peter has imbibed Kant, the two form a perfect partnership, absolving themselves of any social responsibility by retreating into a realm of vague metaphysics so abstracted from the here-and-now as to render it without meaning. Since neither sees the world as it really is, it is a simple matter within the independent fantasies they inhabit to alter politics, faiths, or friends. The "damnation" of a damned world —critical reviews in the service of a corrupt establishment— produces the true poetic damnation, a perversion of morals and of art that turns one into a servant of power oneself. In the realm of Jupiter the Lake Poets are apt approximations of Mercury, time servers able to rationalize all moral distinctions at the same time as they distrust themselves. The depravity they find in the world they have first proved in themselves.

The grace that might have saved Peter—imagination—now deserts him utterly. More and more closed within the self, he becomes increasingly barren. As his own depravity extends, his view of a depraved humanity and his power to deprave humanity intensify. He is poetically and ethically a party to death, his hope, as Hunt says, being "founded in hopelessness." From him comes "A power to infect and to infest" (737), the driving principle behind the plague of hell one must suffer in this world. "Light dies before thy uncreating word," Pope cries in the dark vision that ends *The Dunciad* (IV. 654).[20] The end of Shelley's poem is modeled after that work and draws power from its context. Wordsworth, the chief minister of chaos, is after all a great poet whom fear of chaos has perverted. The presiding genius of the romantic period has donned the mantle of Ahriman, spreading the pestilence that makes all earthly things barren, "uncreating" the beneficent fertility of the world and the word. As the cloud of his dullness extends over the Lake district, it curtails life: "Love's work was left unwrought—no brood / Near Peter's house took wing" (751-52). At the end of the poem—in the section entitled "Double Damnation"—this poet has damned himself, lives in a state of damnation surrounded by the plague of hell. The final line asks, but cannot answer, the question that has compelled the entire satire: "How should it ever pass away?" (772).

That question is implicitly asked of Prometheus in the chief Fury's survey of a world where "all best things are . . . confused to ill" (I. 628). He has no answer to offer either, only pity. The Furies thereupon vanish. The accent similarly falls as Shelley ends the first stanza of his survey of hell in *Peter Bell the Third*:

> There are all sorts of people undone,
> And there is little or no fun done;
> Small justice shown, and still less pity.
> (149-51)

Shelley's early sonnet on Wordsworth begins with a tribute to "the still, sad music of humanity" expressed in his work. With ample cause to condemn the later poet—for his reactionary views, his self-serving alliances, the decay of his genius—what Shelley singles out as fundamental is Wordsworth's loss of compassion emblemized in his evoking the spectre of hell as a moral good: "the chief / Ear in his doctrines' blighted sheaf" is "That 'Happiness is wrong' " (571-73).[21] As in *Lines Written Among the Euganean Hills, The Mask of Anarchy*, and especially in *Prometheus Unbound*, Shelley claims an elemental link between love and imaginative vision. Retreating from compassionate faith in the simple people of the Lakes, Wordsworth loses his fertility, becomes barren and an agent of barrenness.

A week after Hunt's attack on *Peter Bell* in *The Examiner*, he again noticed the poem in reviewing Shelley's *Rosalind and Helen*. Remarking on the contrast between the two works, he emphasizes qualities in Shelley that, by inference, are the virtues *Peter Bell the Third* would inculcate: "The object of Mr. Wordsworth's administration of melancholy is to make men timid, servile, and (considering his religion) selfish; —that of Mr. Shelley's, is to render them fearless, independent, affectionate, infinitely social. You might be made to worship a devil by the process of Mr. Wordsworth's philosophy; by that of Mr. Shelley, you might reseat a dethroned goodness."[22] To isolate oneself from a common humanity, whether out of megalomania like Count Cenci or from false pride like Wordsworth, is to serve all that in human terms the reign of Ahriman represents. The contrary to it is that saving imaginative grace which resists solipsism and affirms a compassionate bond with one's fellows. In that same review Leigh Hunt goes on to apply a term to Shelley that in the modern critical fascination with his metaphysics might seem curious were it not so obviously just: he is, to Hunt, a "Cosmopolite-Poet," in other words, a poet whose chief interest is in the well-being of the polity, not simply of himself or his narrow circle.

And yet, if in his writings of 1819 *Peter Bell the Third* is Shelley's fullest excursion into a contemporary hell, it is also the closest he comes to breaking that necessary demarcation between an objective phenomenon and an internal condition. That the third section surveys a universal condition is true enough, but the form of the poem itself—its genre, its methods, its tone—uncomfortably reflects the very vices Shelley would castigate. The wit has its edge of viciousness; the episodes at times derive from cruel gossip.[23] The moral archness that Shelley decries in Wordsworth supplants the compassion he would demand of himself. There is "Small justice shown, and still less pity."

Mary, in her commentary on the poem, demonstrates her awareness of its flaws in this respect. Even more to the point is Shelley's own rejection of the mode, in a fragment dated by Dowden in 1820 but which, occurring in the Huntington manuscript notebook after materials related to *Julian and Maddalo*, probably reflects the poet's intense concern with the *Quarterly Review*'s attack on *The Revolt of Islam*, thought by Shelley to have been the work of Southey. Since much of Shelley's letter to Charles Ollier of 15 October 1819 is concerned with Southey's failings, it is likely that the fragment, "A Satire on Satires," dates from the same period as *Peter Bell the Third* and demonstrates Shelley's consciousness that his satire compromised his ideals.[24] Indeed, it suggests his very awareness that he had used the terms of hell to attack hell, had himself manipulated "A power to infect and to infest." Satire is an acceptable response, he realizes, only:

> if Despair
> And Hate, the rapid bloodhounds with which Terror
> Hunts through the world the homeless steps of Error,
> Are the true secrets of the commonweal
> To make men wise and just; . . .
> And not the sophisms of revenge and fear,
> Bloodier than is revenge. . . .
>
> (6-12)

Satire can have only a negative impact, can only become a portion of the "uncreating word" whose triumph *The Dunciad* foresees. Shelley states his ethical creed in an aphoristic paraphrase of Beatrice Cenci: "Suffering makes suffering—ill must follow ill" (36).[25] The "stagnant truisms of trite Satire" (50) cannot breed new life or reverse a pitiable degeneration: they beg the necessary question, "How should it ever pass away?"

Satire is a fallen form, the defiant response of a Prometheus who hides Jupiter within his soul. Necessary as it is to discern the "sad reality" of *The Cenci* or "the unconnected exclamations of . . . agony" of *Julian and Maddalo*, to know hell is not to know how to make it pass away. Rather, the opposite: to descend into hell is to surround oneself with its terms, to begin unconsciously employing them and thus to take part in that deterministic chain reaction by which hell is continually being re-created. To conceive the paradise of the liberated Prometheus but to live as yet under the dominion of Jupiter is to share both and possess neither, to be suspended within raging fires that, in *Julian and Maddalo*, cause madness. One can resist the flames of hell only by submitting oneself to the mortal fires of purgatory.

5

PURGATORIAL AND PROPHETIC ODES

I could be content either with the Hell or the Paradise of poetry;
but the torments of its purgatory vex me, without exciting my
power sufficiently to put an end to the vexation.
    —Shelley, Letter to Charles Ollier: 20 January 1821

By the autumn of 1819, when Shelley appears to have penned his sardonic essay, "On the Devil, and Devils," he had immersed himself in the problem of evil in a secular universe.[1] The essay further extends the massive concern with evil expressed in *Prometheus Unbound, Julian and Maddalo, The Cenci,* and *Peter Bell the Third.* The serious perspective from which its humor flashes Shelley states succinctly in the second paragraph:

> The Manichæan philosophy respecting the origin and government of the world, if not true, is at least an hypothesis conformable to the experience of actual facts. To suppose that the world was created and is superintended by two spirits of a balanced power and opposite dispositions, is simply a personification of the struggle which we experience within ourselves, and which we perceive in the operations of external things as they affect us, between good and evil. (*Prose*, 7:87)

Even in such an unfinished *jeu d'esprit* as this, Shelley's complex assumption of traditions is manifest. In form his survey of diabolic incarnations is a parody of Daniel Defoe's *Political History of the Devil,* a hack work designed to support conservative orthodoxy against the modernisms of a radical like Milton.

In spirit and tone, Shelley adopts Paine's stance, debunking Christian conceptions of God and Satan, in *The Age of Reason*.[2] But in his Manichean premise Shelley departs as widely from Paine's simplistic rationalism as from Defoe's pieties. "On the Devil, and Devils" assumes that evil is not to be wished away by syllogisms or good intentions, but is ubiquitous, a significant portion of the human state. Yet the dualistic structure discernible in the earliest of religions and commonly assumed, as Plutarch says, by the wisest of men, is not a transcendental truth.[3] It is "a personification of the struggle which we experience within ourselves," an immanent psychological reality.

Shelley's stress on the psychological basis of evil implies that it can be subverted in the same realm. "A Satire on Satire," recognizing the inefficacy of satire for this purpose, was to have continued, it seems, by exemplifying how a man like Southey might be reformed: not attacked so that he might retreat defensively into self-justification, but presented with the highest and noblest of motives by which to compare his own. The fragment of this presentation is a characteristically Shelleyan assertion of the central form of the good.

> ... Or had the gentle, everlasting, fair,
> And world-sorrounding [sic] element of air
> Soft, liquid, plastic emblem of the love
> Whence it was wrought, with engines which men
> Disdain & anger—such as—hear me Sir. . . .[4]

H. Buxton Forman paraphrases the drift of this fragment aptly: if the "gift of pure air and a natural life had not been fouled and perverted by the mechanical, unnatural, filthy, and evil ways of the sons of Belial, disdain and anger such as Southey dealt in could find no place in the human economy."[5]

Against this pure, creative ether Shelley juxtaposes not mere turbulence, but pestilence—what Coleridge calls "positive Negation."[6] The active assertion of evil is exemplified in Peter Bell's "power to infect and to infest" (737), in Count Cenci's curse of his daughter that inverts natural forces, in the "loathliest weeds" (III. 51) that overwhelm the symbolic garden of *The Sensitive Plant*. Shelley's most concise rendering of Ahriman's power occurs in the first part of the concluding epode of the *Ode to Naples*. There he portrays the tyrannical forces of Austria sweeping down on the infant Neapolitan republic "Like Chaos o'er creation, uncreating" (138). Against this force Shelley concludes his poem with a humanistic transformation of the hymn of all artists, *Veni creator spiritus*, evoking the ultimate creative force in his secular pantheon, "Great Spirit, deepest Love" (149).

The *Ode to Naples* is the third of a succession of odes, following the *Ode to the West Wind* and *Ode to Liberty*, in which Shelley portrays himself as a representative poet, contending with the forces of the universal duality. In a distinctive sense these poems reflect the etymological roots of their generic terms. Ὁδός, meaning way or road, became a literary form through the movements of the dramatic chorus on the Greek stage, alternating between strophe and antistrophe in a danced song. What impels the Shelleyan ode is the need to discover a "way" through the universal contentions he recognizes, to create not just in his poetry but, through his poetry, in his life the realistic equivalent to the structural conventions inherited from literary tradition. Shelley returns to the choric ode for ideological as well as formal principles. The dramatic ode is strongly dialectical in nature, mirroring in the insistent ritual of its strophes and antistrophes the conflicts of purpose dramatized by the actors and felt by the audience. The epode, ἐπῳδός, that is a "way in" is relatively simple to discover in the daily events of men and societies; to create the synthesizing epode that is a "way out" for the universal voice is a test of Promethean intellect, will, and endurance. Between the absolute certainties of heaven and hell lies the no-man's-land of purgatory, the region in which what destroys and what preserves are equivalent, inseparable: a single, dialectical force. The imperative for the skeptical poet is to learn to live in that fluid realm between certainties and from that ground to exert his own weight upon the dialectic.

I

The conclusion of the *Ode to the West Wind*—"If Winter comes, can Spring be far behind?"—is perhaps Shelley's most famous utterance, but in context it operates as an abrupt intrusion, shifting the seasonal locus of the poem. Shelley invokes winter here only by a logical leap, duplicating the implication of the poem's beginning, where the seeds of spring were said to be laid within "their dark wintry bed" (6). However the fame of the last line determines a reader's response, winter is not the subject of the poem. Nor is summer, though it is correspondingly mentioned in the first line of the central section. The poem reflects, and indeed is a precise rendering of, that moment when the rich summer of Tuscany is assaulted by the Alpine storms that introduce autumn.[7] The diametrical corollary, the antistrophe of this movement between seasons, is the initial budding of spring, whose presence runs like an undercurrent in the poem until it surfaces in the final clause. To ask that final question—"can Spring be far behind?"—in midwinter is relatively easy. The answer is less assured, less immediate, when confronted from the perspective of late summer, exactly a half-year distant. The question focuses a universal desire, but its rhetorical nature returns us at the end to the moment between, the central condition of the poem and of the poet, where we began. To be between is to inhabit a region where the preserved summer and destructive autumn poise in an ambience of irresolute oneness; it is to stand firmly upon the cusp of Libra even as it disappears in Scorpio, a most precarious balance.[8] Just a month before, John Keats had dismissed the songs of spring for his own distinctive "deep, autumnal tone" (60) of ripe fulfillment. Nothing could be further from the intent of Shelley's ode. In the *Ode to the West Wind* nothing is to be given up. The moment between is neither life nor death because, like the wind which is its animating symbol, it incorporates both at once.[9]

None of Shelley's brief poems is more carefully textured, nor does any reflect so purely that unique genius in conceptual imagery that Shelley brought to English poetry. The forces of life and death, the elemental duality of human existence, are never simply contrasted, but are insistently conflated throughout the poem. The "Destroyer and preserver" (14) is a single force of universal proportions, moving over "the dreaming earth" (10) at the end of winter as over the dreaming Mediterranean (29) at the end of summer, forcing both earth and water, elemental properties, into activity: into life, into death. This motive force drives the dead leaves (3) and the "sweet buds" (11) equally—the former "Yellow, and black, and pale, and hectic red" (4), the latter "With living hues" (12): each distinct in condition, but alike in movement. At the center of the opening stanza life and death poise in suspended animation: "The wingèd seeds . . . lie cold and low, / Each like a corpse within its grave" (7-8). Life exists in the midst of death, even as in the "Pestilence-stricken multitudes" (5) of decaying leaves death cohabits with life.

In succeeding stanzas Shelley further complicates his understanding of the awesome singularity of the dialectical process symbolized by the wind. In its effect on sky and ocean the wind is characterized both by the calm of its restrained potentiality and the explosion of release. "The locks of the approaching storm" (23) are peacefully suspended above the cloud mass, as the limpid Mediterranean is "Lulled by the coil of his crystàlline streams" (31). Yet, though in both instances suspension figures the fullness of life, it does so from opposite ends of a spectrum. The Mediterranean dreams in utter ease, its surface pulsating, "Quivering" (34), like that of a great hibernating beast, with barely perceptible animation. The poise of the oncoming cloud formation, by contrast, suggests a trancelike state achieved not in lull but through passion—"the bright hair uplifted from the head / Of some fierce Maenad" (20-21): a calm characterized by intense vitality. Similarly, the explosion of energy does not conform to simple expectations of its being a life force. The energy of the storm proceeds from a "solid atmosphere" (27), visiting the earth with wholesale destruction, forcing the Atlantic waves to "Cleave themselves" (38) and the plants of the ocean floor to "despoil themselves" (42). If, then, in the first stanza the activity of life seems inextricably involved in the cessation of activity—death—in ensuing stanzas, paradoxically, cessation images fruition and activity is rendered as destructive. And yet, the objects upon which the wind exerts its force do not alter their symbolic properties as they, too, intermix. The decaying leaves of the first stanza are like the loose clouds of the second and like the "sapless foliage" (40) of the "oozy woods" (39) in the third. The airy "stream" (15) with its "blue surface" (19) in the second stanza prefigures the "crystàlline streams" (31) of the third. The "Black rain, and fire, and hail" (28) descending from the storm, recapitulate the "black, and pale, and hectic red" (4) leaves swept before the storm and look forward to the undersea plants that will "grow gray with fear" (41) when the wind touches the Atlantic. Yet again, the insistent similarity masks inversion: the images of the first and third stanzas are comparable, but in the second the colors otherwise associated with the passive victims are assumed by the active power. The careful development of these image patterns, admirable as it is, is not as remarkable as the way in which their contexts shift. Although one may trace the strands out of which the first three stanzas are woven, sudden contradictions make it impossible to untie the compacted knot they form. The "tangled boughs of Heaven and Ocean" (17) are not more intertwined.[10]

The conflated details of imagery in the first three stanzas support larger allusive patterns as well. The most distinctive is that drawing upon Christian eschatology. Like Wordsworth at the Simplon Pass, Shelley observes in the powers of the wind "Characters of the great Apocalypse" (*Prelude*, VI. 638) in which destruction and creation are aspects of a single act. The "wingèd seeds" (7), like spiritual bodies laid to rest—"Each like a corpse within its grave" (8)—will burst forth when the spring wind "shall blow / Her clarion o'er the dreaming earth" (9-10). At the end of the poem Shelley internalizes, personalizes, this apocalyptic metaphor, explicitly demanding that the power of the wind "Be through my lips to unawakened earth / The trumpet of a prophecy" (68-69). But if the wind gives promise of physical and spiritual regeneration, it wreaks destruction at the same time. The "Angels of rain and lightning" (18) that Shelley discovers in the clouds of the second stanza are messengers of wrath, heralding a "dying year," a "closing night" (24). Through the wind's agency the factious denizens of earth will be gathered at last in the universal church, "Vaulted with all thy congregated might" (26), but the total cosmic order symbolized at this point will be destructive: the edifice "Will be the dome of a vast sepulchre" (25). The "black rain, and fire, and hail" that Shelley foresees desolating the earth are the instruments of God's wrath in Revelation. The allusion is sharpened in the third stanza, as Shelley images the wind as a "voice" (41) from the sky, before which the undersea plants "grow gray with fear, / And tremble and despoil themselves" (41-42), that is, lay down their old vestments. At Armageddon "the seventh angel poured out his vial into the air; and there came a great voice out of the temple of heaven, from the throne, saying, It is done" (Rev. 16: 17).

Still, if the allusions to the Last Judgment are deliberate attempts by Shelley to secularize the inscrutable God who speaks to Job out of the whirlwind and who in the end will have power to summon a universal destruction, other Biblical contexts represent the wind as a symbol of harmony or of vatic force. When "God made a wind to pass over the earth, . . . the waters asswaged" (Gen. 8: 1), and the earth was reborn for the sons of Noah. Shelley's wind "chariot[s] . . . / The wingèd seeds" (6-7) like the whirlwind that propels Elijah's fiery chariot. After his master disappears, Elisha despoils himself like the oozy woods of the third stanza—"he took hold of his own clothes, and rent them in two pieces" (2 Kings 2: 12)—and, following Elijah's example, with his master's mantle cleaves the waters of Jordan "into chasms" (38). The wind as a visionary force passing from mind to mind is likewise exemplified in the famous gathering of Christ's disciples after his death and resurrection.

> And when the day of Pentecost was fully come, they were all with one accord in one place.

And suddenly there came a sound from heaven as of a rushing mighty wind, and it filled all the house where they were sitting.

And there appeared unto them cloven tongues like as of fire, and it sat upon each of them.

And they were all filled with the Holy Ghost, and began to speak with other tongues, as the Spirit gave them utterance. (Acts 2:1-4)

When the multitude expresses surprise and fear at this apostolic gift of tongues, Peter restores calm by reminding them of the divine injunction reported by the prophet Joel:

And it shall come to pass in the last days, saith God, I will pour out my Spirit upon all flesh: and your sons and your daughters shall prophesy, and your young shall see visions, and your old men shall dream dreams. (Acts 2: 17; cf. Joel 2: 28)

The "dome of [the] vast sepulchre," to transpose the model, will house many a "fierce Maenad" of prophetic vision to create life out of the materials of death.

The dual associations of the wind in Christian eschatology —as the power of a wrathful God and as the breath of the Holy Spirit—are duplicated and extended in the other mythologies with which Shelley demonstrates his awareness. The destructive autumn wind he addresses is not Boreas, the north wind, but Zephyr, the benevolent wind of the west in Greek mythology. Boccaccio notes that the west wind "in Latin is called *Javonium,* because it is propitious to birth," and Joseph Spence in his popular *Polymetis* surveys ancient commentators to support his claim that "ZEPHYRUS is the mildest of all the deities of the Winds: the character of his personage is youth, and gentleness. Valerius Flaccus, in speaking of [the] four great deities of the Winds, as employed all together in a storm, adds some character of violence to everyone of them except Zephyrus." Recalling that Zephyrus was married to Flora, who represents the burgeoning of vegetable nature, Spence wryly concludes that "They were perhaps the happiest couple of all those who in the heathen mythology were supposed to have engaged in so bold an undertaking as that of an endless marriage. . . ."[11] In contrast, the spirit bringing life to Shelley's world is not gentle, but rather "wild" (1), "uncontrollable" (47), "impetuous" (62), Maenad-like—a "Spirit fierce" (61).

As in *Prometheus Unbound*, in the *Ode to the West Wind* Shelley assimilates oriental traditions to those central Christian and Greek sources he draws upon. The Phoenician cosmology begins with a great wind breathing upon the waters of chaos. Isaac de Beausobre traces the etymology of this wind, *Kolpiah*, to mean "the voice, or breath, or wind from the mouth of God," and further notes that "It is represented as the husband, because it is the active principle, and matter as the wife because it is the passive principle." To both Phoenicians and Hebrew philosophers the wind is the plastic spirit of God, a "subtle substance, vital in itself, invisible, which insinuates itself in bodies, animating and vegetating them."[12]

In Zoroastrian thought the wind Vayu "is the breath of the macrocosm and therefore also the breath of life that keeps man, the microcosm, alive." Like Shelley's force, the Zoroastrian wind is beyond the antithetical powers of good and evil: R. C. Zaehner describes Vayu as "a mighty, rushing wind, pursuing, overtaking, and conquering the creations both of the Holy Spirit and of the Destructive Spirit."[13] The Manicheans incorporate this force into the dualistic structure of their religion, reversing the values of the Phoenician ontology. The wind that moved upon the watery chaos was dark and humid, producing the corruption of matter. But in the kingdom of light there is a counterwind to the pestilential wind of the dark world. According to Augustine, wind is one of the five elements that operate in each of these worlds.[14]

James Rieger has suggested that Shelley's wind should be construed as a *Quinta Essentia*, the Pythagorean ether, interpenetrating the four elements considered in the poem. The perception is brilliant, but suffers from its self-imposed limitation of source. All the major systems of the near and middle east contain five elements, as opposed to the four of the west. Even Manicheans surround their original man with light, water, fire, air, and wind. Thomas Maurice, terming the Phoenician account of the wind breathing upon chaos a "universal traditionary doctrine which runs through all the cosmogonies of the East," traces it to the Indian veneration for wind as the original element from which the others were created. "The ancient philosophers of India . . . imagined a *fifth* element, formed of the more refined particles of igneous air, which they call the AKASS; that pure, transparent, luminous, aether, in which the planets and other celestial bodies roll. This subtle spirit, this penetrating fluid, they conceive to pervade all bodies, and to be the great principle of vitality and bond of all existence." Volney asserts that the conception of ether as "the grand agent in that spontaneous motion, which in animals is denominated life, and in plants vegetation," allowed the ancient world

> to conceive of the mechanism and action of the universe, as of a homogeneous WHOLE, a single body, whose parts, however distant in place, had a reciprocal connexion with each other; and of the world as a living substance, animated by the organical circulation of an igneous or rather electrical fluid, which, by an analogy borrowed from men and animals, was supposed to have the sun for its heart.

Shelley's wind is thus the same electrical force Berkeley claimed was "equally fitted to produce and to destroy," the force that dominates the physics of *Prometheus Unbound*.[15] The cosmic dance of anarchy in the fourth act is no simplistic utopia, but is fully impelled by the strophe and antistrophe, the creation and destruction, which is the universal rhythm of the wind.

Shelley's insistence on the dual nature of the ethereal fluid likewise has its foundations in Indian, rather than in Greek or Christian, thought. In his first address to the Royal Asiatic Society of Bengal Sir William Jones notes, "To destroy, according to the *Védánti's* of *India*, the *Súfi's* of *Persia*, and many philosophers of our *European* schools, is only to *generate* and *reproduce* in another form." Thomas Maurice, who makes an identical assertion in *Indian Antiquities*, in the *History of Hindostan* quotes from the *Sastra* to link the dialectic with the ethereal fluid: "From the opposite actions of the creative and destructive qualities in matter self-motion first rose. These discordant actions produced the Akass." The dialectic, then, is itself primary, essential: all things partake of it. Maurice notes that Eros in India is of three kinds, the creative, the preserving, and the destructive; and Francis Wilford sees these categories carried even into the Manicheans' view of Christ: "the primeval serpent, who enlightened the minds of ADAM and EVE; the creator, preserver, and the destroyer; the original soul, the preserver of the soul, and the fabricator of the instrument, with which the salvation of the soul is effected."[16]

The characteristic drive of Indian philosophy, personified as well in its mythology, is to subsume radically opposite qualities within a single nature. What Shelley transfers into the complex patterns of the wind's operations in the world is akin to the contradictory yet comprehended facets of Krishna as rendered in Charles Wilkins' original English translation of the *Bhagvat-Geeta:*

> I am the sacrifice; I am the worship; I am the spices; I am the invocation; I am the ceremony to the manes of the ancestors; I am the provisions; I am the fire, and I am the victim: I am the father and mother of this world, the grandsire, and the preserver. I am the holy one worthy to be known; the mystic figure $\bar{O}m$; the *Rĕĕk*, the *Sām*, and *Yăjŏŏr Vēds*. I am the journey of the good; the comforter; the creator; the witness; the resting-place; the asylum, and the friend. I am generation and dissolution; the place where all things are reposited, and the inexhaustible seed of all nature. I am sunshine, and I am rain; I now draw in, and now let forth. I am death and immortality: I am entity and non-entity.[17]

The "Destroyer and preserver" (14) Shelley calls upon to hear him is the combined form of Siva and Vishnu, whose qualities were, from the beginning of English explorations of Indian religion, rendered in those precise terms. But the Indian godhead has a third member, whose presence is missing from this invocation. So, indeed, does the Christian trinity, whose God and Holy Spirit, at least as represented by mythologists, function similarly to Siva and Vishnu. The wrathful force of Jehovah is balanced by the regenerative power of the spring Zephyr, but what is missing—and indeed demanded by the poet—is the creative power of Brahma and of Christ.[18]

Likewise conspicuous by its absence, until the last stanza of the poem, is the volatile and creative element Prometheus willed the human race, fire. Paradoxically, of course, the lack of that element, and the creative principle it signifies, is the creative force behind the poem. The careful recapitulation of the imagery at the beginning of the fourth stanza points explicitly to the flaw that exists when only four of the five elements are in evidence:

> If I were a dead leaf thou mightest bear;
> If I were a swift cloud to fly with thee;
> A wave to pant beneath thy power, and share
>
> The impulse of thy strength, only less free
> Than thou, O uncontrollable!
>
> (43-47)

In this summary of the development Shelley moves to a dead stop. Lacking fire, he lacks all.

And yet fire has been present from the beginning, concealed within the imagery of the initial three stanzas, asking only for its principles to be understood to be released into the poem, the poet, and the world. As Eben Bass has noted, the hues of the dead leaves in line four reproduce colors traditionally associated with the four elements: "Yellow, and black, and pale, and hectic red."[19] Shelley undoubtedly emphasizes these colors to call attention to the importance of elemental imagery to the poem. But it is not enough to say, as Bass does, that we must await the fifth stanza for fire finally to take its due place in the pentagonal structure of first things and of a poem devoted to them. Shelley himself particularly accents the color associated with fire in this fourth line, terming it "hectic red," that is to say, the hue associated with a consumptive fever. Whereas the other colors suggest a nature simply wasting away, "hectic red" seems closer to the principle Robert Frost found exemplified in the midst of winter, in "The Wood-pile": "the slow smokeless burning of decay." As these colors reappear in the storm bursting at the end of the second stanza, fire is itself named as the force of destruction surrounded by "Black rain . . . and hail" (28). And as these powers are seen to explode from a cloud cover of such "congregated might" (26) that it composes a "solid atmosphere" (27), Shelley in his third stanza rights his inverted image, transferring it mirrorlike from the rain-laden sky to "the wave's intenser day" (34). The lulled Mediterranean lies "Beside a pumice isle in Baiae's bay" (32), a gratuitous description unless the particular impact of Shelley's adjective is allowed full force. A pumice isle is one composed of volcanic rock, is created, it would seem, by an explosive eruption from beneath the water and beneath the land supporting it. In the sky one will see "Black rain, and fire, and hail . . . burst" (28)—equivalent to lava, fire, and ash—as on this ocean one *has* seen the same phenomenon in the distant past. In much the same way as the strong volcanic imagery of the second stanza directs our eye to the "pumice isle" of the third, the "sapless foliage" (40) near the end of the third stanza will find its complementary image in the fourth. For if the undersea foliage needs no internal, circulating, vital fluid, but is nourished by the fluid everywhere around, the poet himself does have an internal circulation that is violated. The blood he pours upon the ground is the color of fire—is fire.

The leaves imaged in the first three stanzas illustrate three distinct aspects of a single condition. The autumn leaves appear as "ghosts from an enchanter fleeing" (3), the clouds are "Shook from the tangled boughs of Heaven and Ocean" (17); the undersea flowers and woods "despoil themselves" (42). Different as these acts appear, they represent variations of a fundamental passivity before active force. The wind, as Beausobre recalls the Phoenician ontology, is a husband to whom his material wife is wholly subservient. French materialist mythography similarly bases the duality exemplified in most mythological systems on active and passive contraries: it is for this reason that Dupuis concentrates so strongly on Zoroastrian and Manichean principles. Likewise, contemporary physics, following Newton's legacy both in its atomic and electrical theories, is structured upon a principle of balanced polarity. Antoine Fabre d'Olivet enunciates the elemental theory of polarity that Shelley gradually makes explicit in the *Ode to the West Wind*:

> . . . as a principle of all existence there is but one element brought into action by two contrary forces.
> This unique element is FIRE.
> These two forces are the tangential force and the central force.[20]

The tangential force is active, explosive, always in motion; the central force is passive, attractive, the object of the movement. What Shelley has initially conceived as a divorce between husband and wife is instead the friction from which fire, the creative element, is itself produced.

The force that visited Shelley in the spring of life—" in my boyhood" (48)—was invigorating, allowing him in his visionary desires to be "The comrade of [its] wanderings over Heaven" (49). He lived in a heady dream world, like the Mediterranean "Lulled by the coil of his crystàlline streams," a coil that allowed escape by turning in. The dead stop, the moment between, to which Shelley has come on the verge of a destructive storm presages an inversion of the spiral, winding out, sapping the strength at its center. What had once appeared solely to nourish the life of vision is now seen to support life and death impartially, to intertwine them throughout the world and deep in the self-consciousness seeking to mediate between individual desire and external circumstance. The fourth stanza moves Shelley toward the limbo with which the first act of *Prometheus Unbound* ends, as Beatrice Cenci progressed to the same point of mental space. The paradox exemplified in those instances is again imbedded in the ode's texture of imagery. Never simply articulated, it is nonetheless the pivot upon which Shelley's ode turns defeat into victory, the pivot in which defeat and victory, like the intertwined powers of the wind, are discovered to be identical:

> Oh, lift me as a wave, a leaf, a cloud!
> I fall upon the thorns of life! I bleed!

166

A heavy weight of hours has chained and bowed
One too like thee: tameless, and swift, and proud.
                                            (53-56)

The progression of these four lines, each with the impact of
a separate statement, is extraordinary in intensity. The rich,
symphonic epode that ensues in the fifth stanza is a clear dem-
onstration that the last of these four staccato lines is, in truth,
a declarative statement like the others, that in the moment of
confronting his "chained and bowed" condition, the poet is
liberated, incorporating the power of the wind that had until
this point been considered an external force. The release occurs
through the juxtaposition of verbs—"lift," "fall"—in the first
two lines, the one a cry for preservation, the other an admission
of destruction. In the development of the first three stanzas
the poet has slowly shifted his comprehension of passivity. The
"ghosts from an enchanter fleeing" (3) fear the power of the
wind and pursue a negative path before it. Their attempt to
retain their integrity is vain, for in rejecting the infusion of
magical powers, they are rejecting life and giving themselves
to death. These "Pestilence-stricken multitudes" ("nation" in
the draft), indeed, exemplify that principle of disease that in
the Earth and in Peter Bell, having infected its victim, makes
that victim a contagious instrument of societal infection. The
clouds of the second stanza do not flee, but are instead "Shook
from the . . . boughs" (17) without resistance, to become forces
of destruction empowered by the wind. Compelled by the enchanter, they have assumed the Dionysian power of a "fierce
Maenad" (21), who, like the prototypes of Euripides' *Bacchae*,
may act with an energy as "uncontrollable" (47) as it is violent.
In the third stanza Shelley looks beyond the Mediterranean
awakening from its lulled and lulling fantasies to confront the
far west, the Atlantic realm of death, where he ascertains a
third model of passivity that neither rejects energy nor converts
it into destructive passion. There the waves "Cleave themselves
into chasms" (38) and the blooms "despoil themselves" (42).
They are not so much acted upon by the wind as they are joint

participants in its force, incorporating it through willingly assuming the necessity for their own destruction.

The declarative statements—"Oh, lift me as a wave, a leaf, a cloud! / I fall upon the thorns of life! I bleed!"—demand conjunctive or prepositional links to establish their relationship. Partly because of that very absence, the reader is forced to concentrate on the lines not simply as the emotional climax of the poem, but as its intellectual center as well. The customary gloss, that Shelley prays to be lifted because he has fallen, is dependent upon reading the initial verb as a form of beseechment and the second as a passive complaint. The development of the ode, however, would suggest a far more complex interpretation. Shelley's "fall" is not the simple passivity previously associated with the leaves and the clouds: rather, like the undersea events, it is active, deliberate—a cleaving of the self, a despoiling. He doffs the protective garments and renders himself fully naked to the universal force. "Lift" is then an imperative, a demand that the force assume its complementary function. The wind may lift in order for the fall to occur; it may lift in response to the fall: in either case, to "share / The impulse of its strength" (45-46) is to assimilate preservation and destruction, as an impulse in physical law will produce its reaction, and a cardiac impulse is responsible for the diastole that, in turn, renders the systole possible. The conflation of contrary forces, the poet's active passivity, his willing self-destruction, at last produces fire: "I bleed!" The cry of seeming despair reverberates through the remainder of the poem with the intonations of triumph.

Both the thorns that the poet willingly accepts and the wound from which blood seeps vividly recall the crucifixion of Christ. As a vision in the first act of *Prometheus Unbound* the crucifixion seemed an act without meaning, producing a new cycle of revenge in the world, by which the dead and institutionalized body of Christ, the church, crucified its enemies through the ensuing centuries. In the *Ode to the West Wind* the agnostic Shelley portrays the crucifixion in terms very close to those of Blake, as an ultimate act of willed self-annihilation which produces its corollary in the resurrection. If the fourth stanza con-

cludes with the Friday passion, the question that ends the fifth
stanza and the poem—"can Spring be far behind?"—demands
that Easter follow. More importantly, to give oneself fully to
"passion," to the destructive and preservative powers of the
world, to assimilate four of the five elements, is to empower
as well that missing element and those missing mythological
archetypes—fire, Christ, Brahma. In the gathering coherence of
allusions within the ode a further context of the thorn-blood
metaphor, overlooked perhaps because of the obvious symbol
of the crucifixion, is crucial to the development of the last
stanza. In the Persian variation of natural history, which became assimilated to the myth of Philomela, the nightingale who
sings for her lost and hopeless love presses her breast against a
thorn. Shelley works an elaborate analogy around this legend
at the beginning of *Epipsychidion* (1-12): here it is left in the
realm of implicit allusion. The music that swells in the last
stanza is, however, the music that issues from the nightingale
transforming her pain into beauty, making the very continuity
of her suffering the agent of transfiguration. Shelley concluded
his allegorical fragment "The Woodman and the Nightingale"
with the acknowledgment that suffering is the universal condition of the nightingale:

> The world is full of Woodmen who expel
> Love's gentle Dryads from the haunts of life,
> And vex the nightingales in every dell.[21]
>
> (68-70)

Vexation may not be necessary to creativity, but it can be made
to serve it, just as purgatory is not the realm of the music of the
spheres, but can be made to accommodate a lesser strain. From
the interaction of the five earthly elements sweeping across the
poet as over an Aeolian "lyre" (57), there arises a corresponding "tumult of . . . mighty harmonies" (59). The mightiest of
these tonalities flow from the sudden compounding of fire and
wind, the two elements born from friction, which, united within
the poet, comprise a true igneous fluid, an activating ether, an
electric voice by which to charge the nations of the earth.[22]

The profound recognition that Shelley forces his ode to explore is that death is as inescapable a portion of the emotional and intellectual life as it is of the physical body. The "thorns of life" are ubiquitous, nowhere more concentrated than where one tries to pluck the roses of perfection. The boy can escape into a fantasy world, but the price of creativity in an adult world is destruction. Self-consciousness erodes spontaneity, the vital freshness of mental response, turning the mind inward through a labyrinth of questions and ironies that must be faced. To "seek a repose that ever is the same," Wordsworth's desire in his *Ode to Duty,* is to seal off the labyrinth and, in forestalling one's own destruction, correspondingly to stifle creativity.[23] A poet preys upon himself, participating actively in his own destruction in order to bring new life into objective and separate being. He is a second Christ, the essential fertility figure of a new myth, who spills his blood, like seed, upon barren ground "to quicken a new birth" (64). To be a poet is to accept that responsibility, to redeem ancient myth in a contemporary reality, to affirm the inevitability of martyrdom by others and, more difficult still, by oneself. But if the hearth is to remain "unextinguished" (66), there must be "ashes" amid the "sparks" (67), "withered leaves" (64) as well as seeds. The image of the hearth prefigures the famous "fading coal" metaphor of the *Defence of Poetry,* where Shelley assumes the same paradoxical stance. Personal vision is closed within the self unless one wills the annihilation of both to communicate with others. The poet destroys his own vision, the solace of a mere aesthetic serenity, and, beyond that, the resolved circle of the world's past literature, in order to participate in creating "that great poem, which all poets, like the co-operating thoughts of one great mind, have built up since the beginning of the world" (*Prose,* 7: 124). In his biography of Shelley, Thomas Jefferson Hogg conceives of the poet as both maker and marrer, a sentiment reinforced by Claire Clairmont, who entered the following Shelleyan paragraph into her journal of December 4, 1820:

A great Poet resembles Nature—he is a Creator and a destroyer; he presides over the birth & death of images, the prototypes of things —the torrent of his sentiments should flow like waves one after the other, each distinctly formed and visible yet linked between its predecessor and its follower as to form between them both by beauty and necessity an indissoluble connection. He requires also to possess that power of harmony which like the fire of Vesta should burn perpetually bursting by fits into flame & strength according to the subjects.[24]

The apocalyptic imagery of the poem, internalized by the poet in the final stanza, retains its stern dualistic functions. Not only does "the trumpet of a prophecy" (69) depend on the poet's destruction of himself, but it will entail external destruction as well. The purgatory of his mind will contribute to the purgatorial fires of earth, rendering destruction as a necessary corollary to creation, shedding leaves in order to force new shoots into bloom. In this capacity the poet truly dons the mantle of the Manichean Christ who is "creator, preserver, and destroyer," going forth into a ministry one of whose chief purposes must be to destroy that church which is the anti-Christ and those institutions of oppression which its failure of vision has allowed to flourish.

The *Ode to the West Wind* is probably the most thoroughly misunderstood poem among those Shelley contributed to the standard repertory of English verse. Not only is it a poem without the self-pity commonly ascribed to it; it deliberately eschews self-pity. It is a secularized song of Christian triumph, accepting with bold vision the consequences of thrusting oneself into the midst of the universal duality. By implication, it attests to the extremity of the burden that Beatrice Cenci could not assume but which must be borne willingly before the civilization depicted in the culminating act of *Prometheus Unbound* can be realized. What the virgin Beatrice precisely refused was the necessity for falling upon the thorns of life and bleeding. Her father's vindictiveness was predicated on her resistance: to give herself to the incestuous relationship, to convert rape into an act of love, was beyond Beatrice's imagination, as it was probably beyond the imaginations of those who read Shelley's tragedy then or later. But to embrace one's own violation as the essential requirement for creative life means to Shelley exactly that. Sacrifice is an unavoidable necessity of life in purgatory. Shelley's formulation of this truth in the *Ode to the West Wind* turns upon no mere conceptual or rhetorical cleverness. The enormous implications of his vision he is prepared to accept, as he had had to accept the death of two children in the space of nine months. In no way is life in purgatory easy. It is, however, preferable to life in hell.

II

Although Shelley never alludes to the *Ode to the West Wind* in his correspondence or reported conversations, he apparently thought of it as a central poem in his canon. "The breath whose might I have invoked in song" becomes the destructive and creative power to which the poet freely gives himself in the last stanza of *Adonais*. Less openly but no less surely, he employs the force as a context in his two subsequent excursions into the odal genre, the *Ode to Liberty*, written at the beginning of 1820, and the *Ode to Naples* of the following summer. Both odes are more traditional and refined in structure than the *Ode to the West Wind*. They are also more overt in their political and prophetic stance.

Both odes begin with introductory stanzas derived from the Book of Ezekiel. In the *Ode to Liberty* news of the Spanish revolution inspires the poet's soul, "rapped [by] . . . The Spirit's whirlwind" (11), and "A voice out of the deep" (15) speaks for fifteen stanzas through the poet's words. The introduction to the *Ode to Naples* is more elaborate in its symbolism, beginning with the same lulled stillness Shelley portrayed in *Stanzas Written in Dejection, Near Naples* and in the third part of the *Ode to the West Wind*, and continuing with the extension of a ruffling breeze into a prophetic wind sweeping over all of nature. In each case the wind is accompanied, if not produced, by volcanic force. The spread of revolution in Spain is a series of eruptions "From heart to heart, from tower to tower . . . / Scattering contagious fire into the sky" (3-4). Poised metaphorically above these eruptions, the poet is seized by the displacement of air—"The Spirit's whirlwind"—and is propelled through the "living frame / Which paves the void" (12-13), the igneous, vital fluid of ether. In the *Ode to Naples* Shelley's vantage ground is Pompeii, a mid-point between the earth-bound Kingdom of Naples and the towering monument of natural energy, Vesuvius. Pompeii is a "City disinterred" (1), risen from the grave, not only giving promise of rebirth for other communities buried under tyrannical governments, but suggesting as well that the significant past can be assimilated to the present in a continuum of humanistic achievement. The rustle of "autumnal leaves" suggests "light footfalls / Of spirits passing through the streets" (2-3); not aimlessly driven as in the *Ode to the West Wind*, but pursuing the occupations that make a community of men. Pompeii is an abstract form of Naples: both objectify the condition of the poet, against utter stillness hearing the "oracular thunder" (6) of Vesuvius in his "suspended blood" (7). The stillness is waiting to be charged with energy, its potentiality to be converted into dynamic form.

> . . . the crystal silence of the air
> Weighed on their life, even as the Power divine
> Which then lulled all things, brooded upon mine.
> (20-22)

Brooding here implies not mere intellectual contemplation, but the incubation that transforms one from an embryonic state to nativity, from burial to true rebirth. The imagery recalls Milton's invocation of the Holy Spirit: "thou [who] / Dove-like sat'st brooding on the vast abyss, / And madst it pregnant," a spirit creating life and prophetic vision from the void.[25] As the winds mount in intensity, the poet is borne aloft by a kindred force: "A spirit of deep emotion / From the unknown graves / Of the dead Kings of Melody" (37-39), identified as Homer and Virgil in Shelley's note. These epic forbears are also spiritually

173

"disinterred," transferring their power of vision and song to the receptive fellow poet who brings it to life in his prophecy. The introductory frame of both poems, then, develops a series of analogous conditions. The volcanic eruption, which is the liberation of an enormous natural energy from repression, is reflected in popular revolution; and both acts, by a stretch of the poet's imagination, are made equivalent to the act of poetry itself.

The image patterns of these odes accentuate the same humanistic standard of values as *Prometheus Unbound*. The main body of the *Ode to Liberty* begins with a creation *manqué*, replicating the volcanic symbolism of the introductory stanza:

> The Sun and the serenest Moon sprang forth:
> The burning stars of the abyss were hurled
> Into the depths of Heaven.
>
> (16-18)

The universal convulsion of nature, however, has no significance beyond its assertion of natural force: "this divinest universe / Was yet a chaos and a curse, / For thou wert not" (21-23). Without a complementary eruption within the human breast, without an active assertion of control over society, raw power runs without check "from worst producing worse" (23), a universal, reductive warfare, condensing into the Shelleyan hell: "each heart was as a hell of storms" (30). To quail before this natural warfare is to allow power to consolidate in the hands of those who will establish a specious order—"Anarchs and priests" (43)—who, organizing society to their own ends, make a mockery out of law itself and degrade man to the condition of beasts. They "Drove the astonished herds of men from every side" (45).

The imagery poses sun against clouds, the latter an agency to obscure but never obliterate the former, both manifestations of the neutral power or energy active throughout the cosmos: indeed, the development of the third stanza implies that man has himself wrought the storm clouds of tyranny and religion

174

as a parody of the sun's pavilion spread over the earth. The third source of energy is volcanic, sending forth "Prophetic echoes" (50) of possibility, transformed into "thunder" by "The voices of [the] bards and sages" (80) of Athens:

> A wingèd sound of joy, and love, and wonder,
>   Which soars where Expectation never flew,
> Rending the veil of space and time asunder!
>   (84-86)

The eruption is mental, asserting a power whose purpose is to magnify human nature and re-create the world to humane ends. Athens represents the earthly locus of the "one Spirit vast" which "With life and love makes chaos ever new" (88-89). So the medieval Italian republics, created atop mountains "Like rocks which fire lifts out of the flat deep" (125), assert true law and liberty above the ocean of "multitudinous anarchy" (129). And a similar volcanic eruption, that which occurs at the beginning of the poem and which is now connected through the subterranean channels of a humanized planet, begins the chain reaction that will liberate all men.

Countering the creative images of volcanic eruption are the blood and gold associated with the axis of tyrant and priest. Blood is spilled as sacrifice and in warfare: gold is the measure of individual and corporate power. For a thousand years the "liquid light"—both the rays of the sun and the fiery fluid that bears them, ether—has been "Dyed . . . with blood and tears" (169). Shelley reasserts the Zoroastrian imagery of active evil: his "Galilean serpent" (119) slithers out of a "sea of death" (118). The very conception of monarchy is "the sperm / Of what makes life foul, cankerous, and abhorred" (222-23), as the conception of priesthood was "hurled" from "hell" (229).

In the *Ode to Naples* Shelley's imagery is even more sharply antithetical since it is not a 'progress' poem but a portrayal of a moment suspended in time. The "giant birth" (66) leaping forth from the earth is opposed by a Satanic army, dyeing the heavens "With iron light" (136), the color of blood and warfare, of rust and canker, of the most primitive of the four ages of man.

> The Anarchs of the North lead forth their legions
> Like Chaos o'er creation, uncreating.
>
> (137-38)

The spirit of Athens—described in the *Ode to Liberty* as "with its crest of columns, on the will / Of man, as on a mount of diamond, set" (70-71)—is the prey of this army of uncreation, which spreads, "Trampling our columned cities into dust" (144). Against that marauding anarchy Shelley sets the equivalent of the vision that ends the *Divine Comedy*: "*L'Amor che move il sole e l'altre stelle.*"

> Great Spirit, deepest Love!
> Which rulest and dost move
> All things which live and are, within the Italian shore.
>
> (149-51)

Both the *Ode to Liberty* and *Ode to Naples* move to a polarized standstill as Shelley gathers into position the forces of his Zoroastrian antithesis. On the side of paradise stand love, beauty, liberty, creativity, poetry, commonalty. Arrayed under the banners of hell are hatred, violence, tyranny, destructiveness, religious superstition: a chaos of self-assertion. The terms with which Shelley deals and the forced consolidation of distinct entities reveal an advance over the concerns of *Queen Mab* and *The Revolt of Islam*; and yet, if anything, Shelley appears only to have smoothed off the rough edges and contradictions of his earlier propagandistic art. The black and white division is even more intense for being rendered in brief. The forces seem so wholly codified as to leave no realm between.

Yet it is that realm which the poet occupies, and what makes both odes significant to Shelley's canon is exactly that perception of his role. The parallel Shelley establishes with Ezekiel at the beginning of these odes, as is so often the case, operates as a standard, at points supporting the poet's task, at other points graphically emphasizing his failures. Ezekiel does not want to bear witness to the rebellious nations God singles out for stern chastisement, but as an honest man he has no choice. If he puts sentimental considerations before those of divine justice, he is sharply rebuked. The vision of the divine fire and the four cherubim sustains him, but he must return to the onerous responsibilities of earth "in bitterness and in the heat of my spirit" (Ezek. 3: 14). He does know the source of his truth and the accuracy of his prophecies. Stationed in the present, he employs God's future tense with conviction and assurance.

Shelley lacks both God and assurance. And the apparent vacuum that exists between the polarities of good and evil functions dramatically in both odes to render his isolation acute. The meliorist vision of Shelley's *Ode to Liberty* is far different from that of Collins' poem on the same subject. The card-carrying Whig can end in self-satisfied triumph, with a balanced constitutional monarchy reigning over a commonwealth of free men and prosperous institutions. Shelley's vision reaches its acme in the eleventh stanza with the enlightenment triumphing over its foes, slips in the twelfth with the portrayal of Napoleon, "The Anarch of thine own bewildered powers" (175), as perverting the ideals of Liberty; and then with the question that opens the thirteenth stanza—"England yet sleeps: was she not called of old?" (181)—the poet begins an attempt lasting six stanzas, a full third of the poem's historical vision, to save his vision from collapse. Among the rhetorical strategies he marshals to that end there is scarcely a simple declarative sentence. Rather the poem welters from one rhetorical climax to another, through personification (st. 13), to imperatives and apostrophes (st. 14), optative wishes that kings and priests had never existed (st. 15-16), conditional questions (st. 17), prayer (st. 18). The underlying questions become more and more insistent until they break the self-supported structure of the ode:

> Comes she [Liberty] not, and come ye not,
> Rulers of eternal thought,
> To judge, with solemn truth, life's ill-apportioned lot?
> Blind Love, and equal Justice, and the Fame
> Of what has been, the Hope of what will be?

O Liberty! if such could be thy name
Wert thou disjoined from these, or they from thee:
If thine or theirs were treasures to be bought
By blood or tears, have not the wise and free
Wept tears, and blood like tears?

(261-70)

It is a powerful conclusion, but what Shelley terms "The solemn harmony" (270) that here breaks off is more accurately portrayed in the terms of the internalized west wind: "The tumult of . . . mighty harmonies."

This poet, like Ezekiel, can bear witness to rebellious nations, can set terms of judgment, can even suggest what will be the condition of the rebuilt Jerusalem, but no *telos* supports his vision, no transcendental force insures the truth of his looking forward, nor is there a power able to calm him by the injunction: "be not afraid of them, neither be afraid of their words" (Ezek. 2: 6). Instead, the contradictory impulses that the poet's will to symmetry has kept at bay throughout the poem rush in, overwhelming the last stanza in paradox. Shelley compares himself in his failure to sustain his vision to a swan shot as it flies toward the dawn, a cloud dissolving itself in rain, a candle being obliterated by the coming of dawn, an ephemeral insect dying with the day, a victim of drowning sinking beneath the waves. All images of destruction, they are not equivalent. The dissolving cloud has achieved its end; the beacon in the night is superseded by the bursting forth of greater light. But the beautiful swan, in contrast, is violently thwarted of its life and purpose, and the ephemeral insect carries all with it into universal darkness. The "tempestuous play" (285) of the waves at the end of the poem suggests a nature indifferent to the human values over which the poem has struggled, treacherously converting what had supported the poet's vision into sudden destruction. The five similes reflect the alternatives of the poem without resolving them, at the same time as they suggest that the purgatorial stance of the poet, whatever the outcome of the struggle he organizes into vision, is self-destructive. Less dramatically, but no less powerfully, the *Ode to Naples* breaks off

178

with Shelley, from the vantage of a disinterred ruin—but a ruin nonetheless—watching the progress of armed tyranny and superstition against the defenseless Neapolitan libertarians. The impassioned prayer with which this vision, too, ends is implicitly controverted by the qualifying clause that precedes it:

> Whatever, Spirit, from thy starry shrine
> Thou yieldest or withholdest, oh, let be
> This city of thy worship ever free!
>   (174-76)

As Irene Chayes has argued, the romantic ode is an intrinsically dramatic form, at once the embodiment and the objectification of a spiritual struggle whose acute tensions demand resolution.[26] In his inability to supply that resolution, Shelley seems closest to Keats in his great odes of 1819. But the difference is as important as the similarity. In the tensions between imaginative perfection and earthly mutability Keats discovers a profoundly oxymoronic universe, taking away what it gives, promising relief but deceptively offering only further paradoxes. Shelley's less personal system of values provides him with sharper lines for separating ethical and imaginative goals. In adapting the Zoroastrian duality within a meliorist framework, he knows that the forces of creation must at last surmount those of uncreation. That recognition may be central to all three of the prophetic and political odes of 1819-20, but it is not the real issue. The dramatic impulse of the odes is to find a meaningful stance by which to influence events seemingly beyond one's control, to determine the responsibility of the poet, and to estimate its cost. Shelley's odes all end in poised irresolution, with antitheses sharply defined but the imperative questions unanswered. Their process is not definitive, but educative, both to the reader and the poet who must, in the end, share responsibility for the culmination of the struggle. If the poet is not himself willing to inhabit that realm of purgatorial tensions, neither can he expect his reader to. Shelley portrays himself as accepting the vexation he wishes to be free of, indeed, whetting the vexation in the interests of freedom.[27] Behind the rhetorical flourishes of these odes, behind their moral and cosmological antitheses, is an examplar of visionary courage, demanding that man not beg the questions to which only he can supply the answers, emphasizing that reality does not exist as a thing-in-itself, but is continuously created by human minds and human hearts.

6

THE POET AS LEGISLATOR

His wisdom is the wisdom of a heart overcharged with sensibility, acquiring the profoundest notions of justice from the
completest sympathy, and at once taking refuge from its pain,
and working out its extremest purposes, in the adoption of a
stubborn and loving fortitude which neutralizes resistance.
—Leigh Hunt, Preface to Shelley's *Masque of Anarchy* (1832)

All the poems indeed of Shelley, numerous as they are, resolve
themselves into one of which they may be regarded as so many
separate Cantos. They present to the mind in their different
episodes, their accidental details, or sites or costumes, but one
type, always equally sublime, that of a man who devotes himself, suffers and dies for his fellow beings, a Christ deprived of
his divine attributes, a philosophic Martyr, a Confessor of
Liberty.
—Thomas Medwin, *Life of Percy Bysshe Shelley* (1847)

In 1819 famine and scarcity combined with the inherited
inequalities of the British suffrage, the accruing dislocations of
the new industrialism, and the intransigent conservatism of the
government to drive England to the verge of civil war.[1] The
apocalyptic overtones of Shelley's three odes—especially of the
Ode to the West Wind and *Ode to Liberty*—reflect his sense of
a critical juncture in the moral and political life of the English
people. The very formality of the odes, their use of the high
style and a comprehensive vision, forces the structure of balanced antitheses to unify in the central personality of their
creator, forces as well the analysis of the poet's role as man

between that distinguishes the poems. That compulsion to define his responsibilities immediately derives from the series of political poems Shelley wrote in the early autumn after news of the August massacre at Manchester reached him.[2] Although conceived in the low style, these verses are impersonal, focusing directly on the political tensions of contemporary England. The apocalyptic imagery that Shelley internalizes in his odes is here overt, heralding class war, the eruption of an enormous social energy too long repressed.

There is method to Shelley's employment of this imagery. Although somewhat late in the day, he is relying upon the same general atmosphere that produced Richard Brothers in the 1790s and Joanna Southcote in the early years of the nineteenth century: the intense chiliasm, especially prominent among the lower-class sects, that accompanied the Revolution and Napoleonic Wars and whose urgency was rather fostered than forestalled by the bitter social realities of industrialization. The dualistic psychological and social forces on which Shelley's poetry of this year is founded are starkly evident in contemporary England. They dominate even the slightest of his political verses. "Similes for Two Political Characters" is an impromptu bestiary of diabolic characteristics applied to Lord Sidmouth and Lord Castlereagh. "Lines Written during the Castlereagh Administration" grotesquely reduces the symbolic, violent union of Jupiter and Thetis to an epithalamium—perhaps an anti-epithalamium—celebrating the marriage of Oppression and Ruin, whose aborted issue is British Liberty. Reminiscent of the grotesque meeting of Satan, Sin, and Death in Book II of *Paradise Lost*, Shelley's allegory derives ultimately from the Book of Revelation, where the seven heads and ten horns of the Great Beast are associated with kings (17: 7-14) and it is said of his counterpart, the Whore of Babylon, that "the kings of the earth have committed fornication with her" (18: 3). Stout defenders of king and church had contrived to clothe Napoleon in the garb of the Antichrist: but with the emperor on his lonely island, Shelley has little trouble finding a model closer to home. Even the simple "Song to the Men of England," which achieves a measure of power in its vision of a working force wholly alienated from the products of its labor, extends its imagery of a creativity that is never recompensed to an archetypal anti-creation:

> With plough and spade, and hoe and loom,
> Trace your grave, and build your tomb,
> And weave your winding-sheet, till fair
> England be your sepulchre.
>
> (29-32)

The wages of sin of this magnitude, in other words, is a universal death of the spirit.

In contrast to these poems, which picture the entire state as hell-bent through self-destruction, in others Shelley assumes as fact the logical catastrophe. "A New National Anthem" returns to the symbolic correspondence between the death of a queen and the death of liberty that marks the solemn peroration of *On the Death of the Princess Charlotte.*

> God prosper, speed, and save,
> God raise from England's grave
> Her murdered Queen!
>
> (1-3)

The anthem ends with the "trumpet's clang" (40) and the resurrection of the living dead from the graves consigned them by tyranny. The most compelling of these short poems, Shelley's "Sonnet: England in 1819," is built on the simplest of foundations. The disconnected fragments of Shelley's survey reflect in their form the disunified and discordant nature of a state wherein no element performs its proper function, but from the "old, mad, blind, despised, and dying king" (1) to the "Religion Christless, Godless" (11) contradicts its reason for existence. Those, as Shelley well understands, are the terms for Christian apocalypse, "Are graves, from which a glorious Phantom may / Burst, to illumine our tempestuous day" (13-14). With the exception of the sonnet, these are not poems of weight nor of stylistic consequence: they are written quickly, are written

I met Murder on the way—
He had a face like Castlereagh—
(5-6)

12. "John Bull's Last Kick!" Political Cartoon, 1816. *Courtesy the British Museum*

down, it would appear, to play upon superstitious millenarian expectations Shelley himself did not share. In the presence of political crisis Shelley apparently thought it of some value to remind the religious of their last days.

In contrast, *The Mask of Anarchy* reverts to the more characteristically Shelleyan concern, how to transform what is merely a superstitious tradition whose realization man passively awaits into an active assertion of human creativity. Apocalyptic imagery informs the *Mask* no less than these other verses, but, as its source is elevated from religious dogma to mythological symbol, its purpose is to suggest how humanity may wrest the millenium out of God's hands, purge the Antichrist from its midst, and establish the one true corporate body of human fellowship. The central figure in the pageant of contemporary England is Anarchy, a pervasive and pernicious lawlessness:

> he rode
> On a white horse, splashed with blood;
> He was pale even to the lips,
> Like Death in the Apocalypse.
>
> (30-33)

The equation of Anarchy and Death is organic, a psychological and social reality of the contemporary scene, not merely an obvious extrapolation from the massacre by the undisciplined and unruly yeomanry of Manchester. Anarchy on this level is a disease of the body politic, infecting all aspects of civilized life. Shelley's terms are once again set by the stark context of the Book of Revelation: "And I looked, and behold a pale horse: and his name that sat on him was Death, and Hell followed with him. And power was given unto them over the fourth part of

---

In this 1816 political cartoon by Isaac, Robert, and possibly George Cruikshank, Castlereagh, the foreign secretary and Tory leader in the House of Commons from 1812 until his suicide in 1822, is depicted as a skeletal figure of Death plunging a lance into the heart of John Bull. In his death throes the representative of the British people overturns the regent's chair, the emblem of a constitutional monarchy.

the earth, to kill with sword, and with hunger, and with death, and with the beasts of the earth" (Rev. 6: 8).

I

The implicit assumption of Shelley criticism is that *The Mask of Anarchy* is more significant as ideological statement than as poetic artifact, that, burdened by haste and anger, Shelley lapsed from the power of his opening pageant into simplistic harangue. The biases of New Criticism reinforce this judgment: the patterns of imagery and structure that create the tensions of art are largely absent from the hortatory injunctions comprising the substance of the poem. Shelley's purposes are not suggestive, but declarative; his diction is clean, simple, unambiguous. From one point of view, of course, these are virtues, and Shelley is generally successful in accommodating his vision to the mass audience he wanted to reach. Distinctive evidence of Shelley's continuing effort to broaden his range in the poems of 1819, *The Mask of Anarchy* is his most considerable achievement in the low style, shrewdly coupling its radical politics to a balladlike meter and framing its exhortations within the iconography of chapbooks, penny pamphlets, and folk pageants.[3]

Yet the art of propaganda, especially when conceived for a mass audience, poses for Shelley the same problems he contended with in *The Revolt of Islam*, constraining him from the richest veins of his genius. Shelley was clearly most comfortable in writing for the twenty auditors he thought capable of understanding *Prometheus Unbound:* how could he compete with Cobbett, whom he thought a demagogue, without violating his integrity? without reducing his political vision to the monotone of slogans?[4] "Ye are many—they are few" (155, 372) is a battle cry, but it is scarcely responsible political analysis.

Shelley, however, was quite incapable of deserting his twenty auditors, his "fit audience, though few," even where he attempted to enlarge his appeal. In *The Mask of Anarchy* he occupies that position whose philosophical underpinnings he elaborated in the *Ode to the West Wind*, as a man between, forced to mediate between the claims of time and eternity, of politics and art. New Critical standards of taste, valuable as they are for elucidating many aspects of Shelley's art, in *The Mask of Anarchy* blur precisely those artistic means by which Shelley sought to enlarge the scope of the contemporary struggle he spoke to. The second level of the poem is not organic and self-contained, but contextual, basing its allegorical and oratorical simplicities upon the complex manipulation of generic conventions and semantic ambiguities. If a modern reader easily overlooks this element, one can be certain that Leigh Hunt, to whom the poem was sent for publication, would have immediately grasped Shelley's intent. Hunt, through publication at least, had established himself as the living authority on that "species of dramatic production . . . unknown among us for a long time," the masque.[5]

The Descent of Liberty. A Mask was published by Hunt in 1815 to celebrate "the downfall of the great Apostate from Liberty," Napoleon, and to exhort the freed nations of Europe to commit themselves wholly to the true liberation of their people.[6] Four years later Shelley symmetrically divides twenty-five of his central stanzas between the present condition of the English people, which is slavery, and the characteristics of the freedom denied them. Notwithstanding the baroque embellishments of Hunt's happy vision, in other words, anarchy, not liberty, reigns in England. And more than pious hopes will be necessary to dislodge this tyrant. In reducing the high style of Hunt's literary exercise to a low style reflecting the mundane particularities of human suffering, Shelley implicitly contradicts the ideological assumptions of his mentor. England will be free only when its people refuse the transcendental model inherent in Hunt's vision, only when liberty *ascends* from the people themselves.

If in this sense Shelley controverts Hunt's overly sanguine expectations, *The Mask of Anarchy* as a whole strives to fortify the new generic ground Hunt had broken. Together they stand openly against the main traditions of the masque formed in the early seventeenth century. At that time, more than any other literary type, the masque became the artistic property of the rich and powerful, performed as a ritual enactment of the received order of society and as a recommitment to its structures of authority. The divine machinery with which the masque was invariably invested quietly supported the divine right that the shaky Stuart line claimed to the English throne. And as the hierarchy of a classical heaven complemented (even in its general lasciviousness) the protocol of the Stuart court, so the mixture of forms—drama, song, dance, spectacle—reflected a variety of social forms, each preserving its decorum within the ordered structure of the whole. The lavishness of the entertainment testified to the prosperity achieved through the harmonious interaction of such defined social roles.[7]

In the lengthy preface he attached to *The Descent of Liberty* —"Some Account of the Origin and Nature of Masks"—Hunt is more concerned with defining the elements of the genre than in assessing its social implications. He seems to take it for granted that the swift demise of the form was the natural result of its sycophantic abuses and quotes approvingly from the opening of Beaumont and Fletcher's *Maid's Tragedy*:

> *Lycippus.* What think'st thou of the masque?
> *Strato:* They must commend their king, and speak in praise
> Of the assembly,—bless the bride and bridegroom
> In person of some god. They're tied to rules
> Of flattery.[8]

Hunt makes no connection between the self-congratulatory mode of the spectacle and the distinguishing characteristic he associates with writing in the form—"lawlessness"—but it would seem no mere coincidence that Shelley does.[9] Anarchy is the distinguishing characteristic of oligarchical wielders of power, in the nineteenth as in the seventeenth century. Shelley matches an ironic form to an ironic social vision: the "adoring multitude" (41) flatters the monarch—"Thou art King, and God, and Lord" (71)—but the pageant reflects lawlessness, not order, and offers the "wine of desolation" (49), not a feast of prosperity. To elucidate the pun present from the beginning, the masque of an ordered, harmonious society is a mask.

Shelley's familiarity with masque traditions, if probably not extensive, was at least basic and sound. His knowledge of *The Descent of Liberty* must be assumed, since its reverberations affect *Prometheus Unbound* as well as *The Mask of Anarchy*. He amplifies the ironic conceptions of *The Mask of Anarchy* in *Charles the First*, whose promising first scene, enacted before a masque, establishes its radical perspective with an immediate paraphrase of the satiric lines from *The Maid's Tragedy*. Although *Comus* and the masques in *The Tempest* and the third book of *The Faerie Queene* were obvious paradigms for Shelley, his conception of the form as he re-creates it derives from Hunt's *Descent of Liberty* and from William Beaumont and John Fletcher. Mary's journal records his reading of Fletcher's *Wife for a Month* in 1818 and the *Maid's Tragedy* in July of 1819. His four-volume edition of Jonson, Beaumont, and Fletcher, issued by Stockdale in 1811, omitted Jonson's masques, but, inasmuch as Shelley and Mary were both reading through these authors in the summer and fall of 1819, it is almost certain that Shelley knew Beaumont's *Masque of the Inner Temple, and Gray's Inn*, singled out for praise in Hunt's "Account," and Beaumont and Fletcher's *Four Plays, or Moral Representations, in One* ("The Triumph of Honour," "The Triumph of Love," "The Triumph of Death," "The Triumph of Time"). Although the "Masque of the Inns of Court" in *Charles the First* derives from Bulstrode Whitelock's *Memorials of the English Affairs from the Beginning of the Reign of Charles the First to the Happy Restoration of King Charles the Second* (1682), Shelley's artful manipulation of the form several years earlier suggests the impact of Beaumont and Fletcher, from whom he gained a shrewd understanding of the two principal conventions he exploits in *The Mask of Anarchy*, the triumph and the antimasque.

Hunt's historical account of the masque traces its origins to Italy, the country mentioned in the opening lines of *The Mask of Anarchy*, and to the public pageant and masquerades whose elements are still discernible in the form:

The first appearance of one of them, or perhaps combination of both, undoubtedly took place at Florence, in the time of Lorenzo de Medici, when a party of persons, during a season of public festivity, made their appearance in the streets, riding along in procession and dressed up like reanimated dead bodies, who sung a tremendous chorus, reminding the appalled spectators of their mortality. Spectacles of this nature were clearly the origin of the Trionfi or Triumphs of the Italian poets. . . .[10]

Shelley's attempt to link Anarchy with "Death in the Apocalypse" thus has its roots in this earliest and most common form of the Triumph, the Triumph of Death. The same context is, of course, the ironic assumption of Shelley's last poem, *The Triumph of Life*. But whereas in the later poem he adopts the grand literary vision of Petrarch's *Trionfo della Morte* (or of Quevedo's *Sueños*), in *The Mask of Anarchy* Shelley's prototype is dramatic and pictorial in its immediacy, an allegorical pageant like those portrayed in Beaumont and Fletcher's *Four Plays in One*.[11] His masque begins with a "glorious triumph" (46), a procession symbolizing the victory of anarchy in Britain. By extension it is the triumph of spiritual death.

Of even greater significance for the structure and values of *The Mask of Anarchy* is the tradition of the antimasque. Hunt is silent about it, but it was clearly understood by other contemporaries of Shelley. Schlegel, for instance, commends Ben Jonson's use of this convention:

The peculiarity of Jonson's masks most deserving of remark seems to me to be the anti-masks, as they are called, which the poet himself sometimes attaches to his invention, and generally allows to precede the serious act. As the ideal flatteries, for which the gods have been brought down from Olympus, are apt to become luscious, this antidote on such occasions is certainly deserving of commendation.[12]

The antimasque was generally a parody of the sublime seriousness of the main masque, introducing the grotesque, the vulgar, the chaotic into the pageantry, only to have it superseded by the ritual celebration of harmony that followed. In Beaumont's *Masque of the Inner-Temple, and Gray's Inn* there are two antimasques: the first comprising a dance between four blind Cupids and several metallic-clothed statues who with creaky joints have descended from their niches, and the second depicting a rude peasant dance among whose couples are idiots and baboons. The antimasques here are, at the most, negative models, portraying a confusion of the values to be honored by the nuptials of the Count Palatine of the Rhine and King James's daughter, the Princess Elizabeth.[13]

But if a seventeenth-century antimasque can be seen as a temporary, limited violation of the decorum established by the masque, in the nineteenth century all is reversed. The procession of state, winding with magnificent trappings through England, substantiating with a "cost [of] ten millions to the nation" (77) its ritual authority, is the true source of the grotesque, the chaotic, the vulgarization of society. The pageant is morally an antimasque, even as it embodies all the literary conventions.[14] The disjunction in mode between the two parts of Shelley's poem represents not a simple change of course, but a purposeful transcendence of the black humor of the beginning. "Let a great Assembly be / Of the fearless and the free" (262-63), and there will ensue the main masque, the codification of true authority and harmony through the stripping of the masks of power that conceal its abuse. The masks are ubiquitous, worn not only by the ministers of state but by those who oppose them with their very tactics. The grotesque procession moves through that same landscape Shelley details in *Peter Bell the Third*, where "good and bad, sane and mad, / The oppressor and the oppressed / . . . All are damned" (252-53, 257). In so total an inversion, it is understandable that Hope, that key term of *Prometheus Unbound* and *The Cenci*, "looked more like Despair" (88). Her refusal to run from the spectacle, like the stance of Rousseau and of the narrator in Shelley's later depiction of an inverted triumph, is the first step of self-despoliation, the removal of the false garments.

As in the *Ode to the West Wind*, Shelley's use of apocalyptic imagery is organic to the themes of *The Mask of Anarchy*, not merely an embellishment of its propagandistic tendencies. The antimasque being performed throughout England is more than a dance of death: it is the naturalistic equivalent of the maraudings of the Antichrist, "Tearing up, and trampling down" (52), "Drunk as with intoxication / Of the wine of desolation" (48-49). The Celtic Anarchs depicted in the *Ode to Naples* have nothing over the government of Lord Castlereagh: in England, too, as the Peterloo Massacre exemplified, there is the same raw, destructive power: "Like Chaos o'er creation, uncreating." The answer to the Antichrist, claimed the evangelical proselytizers of a future state, is Christ. Shelley's answer is rather different in its temporal emphasis, but is otherwise remarkably similar, as the *Ode to the West Wind* suggests. But the allegorical form in which this Savior appears is once again that of Lucifer (st. 29), and the abstraction he bodies forth is Liberty.

II

The symmetrical contrast in the twenty-five stanzas of *The Mask of Anarchy* devoted to slavery and to freedom constitutes the clearest outline of the duality around which Shelley organizes the 1819 poems. Slavery is a cycle from which there is no hope for gradual release. It begins with what Marx was to call wage slavery (st. 40) and alienation from the fruits of one's labor (st. 41), is attended by privation and hunger (st. 42-43), is supported by a continuing inflation that devalues meager savings (st. 44-45), and by such economic controls fetters the workman to a system of despair. And should he claim retribution through violence, he only strengthens the moral chains that accrue to the economic ones and begins the cycle once again.[15] Such slavery is synonymous with anarchy, as Shelley suggests in his depiction of contemporary Spain in *A Philosophical View of Reform*:

> [Slavery] is the presence of all and more than all the evils for the sake of an exemption from which mankind submit to the mighty calamity of government. It is a system of insecurity of property, and of person, of prostration of conscience and understanding, of famine heaped upon the greater number and contumely heaped upon all, defended by unspeakable tortures employed not merely as punish-

ments but as precautions, by want, death and captivity, and the application to political purposes of the execrated and enormous instruments of religious cruelty. (*Prose*, 7:16)

Freedom, in contrast, is an open model, whose economic basis is the equitable distribution of the necessities of life and social intercourse (st. 54-55), and whose bases in law are impartial statutes, unrestrained intellectual inquiry, and guarantees against armed force. Once again Shelley attaches corollaries to these mundane premises, as in *Lines Written Among the Euganean Hills*, the *Ode to Liberty*, and in the gathering synthesis of the penultimate stanza (54) of *Adonais*. Freedom is Love (st. 61), is "Spirit, Patience, Gentleness" (258: st. 64), and its beacons are "Science, Poetry, and Thought" (254: st. 63). These swift accretions to the simple premises with which the catalog began are, one must remember, produced through an oracular exhalation of the earth, and the tonalities are those of the Spirit of the Earth in the third and fourth acts of *Prometheus Unbound*. If the earth is no chopper of logic, preferring rather to render life harmonious and whole than to fragment and discriminate, the catalog is more than a blurred collocation of social virtues. The syllogisms that unite these elements into a humane oneness are implicit throughout the poetry of 1819. They become the open framework for the sometimes complex logic of *A Philosophical View of Reform*.

In the first chapter of this treatise, which was later compressed into the substance of the *Ode to Liberty*, Shelley surveys the progress of political liberty in human societies. But it is not until his subsequent analysis of the corruption of contemporary England that Shelley comes to the philosophical center of his systematic document. Convinced that corruption infects all parts of the body politic, Shelley is equally certain that the only solution is through gradualism: "A Republic, however just in its principle and glorious in its object, would through violence and sudden change which must attend it, incur a great risk of being as rapid in its decline as in its growth" (*Prose*, 7:41). This is, of course, the general lesson of the French

Revolution, which Shelley well understood had been used to splinter and suppress the impetus toward reform. He began the second chapter by rejecting as a "specious topic" the principle "that popular violence . . . would be more injurious than the continuance of these abuses" (*Prose*, 7:21). But Shelley does reject violent revolution except as a last recourse, and in doing so he is not content to argue from his personal inclinations toward pacifism. Violent revolution is not consonant with liberty, and liberty cannot be gained through such means. The conclusion to Chapter II, superb in its rhetorical power, contains the essence of Shelley's conception of liberty:

> A civil war, which might be engendered by the passions attending on this mode of reform, would confirm in the mass of the nation those military habits which have been already introduced by our tyrants, and with which liberty is incompatible. From the moment that a man is a soldier, he becomes a slave. He is taught obedience; his will is no longer, which is the most sacred prerogative of man, guided by his own judgement. He is taught to despise human life and human suffering; this is the universal distinction of slaves. He is more degraded than a murderer; he is like the bloody knife which has stabbed and feels not: a murderer we may abhor and despise; a soldier is by profession, beyond abhorrence and below contempt.
>
> (*Prose*, 7:41)

The core of political and personal liberty in this new Godwinian vision is free will. It is the essential characteristic of being human, the fundamental right of man, the fundamental basis for a just society. The logical implications of this philosophical premise are, for Shelley, far-reaching. A meaningful reform cannot be effected without a total commitment to the dignity of the individual will, and that abstract commitment is equivalent to love, which Shelley defines in *A Defence of Poetry* as "a going out of our own nature, and an identification of ourselves with the beautiful which exists in thought, action, or person, not our own" (*Prose*, 7:118). Intellectual liberty must thus depend on love for its continuance, and the political liberty that is its extension can be achieved only through a politics of love. By 1819 Shelley has outgrown the flower-bedecked ships of *The Revolt of Islam*: to undertake such a politics is neither pleasant nor easy, but an unavoidable necessity that is lifelong in its commitment.

Godwin, rejecting war and, indeed, all associations that demanded the submission of the individual to a collective will, could advocate only discussion as a means of change. Shelley's assessment of evil as an active moral and political force whose overriding tendency is to destroy the integrity of the will makes it imperative that a counterforce that dignifies the will be discovered. The position that Shelley advocates in *The Mask of Anarchy* and reiterates in *A Philosophical View of Reform* is not only consonant with his philosophical premises, but has become, with its admitted drawbacks, a major dimension in the politics of the world: passive resistance. Had the assembly at Peterloo stood its ground before the yeomanry, "it is not to be believed that they would massacre an unresisting multitude of their countrymen drawn up in unarmed array before them, and bearing in their looks the calm, deliberate resolution to perish rather than abandon the assertion of their rights" (*Prose*, 7:49). Later generations might be less confident in their beliefs than Shelley, but it would be a gross error to dismiss this assertion as donnish. If one is to preserve one's faith in the ideals of human fellowship, one must act so as to create from belief the actuality that it shadows forth. It is not a man who raises his sword against unarmed petitioners, it is the role, and to attack the role is the only means of redress if one refuses to attack the man. The masquers who support anarchy are reduced to their common humanity when stripped of their disguise.

The psychological warfare Shelley advocates is not a simple assertion of individual rectitude against the power of the state, like Thoreau's civil disobedience. It is an active and primarily educative force similar to that of Gandhi. The Indian sage based his philosophy of passive resistance on the concept of *Satyagraha*—or self-suffering. As Shelley examines the personal demands of the public posture in the *Ode to the West Wind* and, implicitly, in *The Cenci*, it is clear that he means much the same thing. One pays tribute to the dignity of another's will only at the continuing expense of one's own. As the mythological exemplar of this ethos in the modern world is the crucified Christ, alluded to pointedly in the definition of love in *The Mask of Anarchy* and in the personal commitment of the *Ode to the West Wind,* so the figure who stands at the summit of Shelley's syncretic conflation in 1819 is Prometheus, whose logical leap conveys him into the mental perspective necessary for passive resistance rather than hateful defiance. No other stance is compatible with true liberty, which ceases to exist when the mind defines its attitudes in a reactionary manner, implicitly giving greater credence to the authority from which it revolts than to the assertion of its own values. Thus Jupiter rules, and thus Prometheus remains in the chains of mental servitude, asserting defiance rather than liberty. The neurotic syndrome in which he has locked himself has been wisely characterized by Erich Fromm:

> The courage of the authoritarian character is essentially a courage to suffer what fate or its personal representative or "leader" may have destined him for. To suffer without complaining is his highest virtue—not the courage of trying to end suffering or at least to diminish it. Not to change fate, but to submit to it, is the heroism of the authoritarian character.[16]

Shelley's choice of Prometheus, instead of Christ, as an exemplary model reflects more than a desire to refrain from religious controversy. The ethical verities of Christ's teaching are encompassed by transcendental truths, whereas Prometheus' gift of knowledge is symbolically a humanization of truth, and his liberation from Jupiter constitutes a final break with the transcendental as the source of authority. The progress of liberty in human societies, as expressed both in *A Philosophical View of Reform* and in the *Ode to Liberty*, is the progress of secularization, of philosophical skepticism. For Shelley the pivotal figure in modern thought is Francis Bacon, whose inductive theory entirely altered man's relation with the external world and laid the basis for the enlightenment. Locke followed Bacon by translating induction from natural to psychological processes. To Shelley the syllogistic extension was irresistible. "Berkeley and Hume, [and] Hartley [at a] later age, following the traces of these inductions, have clearly established the certainty of our ignorance with respect to those obscure questions which under the name of religious truths have been the watchwords of contention and the symbols of unjust power ever since they were distorted by the narrow passions of the immediate followers of Jesus from that meaning to which philosophers are even now restoring them" (*Prose*, 7:9). Clearly, Shelley's philosophical line leads directly to that urbane writer of "very acute and powerful metaphysical criticism," with whom Shelley visited in Rome in the spring of 1819, the skeptical Sir William Drummond.[17] Like Drummond, Shelley sees two equally pernicious, if opposite, philosophical reactions in the modern age, the attempt of Kant to resurrect transcendental ideas unrelated to human values, which is sharply criticized in *Peter Bell the Third*, and the effort of French materialism to substitute for the transcendental power of God the objective processes of natural law. "They told the truth," Shelley admits, "but not the whole truth" (*Prose*, 7:9). Like their countrymen at the end of the eighteenth century, the French materialists overthrew a king only to embrace an emperor. Indeed, if political and social forms give body to the abstract formulations already conceived by metaphysics, as Shelley asserts, it was natural enough for Napoleon to construct an empire on the philosophical foundations that prepared his way. The truth omitted by the materialists was cardinal, was man's capacity to create his own reality upon the basis of natural law, to exercise vigorously that intellectual freedom which is his birthright.

Philosophy can open the apertures of the mind, but it is only an instrument, not a regenerative faculty. Asia must join Prometheus in order for a new Genesis to occur. As described by the Chorus of Spirits in the last act of *Prometheus Unbound*, such a creation is a continuous propensity of the liberated mind:

> And our singing shall build
> In the void's loose field,
> A world for the Spirit of Wisdom to wield;
> We will take our plan
> From the new world of man,
> And our work shall be called the Promethean.
> (IV. 153-58)

Imaginative vision is at once the result, the process, and the instrument of mental liberation, exemplifying the active assertion of free will in a humanized environment, embodying philosophical abstractions in symbolic forms, exploding the sterile casings of superstition into vital, mythological significance. The poetic faculty illuminates "the highest perfection of moral and intellectual nature" as well as "the dark and secret caverns of the human heart," mediating between "idealisms of moral excellence" and the "sad reality" of an unregenerate world.[18]

The progress of liberation in the world Shelley sees as a progress of skepticism: it is also the progress of poetry. Chapter I of *A Philosophical View of Reform* returns continually to art as the index of a culture, as does the compressed survey of the *Ode to Liberty*. Chaucer exists not because of his patron, Richard II, but because of his Italian mentors, who are themselves nursed into art by republican societies. Milton is both creator and creation of the mental currents that took concrete political form in the Commonwealth. And the ferment of Romantic art is closely tied to the universal revolutionary impulse, even where the writers' politics are reactionary. The first chapter of *A Philosophical View of Reform* reaches its climax in its consideration of this phenomenon, leading Shelley to the original statement of one of his profoundest insights, as well as of his most famous prose utterance:

> It is impossible to read the productions of our most celebrated writers, whatever may be their system relating to thought or expression, without being startled by the electric life which there is in their words. They measure the circumference or sound the depths of human nature with a comprehensive and all-penetrating spirit at which they are themselves perhaps most sincerely astonished, for it [is] less their own spirit than the spirit of their age. They are the

priests of an unapprehended inspiration, the mirrors of gigantic shadows which futurity casts upon the present; the words which express what they conceive not; the trumpet which sings to battle and feels not what it inspires; the influence which is moved not but moves. Poets and philosophers are the unacknowledged legislators of the world. (*Prose, 7, 20*)

Shelley uses the word 'legislator' with an exact sense of its contemporary meaning: signifying not a parliamentarian disputing over methods of rule, but a law giver, like Zoroaster or Moses, who illuminates the essential nature of man and of his society and whose imaginative conceptions explore the potentiality inherent in the human race. The freedom that a poet exercises within the dual confines of the limits of language and of human possibility is microcosmic of that by which humanity converts itself into integrated societies. The cosmic masque that Shelley added to *Prometheus Unbound* at the end of 1819 builds its sublime structures of poetry and of social vision upon a simple equation. The imaginative act is the essential social act. A defense of absolute liberty, Act IV of *Prometheus Unbound* is simultaneously a defense of poetry.

III

The tendency to think in terms of dualities is distrusted by the modern industrial state, which, like that of the eighteenth century, prefers the stable values of philosophical and cultural monism to the apocalyptic urgings of contending factions. The revolutionary politics and poetics of Shelley are built upon a dualistic foundation. In psychological terms this may translate into a continuous dialectical process, but in respect to society Shelley everywhere sees the clash of antithetical forces. His compulsion to syncretize issues in a remarkably unified vision may appear, to a later time, of less moment than his compulsion to divide. And yet, of course, the two are inextricably involved. What Shelley attempts in the poems of 1819 is to transform the simple dualities of *Queen Mab* and *The Revolt of Islam* into a structure that is true to human life, compassionate of human failings, but insistent on fundamental human values. It hardly need be acknowledged that all Austrians are not Celtic Anarchs nor all Neapolitans virtuous democrats, but that is not to say that a sharp distinction should not be drawn between the forces of anarchy and of democracy.

Liberty is not a right guaranteed by a transcendental power; rather it is a concept, born in the human mind, which can be imposed on the institutions of society or on the edifice of natural law only by an act of deliberate will. Ultimately, the Shelleyan duality is that to which all ontological and ethical questions reduce: that between free will and determinism. In politics, it is manifested in the contention of freedom and tyranny, in whether the prerogatives of power are invested in all men or in a special oligarchy who, by claiming the right to frame laws that perpetuate their own rule, breed anarchy. The contest in society as a whole is between equality and those hierarchical forms that create classes. Indeed, to Shelley all social forms that become institutionalized lose the human perspective by which they were first generated and transform those who live by them into what Beatrice Cenci calls "Cruel, cold, formal man" (V. iv. 108) or what Camillo sees in Clement VIII: "a marble form, / A rite, a law, a custom: not a man" (V. iv. 4-5). Shelley follows Pope in extending the duality into the realm of art in *Peter Bell the Third*, and he explores the artistic ramifications most profoundly in *Adonais*, where he attaches customary bestial imagery to those critics who serve the interests of the state rather than of genius. The creative faculty is the essential manifestation of man's free will, shaping from the impressions, nuances, desires of the moment a new and unified vision of reality. In contrast, the time-serving critic is a parasite, uncreating the creations of others, destroying the urges of life with the blight of his own spiritual death. In the realm of the individual psyche, which in Shelley's "intellectual philosophy" is the basis for all knowledge, the duality operates at its subtlest and most critical level. Failure to discriminate between free will and will is finally responsible for all the tyrannies of the world, as *Prometheus Unbound* attests. The former is predicated on the liberty of all beings, the latter only on that of oneself. Free will rejects institutions, whereas will thrives on them for the sake of power, paradoxically subjecting itself to a psychological tyranny by denying its individual integrity before an external source of reality.

A fundamental tenet of Shelley's art is the organic connection between all aspects of human endeavor. Aesthetics and politics are facets of a single reality, and a unified poetic or philosophical vision must encompass both. Inclusiveness is as imperative to such a vision as is discrimination, and thus the political radical, anatomizing contemporary tensions, is a traditionalist as well, assimilating the myths of eastern and western culture, gathering the sweep of history into the structure of the present. Shelley shares the universal Romantic impulse to revert to the cultural ideals, if not the political forms, of Renaissance humanism. Secularizing its Christian values, he likewise adopts the dualistic vision central to it, but reduces it from a transcendental to a psychological reality. In such a setting Shelley transposes Milton's vision of *Paradise Lost* and *Paradise Regained*—lost through the acquisition of moral knowledge, and regained through an exemplary resistance to the temptations of Satan—into a myth that represents the codification of tyranny through self doubt and the re-creation of true liberty through the rejection of transcendental authorities. In a similar vein the Dantean journey is recapitulated as psychological process, with the inferno, purgatory, and paradise being converted into the mental states each reflects. Shelley, however, reverses the cosmic model of Dante: at the center is not a Satanic monster frozen in its denials but the creative spirit of man which can circumscribe the universe only if it never allows the primal force to be divorced from the emanating center.[19]

The body of writings Shelley composed during 1819 represents a coming of age not only in poetic terms, but in philosophical and critical understanding as well. The *annus mirabilis* is a direct result of Shelley's comprehension of the potentiality inherent in the skeptical idealism which he had come to see as underlying all attempts to conceptualize the unknown. From the simplest of philosophical bases—that the mind creates the reality in which it exists—Shelley proceeds to extend its ramifications in poetry the variety of whose forms and styles is dazzling. In the space of little over a year he creates distinguished versions of the ode, tragedy, debate, satire, sonnet, masque, song, political broadside, and, arching over the year, that sublime dramatic comedy which, beginning in tragedy, ending as masque, and incorporating dozens of distinct lyrical forms, defies all genres and seems, at least, to subsume all forms. In each case Shelley exhibits a distinctive awareness of the decorum of the genre he employs—its conventions, audience, stylistic proprieties, ideological ramifications—yet in each case he subjects the genre to the idealist premise from which he begins. Tragedies are effected by human attitudes; the dialectical structure of an ode emanates from a human predicament. In every poem Shelley re-creates the genre by demanding that its proprieties directly relate to its themes, that formal conventions serve the content that invests them with meaning. Not since Milton had there been such a concerted effort to recreate the genres of poetry as Shelley undertook in 1819, and odious comparisons need not be indulged by the simple observation that not even Milton attempted so much in so brief a span.

The diversity of form and of idea in the poems of the year, though unified by an arching scheme, attains that breadth of dimension and purpose that one associates with the epic. As Shelley clearly defines his mentors during this period as Dante and Milton, both of whom revolutionized the epic form, by concentrating his genius upon the creation of virtuoso forms —moving with admirable *sprezzatura* from form to form, from condition to condition, writing in the high style with one hand and in the low style with the other—he revises their visions within a structure of poems whose manifest unity of idea is balanced by diversity of effect. Shelley may well have felt that he had theoretical justification for investing such a loose confederation of distinct forms with an arching epic purpose. In 1818 he had briefly considered writing a tragedy on the life of an epic poet he greatly admired, Torquato Tasso. Corresponding with Peacock in August of 1818, Shelley recalled "this proud, though sublime, expression of Tasso" to which great poets aspire: *Non c'è in mondo chi merita nome di creatore, che Dio ed il Poeta*—no one in the world merits the name of creator but God and the Poet.[20] It is likely that Shelley also recalled the context for this statement in Tasso's *Discourses on the Heroic Poem*, at least as represented in the standard English biography of his time, John Black's *Life of Torquato Tasso*. There Tasso conceives the end of epic poetry to be the recreation of the world in a heterocosmic form:

> I for my part, (says Tasso, in one of his juvenile *Discourses on Heroic Poetry*,) am of opinion that unity of action is both necessary in a heroic poem, and possible to be obtained. For as, in this wonderful operation of the Almighty, which is denominated *the world*, we behold the heaven adorned with such variety of stars, and (descending downwards) the air and sea full of birds and fishes, and the earth a habitation of tame and of ferocious animals: As we behold streams, and fountains, and meadows, and woods, and plains, and mountains; on one hand fruits and flowers; on the other ice and snows; here, habitations and cultivated fields, there, solitudes and horrid wastes; yet still it is one world which includes in its bosom so many diversities; *one* is its form and essence; *one* the mode by which all its parts are with discordant concord connected and conjoined, without any thing wanting, yet with nothing superfluous or unnecessary: Thus I judge, that, by an excellent poet, (who for no other reason is called divine, but because he seems to partake of divinity, by the similarity of his operations to those of the Sovereign Artificer,) by an excellent poet, may be formed a work in which, as in a little world, we may read of armies in array, of land and naval fights, of sieges, skirmishes, jousts, and duels; in one place, descriptions of thirst and famine; in another of tempests, prodigies, and conflagrations. Here, we may find celestial and infernal councils; there, seditions, discords, wanderings, adventures, and enchantments; with deeds of cruelty, audacity, or generous courtesy; with happy or hapless, joyful or joyless incidents of love. Yet, still the poem, which contains such variety of matter, may have unity; *one* may be its form and fable, and all this diversity may be so disposed, that the latter parts may correspond with the former; each may regard the other, and every event have such a necessary, or probable dependence on a preceding one, that the alteration or removal of a single member would bring ruin on the whole. This simple variety will be laudable too from its diffi-

culty; for it is an easy matter, and a thing of no industry, to introduce a great diversity of accidents in a multitude of separate actions;
but that in a single action the same variety should be found, *Hoc
opus, hoc labor est.*[21]

Whether Shelley was guided by such a conception of the epic
creation as Tasso's, in effect he achieves much the same ends.
To view the poems of this year as part of a single structure is to
grasp after the insubstantial form that subsumes the integral
poems, an exact equivalent for that process by which the sym-
bolist, based in a human reality of a particular time and place,
aspires to the infinite. If Shelley did not deliberately predicate
a subsuming form in the poems of 1819, it is difficult to conceive of a more characteristic Shelleyan invention than the
merging of form and content on a conceptual level.

This diversified, open-ended unity of the 1819 poems is the
poetic extrapolation of the ideological stance Shelley holds to
throughout, an exact embodiment of his skepticism. Poem after
poem investigates the nature of truth, and yet nearly all end
in conditional assertions or interrogatives. It is easy to overlook
the fact that Demogorgon's enunciation of Shelleyan faith at
the end of the drama is appended to a conditional clause suggesting the ease with which liberated man might revert to
tyranny. A similar suggestion of human limitation punctuates
the close of the third act. *The Cenci* ends with Beatrice's enigmatic "Well, 'tis very well," whose untruth, at least in any
simple sense, is manifest almost to the point of absurdity. The
Ode to the West Wind concludes with a question, and the *Ode
to Liberty* collapses into similes of failure following the series
of impassioned questions leading to its climax. Likewise, *Peter
Bell the Third*, describing the pestilence of uncreation pressing
over England, offers no answer to its final line: "How should it
ever pass away?" Even *The Mask of Anarchy*, so simple and
assured in its energies, builds to a vision of the victorious people
that is possible but by no means probable. And where Shelley
does not end with a conditional or questioning syntax, he is
wont to break off in sudden inconclusiveness, as in *Julian and
Maddalo*. It is curious that a poet with so little certainty ever

got the reputation of being an easy optimist. Even where, as in *Prometheus Unbound*, Shelley's faith in human nature is most steadfast, purgatorial questions intrude.

But then, the point of skepticism is to free one from those external forms that settle questions by tyrannizing the mind. And if some men create hell, others strive for paradise, and many inhabit the contentious realm between, there is no state of life that is not conditional. The concomitant of skeptical flexibility is the responsibility to maintain a humane openness —like Boccaccio, whom Shelley praises in September, 1819, as an ideal writer: "He is a moral casuist, the opposite of the Christian, Stoical, ready made and worldly system of morals."[22] To resist the rigidity of preconceived forms is not to abandon values, but to test them repeatedly, to invest them with significance as they are continually re-created.

For Shelley skepticism is the true *via media* between a self-righteous conviction reliant on inhuman rigidity and the abject doubt that denies all assurance. Doubt, indeed, is the obverse of superstition, unable to affirm values without a transcendental injunction. It is the condition in which Prometheus imprisons himself while depending upon Jupiter to structure the cosmos. But skepticism, as Shelley represents it, is true faith, based upon the firm conviction that, since the mind structures reality, the mind can create paradise, as it has created hell, upon the plastic forms of the natural world. Shelley's conflation of religions in the poems of 1819 reduces them to the human standards from which they have strayed. It represents an act of faith, whose piety perhaps need not be emphasized, but whose depth of vision and solemnity of purpose are reminiscent of the great religious poets of western culture. Acknowledging in the preface to *The Cenci* that "Imagination is as the immortal God which should assume flesh for the redemption of mortal passion," the poet who paradoxically began his career by admitting to the "Necessity of Atheism" testifies to the faith that informs his major works. In justifying that faith for later generations, Shelley proved himself the greatest religious poet in the English language between Blake and Yeats.

Notes

Notes

Preface

[1]Notebook 2 begins (pp. 3v-6v) with a draft for *Prometheus Unbound*, II. iii. 54-99, the chorus of spirits leading Asia and Panthea to their encounter with Demogorgon. Several loose sheets (pp. 6ar-6cr), now in the Pforzheimer Library, continue the chorus, followed by a draft of the dedication to Hunt that prefaced *The Cenci* and an unused stanza for *The Mask of Anarchy*. The Huntington notebook is then given over to the pressing claims of *The Mask*, which is followed by the last stanza of the spirit chorus with which the notebook began. In Notebook 1 another brief sequence from the second act of *Prometheus Unbound* (II. v. 98-103) suddenly interrupts (pp. *26r-*25v) the composition of Act IV. 381-99. An interruption alike in its suddenness occurs in the intermediate holograph of *The Mask of Anarchy*, printed by H. Buxton Forman as a Shelley Society facsimile: on p. 16v we suddenly come upon a sketch for *Prometheus Unbound*, IV. 325-31. One cannot, of course, depend absolutely on notebook sequence, for Shelley, like all of us, could at any time and any place seek a spare page on which to jot his thoughts. Still, in combination these particular instances strongly suggest a poet laboring on three separate works at the same time. And incidentally they remind us, against the popular opinion, that Act IV of *Prometheus Unbound* was no mere afterthought.

Chapter 1. Epic Ventures

[1]*Clairmont Journals*, pp. 86-87.

[2]*Letters*, 2: 1.

[3]*To Constantia* was published under a pseudonymn in the *Oxford University and City Herald* for 31 January 1818, and not discovered in this pure text until quite recently. See Judith Chernaik, *The Lyrics of Shelley* (Cleveland: Press of Case Western Reserve Univ., 1972), pp. 195-97.

[4]The *Examiner* reviews of 1 December 1816 and 18 January 1817 are reprinted in Newman Ivey White's compilation, *The Unextinguished Hearth: Shelley and His Contemporary Critics* (Durham: Duke Univ. Press, 1938), pp. 108-09. The first favorable notice after Hunt's seems to have been that in *Blackwood's Edinburgh Magazine* for November, 1819: there, umbrage is taken with other journals who have "entirely overlooked, or slightly noticed, or grossly abused" this promising poet (*The Unextinguished Hearth*, p. 114).

[5]*Letters*, 1:577.

[6]Thomas Medwin, *The Life of Percy Bysshe Shelley*, ed. H. Buxton Forman (London: Oxford Univ. Press, 1913), p. 238.

[7]The subject deserves greater attention than it has received. Among full-length accounts are Brian Wilkie, *Romantic Poets and Epic Tradition* (Madison: Univ. of

Wisconsin Press, 1965); Karl Kroeber, *Romantic Narrative Art* (Madison: Univ. of Wisconsin Press, 1960); and, for critical attitudes toward the form, Donald Foerster, *The Fortunes of Epic Poetry; a Study in English and American Criticism, 1750-1950* (Washington: Catholic Univ. of America Press, 1962), esp, pp. 30-82. Pertinent as well is Professor Kroeber's essay, " 'The Rime of the Ancient Mariner' as Stylized Epic," *Transactions of the Wisconsin Academy of Sciences, Arts, and Letters* 46 (1957), 179-87. See also note 12, below.

[8]*The Letters of Charles Lamb To Which Are Added those of His Sister Mary Lamb*, ed. E. V. Lucas (London: J. M. Dent, Methuen, 1935), 1:85.

[9]*The Letters of Samuel Taylor Coleridge*, ed. Earl Leslie Griggs (Oxford: Clarendon Press, 1956-71), 2:963.

[10]Review of Hayley's *Memoirs* in *Quarterly Review* 31 (1825), 283.

[11]Byron, *Don Juan*, III.97.

[12]On Milton's strong influence on the epics of this period, see my essay in Joseph Anthony Wittreich, Jr., ed., *Calm of Mind: Tercentenary Essays on "Paradise Regained" and "Samson Agonistes"* (Cleveland: Press of Case Western Reserve Univ., 1971), pp. 133-62: "The Mental Pinnacle: *Paradise Regained* and the Romantic Four-Book Epic"; as well as the introduction to Professor Wittreich's *Romantics on Milton* (Cleveland: Press of Case Western Reserve Univ., 1970). Sophisticated treatment of the important issues of epic theory and genre, centered in Blake's epic prophecies, is to be found in Professor Wittreich's two essays: " 'Sublime Allegory': Blake's Epic Manifesto and the Milton Tradition," *Blake Studies* 4, ii (1972), 15-44; and "Opening the Seals: Blake's Epics and the Milton Tradition," in Stuart Curran and Joseph Anthony Wittreich, Jr., eds., *Blake's Sublime Allegory: Essays on "The Four Zoas," "Milton," and "Jerusalem"* (Madison: Univ. of Wisconsin Press, 1973), pp. 23-58.

[13]William Hayley, *An Essay on Epic Poetry* (1782), ed. Sister M. Celeste Williamson, SSJ (Gainesville, Fla.: Scholars' Facsimiles and Reprints, 1968). Hayley's importance to Blake's biography has been much stressed: for his impact on the writings, see Professor Wittreich's essay, "Domes of Mental Pleasure: Blake's Epics and Hayley's Epic Theory," *Studies in Philology* 69 (1972), 201-29.

[14]*Paradise Lost*, IX. 14. In *Paradise Regained* Milton emphasizes that the deeds of Christ in the wilderness are "Above Heroic" (I. 15).

[15]"Carmen Triumphale, for the Commencement of the Year 1814" and "Carmina Aulica, written in 1814, on the Arrival of the Allied Sovereigns in England" were greatly ridiculed by such contemporaries as Francis Jeffrey and Leigh Hunt.

[16]One must, of course, recall that minor authors, especially those with government annuities, employed the form for jingoistic purposes: the prime example is *Alfred* (1801) by the Poet Laureate Henry James Pye. But even among minor authors the political character of the epic is manifest: George Cocking's *War* (1781), on the American Revolution; James Ogden's *The Revolution* (1790), on the Glorious Revolution of 1688; John Ogilvie's *Britannia* (1801), on the foundations of the British state.

[17]David V. Erdman, ed., *The Poetry and Prose of William Blake* (Garden City, N. Y.: Doubleday, 1970), p. 693.

[18]"The Reason of Church-Government," in Don M. Wolfe, et al., eds., *Complete Prose Works of John Milton* (New Haven: Yale Univ. Press, 1953), 1:815.

[19]Charles Kegan Paul, *William Godwin: His Friends and Contemporaries* (London: H. S. King, 1876), 1:69.

[20]*Letters*, 1:220.

[21]*The Young Shelley: Genesis of a Radical* (New York: Macmillan, 1950), p. 241.

[22]Ibid., pp. 243-45.

[23]The first reprinting of *Piers Plowman* since the sixteenth century was issued in the same year that Shelley brought out *Queen Mab*, and it is thus difficult to conceive of its having had an influence on the poem: see *Visio Willi de Petro Ploughman*, edited (with modern paraphrase) by Thomas Denham Whitaker (London: John Murray, 1813). As for *Night Thoughts*, one should recall that Blake not only attempted a recasting in *The Four Zoas*, but preceded that apocalyptic vision with an extraordinary pictorial interpretation consisting of 537 designs to the poem.

[24]Cameron, *The Young Shelley*, pp. 274, 407, n128.

[25]*Kubla Khan*, it is true, was not published until 1816, but the echo seems so assured that one can only surmise that Shelley had come upon a copy of the poem, perhaps through Southey during his stay at Keswick from November 1811 to January 1812.

[26]*Letters*, 1:201, 324.

[27]*Letters*, 1:218.

[28]*Letters*, 1:558.

[29]On this note it is significant that Shelley immediately invokes the legend of the Wandering Jew for metaphorical support after the poet has died: *Alastor*, ll. 675-81.

[30]Wilkie (*Romantic Poets and Epic Tradition*, pp. 139-43) has a perceptive discussion of the importance of eloquence to the heroic values of the poem.

[31]That the site of Paradise appears to shift radically between the first and last cantos is the result of recondite learning, not carelessness. In Canto I the Woman conveys the questioning poet toward the north pole—an archetypal journey inverted the same year in the nightmare quest of Dr. Walton, Victor, and the monster in the closing pages of *Frankenstein*—but in Canto XII Laon, Cythna, and the child journey up a river until it joins with three others in a great lake, which appears to be the legendary Lake Mansarovara north of India. Francis Wilford, in his essay "On Mount Caucasus," claims that the four rivers of Eden issue from this lake, identifies them with the major rivers of Asia, and locates the lake near Bamiyan in the Indian Caucasus. Shelley's awareness of Wilford's claims is examined in the succeeding chapter. In the context of *The Revolt of Islam*, it is sufficient to note that, however incongruous the geography appears, it has strong mythological authority. "The great *Mána-sarovara*, which proceeded from the heart of BRAHMÁ, is on [Mount] *Méru*, and the four great rivers issue from it." Mount Meru is, of course, the Indian Paradise; its top is, like that of Olympus, the abode of the gods. "By *Méru*," Wilford explains, "they [the *Puránás*] understand in general the North pole, but the context of the *Puránás* is against this supposition. In these sacred books, *Méru* is considered solely as a point to the North of *India*, from which four large rivers issue, and flow toward the four cardinal points of the world: and we frequently read of countries and places said to be to the North of *Méru*. . . *Méru* is not the North pole. . . [but] it is the zenith, and center of the known world." See Francis Wilford, "On Mount Caucasus," *Asiatic Researches: or, Transactions of the Society Instituted in Bengal*. . ., 6 (London, 1801) 463-64, 486-91; and, for the quoted passages, "On the Geographical Systems of the *Hindus*" (Part 1 of "An Essay on the Sacred Isles in the West"), *Asiatic Researches* 8 (London, 1805), 323, 286, 308. Meru's position at the North pole is likewise asserted in Edward Moor's *Hindu Pantheon* (London, 1810), p. 259, which Shelley owned, and is mentioned in a note to Southey's *Curse of Kehama* (*Poetical Works* [London, 1838], 8:235-36); Southey also gathers together a number of Wilford's comments on the four rivers descending from the mountain (*Poetical Works*, 8:261-62). Meru is understood as well to be identical with Meros, the birthplace of Dionysus. As for the tradition of locating paradise in so unlikely a spot as the North pole, the far north was extensively argued to be the original seat of man by Jean-Sylvain Bailly, whose theory Shelley mentions in a footnote to *Queen Mab*, VI. 45-46.

[32]Carlos Baker (*Shelley's Major Poetry: The Fabric of a Vision* [Princeton: Princeton Univ. Press, 1948], p. 79) sees not only *Thalaba*, but Peacock's draft of *Ahrimanes* as influencing the poem. Cameron tempers this second view, arguing strongly for a mutuality of influence (*Shelley and His Circle* [Cambridge: Harvard Univ. Press, 1970], 3:237, 240-43). Shelley warmly admired Southey's eastern epic-romances. Medwin claims that in 1809 Southey was his favorite poet: "He had read *Thalaba* till he almost knew it by heart and had drenched himself with its metrical beauty. . . . But he still more doted on *Kehamah*" (*Life of Percy Bysshe Shelley*, p. 44). In 1811 Shelley declared that "The Curse of Kehama. . . is my most favorite poem" (*Letters*, 1:101), and later, in writing to Hogg, cited the versification of *Thalaba* (with that of *Samson Agonistes*) as authority for his experiments in *Queen Mab* (*Letters*, 1:352). Both Mary and Claire record Shelley reading aloud *The Curse of Kehama* and *Thalaba* in September of 1814 (*Clairmont Journals*, pp. 44-46; *Mary Shelley's Journal*, pp. 15-16).

[33]Loath as one is to perpetuate biographical fallacies in Shelley criticism, their particular applicability to *The Revolt of Islam* is suggestive of the extent to which Shelley's personal fantasies color the poem. The equation of Mary and himself with his heroic subjects is only the most obvious. Mary's notes remark on the tribute to Shelley's tutor Dr. Lind in the figure of the Hermit. Shelley also makes the first of his public apologies to Thomas Jefferson Hogg, who is cast as the misunderstood friend of Laon's youth. And with the numerous attacks on the villainy of the old, one cannot help picturing that crafty, taciturn Whig politician, Sir Timothy Shelley, in the sultan, or the Oxford orthodoxy in the inquisitorial Iberian priest. It hardly need be added that Shelley's impulse to give everyone his due does not strengthen his poem; but, on the other hand, it cannot be denied that Spenser and, especially, Dante provide distinguished authority for making cosmic issues from personal relationships.

Chapter 2. The Key to all Mythologies

[1]A. *Course of Lectures on Dramatic Art and Literature*, trans. John Black (London, 1815), 1:16-17.

[2]Ibid., 1:112-13.

[3]Ibid., 1:113.

[4]See *Mary Shelley's Journal*, pp. 94-95.

[5]Ibid., p. 95.

[6]Newton's views of Prometheus are expressed in *The Return to Nature, or, A Defence of the Vegetable Regimen* (London, 1811), pp. 7-13. Horace interprets the introduction of fire to pertain to human fevers in *Odes*, I. iii.

[7]Earl Wasserman's reading of this epigraph is shrewd and convincing: *Shelley: A Critical Reading* (Baltimore: Johns Hopkins Univ. Press, 1971), pp. 282-83. Arrogant epigraphs (and prefaces) are so common in the Renaissance epic as to constitute a minor convention. To aspire to things unattempted yet in prose or rhyme is Ariosto's desire, as after him it is Spenser's and Milton's. Wordsworth, in "Home at Grasmere," the first part of his unfinished epic *The Recluse*, adopts the same posture, as does Blake in the prefatory remarks he appended to *Milton* and *Jerusalem*.

[8]Of the 2610 lines of the first edition of *Prometheus Unbound*, 1267 precede Act II, Scene iv, 32, the start of this 78-line speech; and 1265 follow line 109, its end. Shelley's careful attention to the numbering, documented in Lawrence Zillman's variorum edition of the drama, would seem justified less as idle busy work than as concern for structural balances: it would also seem likely that Shelley finally counted all his lines rather than missed several, as Zillman argues (*Shelley's "Prometheus Unbound": A*

Variorum Edition [Seattle: Univ. of Washington Press, 1959], pp. 260, 300-01). This argument, of course, assumes that Shelley viewed his four-act structure as an entity, the position maintained throughout this study.

[9]That the balance of power shifted to the gods because of defections by principal Titans like Oceanus and Clymene is central to Keats's conception of *Hyperion*. The political dimensions of Prometheus' struggle are illuminated by a French rendition, in which as leader of the cult of Heaven and Earth, he is jealously distrusted by fanatics of Cronos and offers his services to their enemies, the cult of Zeus. After a ten years' war the latter triumph, but Prometheus discovers that the new rulers wish to exterminate the followers of Heaven and Earth, and for warning his old associates he is imprisoned in chains. See Guillaume, le Baron de Saint-Croix, *Recherches Historiques et Critiques sur les Mystères de Paganisme* (1784), 14-19; rev. Baron Silvestre de Sacy (Paris, 1817), 1:18-25.

[10]Ahasuerus ends his long catalog of crimes committed in the name of God with a vision of the crusades, where "blood-red rainbows canopied the land" (*Queen Mab*, VII. 234). As there are two versions of the "earthly" cosmology in Act I, a reflection of Asia's account is intimated earlier in the second act when the fauns return to their labors, anticipating the "wise and lovely songs" of "thwart Silenus" (II. ii. 91, 90) as their reward. What they will hear, of course, is the cosmology Silenus sings the shepherds in Virgil's Sixth Eclogue.

[11]*PMLA* 40 (1925), 172-84.

[12]Robert Ackerman, "Writing About Writing About Myth," *Journal of the History of Ideas* 34 (1973), 154. Shelley scholarship owes a pronounced debt to Earl Wasserman whose various essays, collected in *Shelley: A Critical Reading*, have emphasized the great importance of mythological syncretism to Shelley's work. The most useful treatment of this material in terms of the Romantic movement is by Albert J. Kuhn, "English Deism and the Development of Romantic Mythological Syncretism," *PMLA* 62 (1956), 1094-116: his accents, however, fall on Blake, as do those of Florence Sandler in "The Iconoclastic Enterprise: Blake's Critique of 'Milton's Religion,'" *Blake Studies* 5, i (1972), 13-57. That Edward B. Hungerford collected considerable material pointing to the significance of the Indian Caucasus, then transposed *Prometheus Unbound* to the Georgian Caucasus for purposes of discussion, is a marvel of modern scholarship, but is perfectly in accord with his flippant approach to the subject in *The Shores of Darkness* (New York: Columbia Univ. Press, 1941). The impact of the collection edited by Burton Feldman and Robert D. Richardson, *The Rise of Modern Mythology, 1680-1860* (Bloomington: Indiana Univ. Press, 1972) has not yet been felt, but the extracts it contains and the extensive bibliography appended to it should greatly simplify the labors of future scholars. The strong bias of that anthology, however, is occidental. Until this present study there has been virtually no scholarship tracking the English Romantic poets on their forays into the orient, and this volume, unable to consider such works of Shelley's as *The Indian Girl's Song* or that idyll known as *Fragments of an Unfinished Drama*, both of which exhibit knowledge of eastern tonalities and versification, cannot claim to have exhausted even Shelley's debt, let alone those accrued by other poets of the period. Here, too, there is a significant need for future scholarship.

[13]*Letters*, 2:70-71.

[14]*Genealogie Deorum Gentilium* (Bari: Laterza, 1951), 1:196-202, esp. p. 198. This book has never been completely translated into English, although Charles C. Osgood has provided an extract in *Boccaccio on Poetry: Being the Preface and the Fourteenth and Fifteenth Books of Boccaccio's Genealogia Deorum Gentilium* (Princeton: Princeton Univ. Press, 1930). In Banier's *Mythology* (London, 1739-40), see 2:282-83. Other euhemerist interpretations include those of Saint-Croix, note 9 above, and Fabre

d'Olivet, note 70 below; Jean Sylvain Bailly, *Histoire de L'Astronomie Ancienne Depuis Son Origine Jusqu'à L'Etablissement de L'Ecole D'Alexandrie* (Paris, 1775), pp. 187-88; and Jean Joseph Lionnois, *Traité de la Mythologie, ou Explication de la Fable par l'Histoire et les Hiéroglyphes des Egyptiens*, 5th ed., rev. (Nancy, 1805), pp. 29-30. The first commentary to make Prometheus an ancient Egyptian king is that of Diodorus Siculus in the *Library of History*, I. 19. 1-4.

[15]So Boccaccio, *Genealogie*, 1:198. Francis Bacon in *The Wisedome of the Ancients* (1619; facs. New York: Da Capo, 1968) sees Prometheus as providence, p. 124; Alexander Ross, *Mystagogus Poeticus, or The Muses Interpreter: explaining the historicall Mysteries, and mysticall Histories of the ancient Greek and Latine Poets*, 3rd ed., rev. (London, 1653), quotes Tertullian that "God is the true *Prometheus*," p. 369; John Turner, *An Attempt Towards an Explanation of the Theology and Mythology of the Antient Pagans* (London, 1687), designates Prometheus a sun god representing a pagan conception of the Supreme Numen: "the same things are attributed to him, which are ascribed to God in Scripture" (sig. g^{2a}), especially his instruction of Deucalion (Noah) to avoid the flood.

[16]This is the thesis of the most influential of English syncretists, Jacob Bryant, in *A New System, or An Analysis of Ancient Mythology* (London, 1774-76), 2:273-74, which is reiterated in Lionnois, *Traité de la Mythologie*, p. 31, mentioned briefly in Thomas Maurice's *The History of Hindostan; its Arts, and its Sciences, as Connected with the History of the Other Great Empires of Asia, during the most ancient periods of the world* (London, 1795), 1:496, and expanded by George Stanley Faber, *The Origin of Pagan Idolatry ascertained from Historical Testimony and Circumstantial Evidence* (London, 1816), 2:193-94. This conflation had been early attempted in additions to Natalis Comes' *Mythology* when it was published in Paris in 1627 (see pp. 306-07).

[17]Prometheus is identified as Mind by Eusebius and Syncellus, according to Faber, *Origin of Pagan Idolatry*, 1:172. The Neoplatonic version of the myth can be found in Claudian, "Panegyric on the Fourth Consulship of the Emperor Honorius," 225-54, which is the basis for Thomas Taylor's glosses on Prometheus in the notes to his edition of Pausanias, ordered by Shelley in 1817 ([London, 1794], 3:240-41; reprinted in *The Six Books of Proclus the Platonic Successor. . . by Thomas Taylor* [London, 1816], 2:230-31). The Renaissance humanist is Natalis Comes, *Mythologie* (Paris, 1627), pp. 296-307, especially p. 302. For Prometheus as martyred liberator, see John Cam Hobhouse, *Historical Illustrations of the Fourth Canto of Childe Harold* (London, 1818), pp. 444-45: the passage actually occurs in the concluding "Essay on Italian Literature," the ideas of which were supplied by Ugo Foscolo, then a resident of England.

[18]George Sale, *The Koran. . . to which is prefixed a Preliminary Discourse* (London, 1734), p. 458*n*. The Hebrew derivation, attributed to Eusebius, can be found in the midst of the lengthy account of Prometheus in Samuel Shuckford, *The Sacred and Profane History of the World Connected*, 2nd ed. (London, 1731-40), 3:98; *Asa-Devi* and *Hásyá* figure in Francis Wilford, "On Mount Caucasus," *Asiatic Researches* 6 (London, 1801), 495, 504; and a later essay records that the Greeks pronounced *Isa* as *Asos, Asioi* (*Asiatic Researches* 8 [1805], 279). The account of the *Asæ* is contained in one of the pieces appended to Wilford's "Essay on the Sacred Isles in the West," entitled "Origin and Decline of the Christian Religion in India," *Asiatic Researches* 10 (London, 1811), 28-29. The Zoroastrian contexts of *Asha* are delineated in Jacques Duchesnes-Guillamin, *Symbols and Values in Zoroastrianism: Their Survival and Renewal* (New York: Harper & Row, 1966), pp. 25-28, and in R. C. Zaehner, *The Dawn and Twilight of Zoroastrianism* (London: Weidenfeld and Nicolson, and New York: Putnam, 1961), p. 64. Wilford also derives Bacchic Nysa from Nicæa, a nymph who is also called Asyaca in the Puranas: "On Mount Causasus," *Asiatic Researches* 6:496.

[19]Shelley could easily have found Varro's assertions in *De Lingua Latina* (V. 31) or as gathered by Boccaccio (*Genealogie*, 1:187) or by Lemprière (*Classical Dictionary.* 7th ed. [London, 1809], "Asia"). This interpretation accords with the discriminations made by Frederick A. Pottle in "The Role of Asia in the Dramatic Action of Shelley's *Prometheus Unbound*": see George M. Ridenour, ed., *Shelley: A Collection of Critical Essays* (Englewood Cliffs, N.J.: Prentice-Hall, 1965), pp. 133-43.

[20]Bacon's allegorization occurs in his *Wisedome of the Ancients*, p. 139. For fire and water as sexual symbols, see Plutarch's *Roman Questions*, 1. Numerous classical authors acknowledge the Persian deities as fire, water, and earth: e.g. Diogenes Laertius, *Lives and Opinions of Eminent Philosophers*, I.6; Herodotus, *History*, I.131. The creation of Ormusd from fire and water is mentioned in Claude Emmanuel Joseph Pierre de Pastoret, *Zoroastre, Confucius et Mahomet, comparés comme Sectaires, Législateurs et Moralistes; avec le Tableau de leurs Dogmes, de leurs Lois & de leurs Morales*, 2nd ed. (Paris, 1788), p. 19. The Indian derivation is asserted by Thomas Maurice, *Indian Antiquities* (London, 1800), 2:58. One might note as well that the Indian Venus, Laxmi or Sree, is the daughter of Varuna, god of the oceans, and is the consort of Vishnu, the preserver: see "Lachsmi," in Edward Moor's *Hindu Pantheon* (London, 1810), pp. 132-44, and Faber, *Origin of Pagan Idolatry*, who defines Lachsmi as the white goddess Isi (3:46-47). Wilford, his source, terms the white goddess Leuco-thea, identifies her with Minerva, and remarks that she lives with the daughters of Nereus at the bottom of the sea: "ŚWETÁ DEVÍ: *or the* WHITE GODDESS," ch. 3 of "Essay on the Sacred Isles in the West," *Asiatic Researches* 11 (1812), 130. In François Noël's standard French textbook, *Abrégé de la Mythologie Universelle* (Paris, 1815), Asia is likewise asserted to be a surname of Minerva, and the Asiae to be nymphs in the service of Diana (p. 84).

[21]The definition of Panope is taken from Lempriere's *Classical Dictionary*; the other references are to Hesiod, *Theogony*, 250, and Apollodorus, *The Library*, 1.ii.7.

[22]*Panthea, or The Captive Bride: A Tragedy* (London, 1789); *The History of Hindostan*, 2:154-55.

[23]Comes, *Mythologie* (1627), p. 917; and on the Ionides, see the standard handbook, originally published in 1727, Pierre Chompré's *Dictionnaire Abrégé de la Fable* (Avignon, 1817), p. 228. Faber (*Origin of Pagan Idolatry*, 3:408) explicitly relates the homonymn, remarking that the cult of Ionism or Hellenism worshipped the *yoni*. Charles François Dupuis—*Origine de Tous les Cultes* (Paris, 3 [1795], 2:119)—notes the connection between the Bacchic "Io" and the daughter of Inachus. It should be recalled as well that the first of the Hours whom the sun engendered was named Eone.

[24]Plutarch appears to have been the first who placed a strong claim for Isis (Io) as the daughter of Prometheus: *Moralia*: "Of Isis and Osiris," III. 37. Boccaccio's treatment of Isis follows immediately upon his section on Prometheus (*Genealogie*, 1:203-04): his separate account of 'Ione' is in *Genealogie*, 1: 357-60. Whatever Boccaccio's reasons for separating these figures, the identification of Io and Isis is a commonplace of mythology, even among classical authorities. Faber (*Origin of Pagan Idolatry*, 3:46-47) identifies Isis with the Indian Isi, and Lionnois (*Traité de la Mythologie*, pp. 479-80) sees her as the type both of the popular and celestial Venus. Isis is identified with the Hebrew Isha, the ancient name for woman, by Noel Antoine, Abbé Pluche, *The History of the Heavens, considered according to the Notions of the Poets and Philosophers, compared with the Doctrines of Moses*, trans. J. B. de Frevel (London, 1740), 1:50: Isha is, of course, related to Aish, noted as a cognate for Asia in note 18 above. The translation of Isis into the moon is discussed in Faber, *Origin of Pagan Idolatry*, 3:17, as being equivalent to the transfiguration of the Delphic Sibyl into that body: the association of Io, Isis, the moon, and fertility symbols can

be found in Dupuis, *Origine de Tous les Cultes*, 1:395-401. Similar connotations, it should be noted, surround Iona, the heroine of Shelley's *Swellfoot the Tyrant*.

[25]*Indian Antiquities*, 4:245-391; reprinted in *A Dissertation on the Oriental Trinities in 1800* and, with additions, again in 1801. The other reference is to Faber, *Origin of Pagan Idolatry*, 3:3-5. A similar relationship between the three nymphs is suggested in Earl Wasserman's early note, "Myth-Making in *Prometheus Unbound*," *Modern Language Notes* 70 (1955), 182-84. An interesting analog to Shelley is provided by Keats, whose Endymion must discover that Cynthia, Proserpine, and Diana are three aspects of one goddess.

[26]On the Graces, see Boccaccio, *Genealogie*, 1:144, 276-77, and for the Hesperides, 1:188. Comes offers commentary on the Graces, pp. 390-93, the Hours, pp. 394-95, and the Nymphs, pp. 455-58. The description of the Hours comes from [Thomas Blackwell's] *Letters concerning Mythology*, a hallmark of allegorical mythography (London, 1748), p. 88. For the triple Hecate and triple Diana, see Lionnois, *Traité de la Mythologie*, pp. 476-77, and Pluche, *History of the Heavens*, 1: 122-23; and, for commentary on the various mythological personifications of the moon, Alexander Ross, ΠΑΝΣΕΒΕΙΑ: *or, A View of all Religions in the World*, 3rd. ed., rev. (London, 1658), p. 141.

[27]*A New System, or An Analysis of Ancient Mythology* (1774-76), 2:42, n22. An interesting analogy to Shelley's conception of the Furies is contained in Maurice's elaboration of one of the famous Zoroastrian or Chaldean oracles, "The Furies are Stranglers of Men": "Psellus, commenting upon it, says, that the dæmons who torment mankind, being the vices and passions of men personified, torture them for their crimes, and, in a manner, STRANGLE them. The exhibition of the contests of these good and evil genii seems formerly to have constituted as favourite a portion of the dramatic productions of India, as our VICE, and other mythologic characters, used to be in the ancient dramas of Britain": *Indian Antiquities*, 4:284. The harpies of classical mythology are, of course, also three in number.

[28]On the birth of the three Fates, see Boccaccio, *Genealogie*, 1:18, and *Letters concerning Mythology*, p. 55, where Blackwell on the basis of this account calls the Fates "the Daughters of *Necessity*." Francis Wilford's exposition is found in "ŚWETÁ DEVÍ; *or the* WHITE GODDESS," *Asiatic Researches* 11 (1812), 110-43.

[29]See Walter Sidney Scott, ed., *The Athenians, Being Correspondence Between Thomas Jefferson Hogg and his Friends Thomas Love Peacock, Leigh Hunt, Percy Bysshe Shelley, and Others* (London: Golden Cockerel Press, 1943), pp. 36, 39-40. For commentary on Demogorgon, see Wasserman—*Shelley: A Critical Reading*, pp. 332-33—and the brief notes of Henry G. Lotspeich, "Shelley's 'Eternity' and Demogorgon," *Philological Quarterly* 13 (1934), 309-11, and Albert J. Kuhn, "Shelley's Demogorgon and Eternal Necessity," *Modern Language Notes* 74 (1959), 596-99.

[30]*Rhododaphne*, in *Works*, 7:94: in this note he also remarks that Natalis Comes reproduces Boccaccio's account. According to the sale catalog of his library, Peacock owned Bassano's Italian translation of Boccaccio, *La Geneologia de Gli Dei de Gentili* (Venice, 1574) and the *Comitis Mythologia* published in Venice in 1581. (The catalog, 11 and 12 June 1866, issued by Sotheby, Wilkinson, and Hodge, is reproduced in *Sale Catalogues of Libraries of Eminent Persons*, ed. A. N. L. Munby [London: Mansell, with Sotheby Parke-Bernet, 1971], 1:153-201.) See also *Bell's New Pantheon; or, Historical Dictionary of the Gods, Demi-Gods, Heroes, and Fabulous Personages of Antiquity* (London, 1790), 1:228b-29a; Banier, *Mythology*, 2:549-51; and—as Nature—Chompré, *Dictionnaire Abrégé de la Fable*, p. 131, and Lionnois, *Traité de la Mythologie*, p. 184. Kenneth Cameron notes a reference to Demogorgon in a work Shelley used as a source in his early poetry, *The Tales of the Genii*, translated from the Persian

by Sir Charles Morell (James Ridley): see *Shelley: The Golden Years* (Cambridge: Harvard Univ. Press, 1974), p. 646, *n*41.

[31]Wasserman, p. 335; Boccaccio, 1:15, 30-31, and for the genealogy of the Titans, 1:154. Without citing a source, J. Macmillan Brown asserts that medieval traditions place Demogorgon in the Himalayas where he presides as king over the elves and fays (*The "Prometheus Unbound" of Shelley* [Christchurch, Wellington, and London: Whitcombe and Tombs (1905)], p. 84). Numerous other associations of Shelley's drama with the Indian Caucasus are treated below.

[32]Boccaccio (*Genealogie*, 1:15-16), describing Demogorgon and Eternity in their cave, may well have influenced Shelley's portrayal of the cave to which Prometheus and Asia retire to preside over a regenerate cosmos. An extensive account of Demogorgon, extracted from numerous authors, can be found in Michel de Marolles, *The Temple of the Muses; or, the Principal Histories of Fabulous Antiquity* (Amsterdam, 1753), somewhat abridged from the French original—*Tableaux du Temple des Muses* (1676)— whose account of Demogorgon and Eternity precedes a subheading entitled "Les premiers principes des choses sont imperceptibles" (p. 6), of which an apt translation might be Shelley's "the deep truth is imageless" (II. iv. 116). Variations of the demiurgic soul are taken from Maurice, *Indian Antiquities*, 5:58-59, which also has an exposition of the serpent Cneph as eternity, 4:302-03 (for Shelley's knowledge, see *Prose*, 7:103). Maurice returned to this subject at some length in *Observations on the Remains of Ancient Egyptian Grandeur and Superstition, as Connected with Those of Assyria* ... (London: John Murray, 1818), pp. 80-81, 88-89. A long section of Dupuis's *Origine de Tous les Cultes* is devoted to the mystery cults (2^2:1-259). John Robison's fanatical attack on Masonry—*Proofs of a Conspiracy Against all the Religions and Governments of Europe*, 4th ed., rev. (Dublin, 1798)—suggests that French Masonic rituals were designed to achieve a oneness with the 'Soul of the World' (pp. 44-45) and that the German Illuminati, the subject of Hogg's *Memoirs of Prince Alexy Haimatoff*, patterned their rites after Mithraic models (pp. 136-37). Warburton's famous discourse on the pagan mysteries occurs in *The Divine Legation of Moses Demonstrated*, in his *Works* (London, 1788), 1:166-336. This enlargement on Wasserman's analysis of the Virgilian contexts of the second act of *Prometheus Unbound* is not meant to impugn so worthy an explication, but rather to suggest that it should be subsumed by a larger pattern of meaning that Shelley surely knew: see *Shelley: A Critical Reading*, pp. 310-15, 320-23.

[33]Ross, *Mystagogus Poeticus*, pp. 367-70; Wasserman, *Shelley: A Critical Reading*, p. 293.

[34]*Blackwood's* ended its review with the injunction that it was high time Shelley "learned to 'fear God and honour the king,'" and the *Quarterly* devotes several columns to countering Shelley's impiety: see Newman Ivey White, *The Unextinguished Hearth: Shelley and His Contemporary Readers* (Durham: Duke Univ. Press, 1938), pp. 231, 248-49.

[35]Shelley's familiarity with Gnostic doctrine when he wrote *Queen Mab* can be discerned in VII.174-76. The Gnostics universally conceived of the Creator as evil, to be identified with the devil: see, for instance, Isaac de Beausobre, *Histoire Critique de Manichée et Manicheisme* (Amsterdam, 1734), 2:14-15; and Nathaniel Lardner, *The Credibility of the Gospel History*, in *Works* (1788), 3:494. Lardner, in his *History of the Heretics of the Two First Centuries after Christ ... with Large Additions by John Hogg*, repeats Irenaeus' observation "Marcion taught that when Christ descended to hell, he delivered many wicked people, but left there the patriarchs, and many other good men of the Old Testament." This is explained by Theodoret: "Cain and the people of Sodom, and other wicked people, came to the Lord Jesus in hell, obtained salvation, and were taken by him into his kingdom: but Abel, and Enoch, and Noah,

and the patriarchs, and the prophets, were not delivered, because they would not come to him" (*Works*, 9:377). Some Gnostic sects conceived of Jesus as the Tree of Knowledge and as the serpent (Beausobre, 1:246, 2:453-58; and John Laurence Mosheim, *An Ecclesiastical History, Ancient and Modern*, trans. Archibald Maclaine [London, 1811], 1:135). Aside from these texts, Shelley might well have been familiar with the numerous writings of Joseph Priestley on Christian heretics, notably *An History of Early Opinions Concerning Jesus Christ, Compiled from Original Writers: Proving that the Christian Church Was at First Unitarian* (London, 1786). On the centrality of Gnostic traditions to another poet of the age, see my essay "Blake and the Gnostic Hyle: A Double Negative," *Blake Studies* 4:ii (1972), 117-33.

[36]Cicero was apparently the first writer to equate the sidereal Venus and Lucifer (*De Natura Deorum*, II. 25); Shelley uses this continuously as a symbol. It informs the first canto of *The Revolt of Islam*, where the woman narrator, reminding the poet of the evening star, details the process by which she becomes ideologically inspired as falling in love with the morning star, Lucifer. Much subtler is the reunion of Adonais with Urania, where the soul of Keats becomes assimilated with Vesper in the 46th stanza of *Adonais*.

[37]Jacob Bryant and Thomas Maurice both treat Prometheus as Noah, but their list is hardly exclusive: others thought to be Noah are Apis, Atlas, Athena [as Nous], Chronos, Deucalion, Dionysus, Fohi, the Indian Ganesis, Ianachus, Janus Bifons, Neptune, Oannes, Osiris, Poseidon, Satyavrata, Theuth, Xisasthrus, Xuthus, and Zuth.

[38]Joseph Raben's "Shelley's *Prometheus Unbound*: Why the Indian Caucasus?" (*Keats-Shelley Journal* 12 [1963], 95-106) is a useful starting point for this consideration, but its sources are too limited to justify its sweeping conclusions.

[39]The exploits of Alexander the Great in the Indian Caucasus are detailed by Arrian in his *Anabasis Alexandri* and in the *History of Alexander* by Quintus Curtius Rufus, and are mentioned in Strabo's *Geography* (11. 5. 5; 15. 1. 8-9). On British imperialism during the Napoleonic Wars, the following comment in the *Quarterly Review*'s notice of Lieutenant Henry Pottinger's *Travels in Beloochistan and Sinde* (April, 1816) should suffice: "We are indebted for these volumes [on eastern cultures] . . . to the restless ambition of Buonaparte, whose views on the Eastern world, after the peace of Tilsit, could neither be mistaken, nor treated with indifference by the British government at home, or its representatives in India: the latter of whom, with a laudable zeal, and in the proper spirit of military precaution, anticipated every measure that the former could have desired, by the mission of Sir J. Malcolm to Persia, of Mr. Elphinstone to Caubul, or Mr. Smith to Sinde, and of our present travellers through Beloochistan" (15, 86). Shelley read Mountstuart Elphinstone's *Account of the Kingdom of Caubul* in July-August of 1817 and perused both ancient histories of Alexander in the same year.

[40]*The History of the World*, in *The Works of Sir Walter Raleigh* (Oxford, 1829), 2:230. On the basis of this distinction, Raleigh construes Bacchus, who journeyed from the Indian Caucasus to Greece, as identical with Noah. The westward drift of civilization is a prime impetus to mythographers: Faber, for instance, sees the Sacae as the original of the Saxon race: *Origin of Pagan Idolatry*, 2:272. An even closer analogy is provided by the Abbé Paul Ives Pezron's claim that Japhet's eldest son Gomer fathered the Gomerians, later termed the Sacae, who descended from the region of the Indian Caucasus to become the Titans of Greece and thus the ancestral race of Europe (*The Antiquities of Nations; more particularly of the Celtae or Gauls, Taken to be Originally the Same People as our Ancient Britons*, trans. D. Jones [London, 1706], pp. iv-v).

[41]Comes' *Mythologie*, as augmented by Baudoin (Paris, 1627), has an added passage identifying Prometheus with Noah and designating Caucasus as Ararat: pp. 306-07;

the supposition is given strong support in the seventeenth century by Bishop Patrick's commentary on Genesis, is similarly defended by Samuel Shuckford (*The Sacred and Profane History of the World Connected*, 1:98-104), and given prominence as an acceptable theory in the *Universal History, from the Earliest Account of Time* (London, 1747-54), 1:245-46. The latter work Shelley cites in a footnote to *Swellfoot the Tyrant*. The references in this passage are to Maurice, *Indian Antiquities*, 5:100-01; Wilford, "On Mount Caucasus," *Asiatic Researches* 6 (1801), 455-536; and Faber, *Origin of Pagan Idolatry*, 1:333-34.

[42]Arrian notes that "all the important rivers of Asia rise from Mounts Taurus and Caucasus" (*Anabasis Alexandri*, V. 5. 4; trans. Iliff, 2:19), and Quintus Curtius Rufus (*History of Alexander*, VII, 3. 19-23) makes much the same assertion. Bailly, as hypothetical guide, offers Voltaire this view from the summit of Caucasus: "You are at the very source of fertility: it is produced by the waters which collect around us. Here is the grand reservoir of the largest quarter of the globe. Look towards the south—you see the course of the Indies [Indus], which still remembers to have been crossed by Alexander; the Ganges, in which the Indians perform their ablutions:—upon the right, the Ghoango, where the Yellow River of China proceeds towards the sea of Japan: but if you turn your eye towards the north, where my steps conduct you, you will see the Oby, accompanied by the Irtiz, the Jenisea, and the Lena, in their descent to the Frozen Ocean" (*Letters Upon the Atlantis of Plato, and the Ancient History of Asia: Intended as a Continuation of Letters upon the Origin of the Sciences, addressed to M. de Voltaire*, trans. James Jacque [London, 1801], 2:174). In the *Quarterly Review* notice of recent works on "The Himalaya Mountains, and Lake Manasawara" (17 [July 1817], 428) it is remarked that "the sources of the two great branches of the Ganges and the Indus [are] within four or five miles of each other." For the link between the rivers of Caucasus and those of Eden, see ch. 1, note 31. Reuben Burrow ("A Proof that the Hindoos Had the Binomial Theorem," *Asiatic Researches* 2 [1799], 487) amplifies Bailly by claiming that "the four sacred rivers of *Eden* went through *India, China, Siberia*, and into the *Caspian Sea*, respectively."

[43]Faber, *Origin of Pagan Idolatry*: "the ancestors of the classical mythologists emigrated from the region of the Indian Caucasus" (1:397). Faber sees the nation of Cush extending from India to the Mediterranean (1:83-85); see also 3:570-75, and, for Peruvian and Mexican derivations, 3:251-52. Maurice discusses American links in *Indian Antiquities*, 5:20, following Shuckford's suggestion, *Sacred and Profane History*, 1:104. Bailly, defining the Persian Devas as the original Titans and Prometheus as an ancient Persian mythic hero, locates them all on "the summit of Caucasus, whence the Atlantides descended, as well as the worship of the sun, and where the Persians took their origin and the beginning of their history" (*Letters Upon the Atlantis of Plato*, 2:225).

[44]The voyage of the poet is, of course, an archetypal journey toward what Jung, using Longfellow's *Hiawatha* as an improbable model in chapter 7 of *Symbols of Transformation*, terms 'the dual mother,' who offers her womb for bestowing death as well as life. There exists, however, a remarkably close, contemporary analogue to the poet's travels, the lengthy narration of Adim and Evehna, journeying from their home in Atlantis to the birthplace of humanity in the Caucasus, in Antoine Fabre d'Olivet's *Lettres à Sophie sur l'Histoire* (Paris, 9 [1801]), 1:203-84.

[45]*Quarterly Review* 22 (January 1820), 352. Linking the Edenic and Noachian contexts of Caucasus, Faber reminds his readers of the legend that both Adam and Noah are buried in a sepulchre there: *Origin of Pagan Idolatry*, 1:334-35. The Abbé Lambert, deriving Indian religions from the Old Testament, suggests that the veneration paid Caucasus recalls its original, Mount Sinai: Claude François Lambert, *A Collection of Curious Observations on the Manners, Customs, Usages . . . of the Several Nations of Asia, Africa, and America*, trans. John Dunn (London, 1750), 1:20. It is exactly this

sort of tendentious Christian propaganda that Thomas Blackwell, in a mock argument proving the identity of Moses and Bacchus with Romulus, attacks (*Letters concerning Mythology*, pp. 235-38), and a similar parody, conflating Descartes and Democritus, is spun by the usually humorless Bailly in *Essai sur les Fables, et sur leur Historie* (Paris, 7 [1799]), 1:19-21. William Godwin, seeking to provide an alternative to the standard Christian bias of mythological handbooks, published—under the pseudonymn Edward Baldwin—*The Pantheon: or Ancient History of the Gods of Greece and Rome* in 1806. Whether Shelley knew Godwin's book, he adopts the same skeptical attitude in his use of mythology. Yet, it should be obvious that, however much Scripture led eastern mythologists astray, they were compelled by very real discoveries. When Maurice, for instance, sets as the goal of his labors "the derivation of all languages from one primæval tongue, as well as of all nations from one great family" (*Indian Antiquities*, 6:20), he is working within the slowly developing comprehension of what today we know as the Indo-European language group. The foremost linguists of this period laid the conceptual foundation for later and more refined analysis: in England Sir William Jones discriminated false from true etymologies and fostered the study of Sanscrit, and in France his counterpart Silvestre de Sacy greatly furthered the study of comparative languages. As linguistic research masqueraded under the guise of scriptural exegesis, so did the psychology of symbolism. Faber's *Origin of Pagan Idolatry* is built upon what for the time was a remarkable thesis, that all ancient religious imagery reduced to phallic and vulvaic symbolism, which he explained with donnish inspiration as the race memory of Mount Ararat and the ark.

[46]For associations of Mount Meru and its significance for *The Revolt of Islam*, see ch. 1, note 31. Wilford specifies the location of the sacred mountain in "Of the two Tri-Cu′t′a′d′ri, or Mountains with three Peaks. . . ," *Asiatic Researches* 10 (1811), 127: repeating his assertion are Faber, *Origin of Pagan Idolatry*, 1:331-34, 2:198, and Sir William Drummond, *Origines; or, Remarks on the Origin of Several Empires, States, and Cities* (London, 1824), 1:325 (a work, of course, published after Shelley's death, but whose author he greatly admired and whom he visited in Rome on 22 April 1819). Wilford's explication of the sexual symbolism of Meru is in "On the Geographical Systems of the *Hindus*," *Asiatic Researches* 8 (1805), 273, and the passage is repeated in Moor's *Hindu Pantheon*, p. 389. For Pir-pangial, see Abbé Lambert, *A Collection of Curious Observations*, 2:117-18, and Bailly, *Letters Upon the Atlantis of Plato*, 1:115.

[47]Byron glosses "Kaff" as Mount Caucasus in his note to *English Bards and Scotch Reviewers*, l. 1022. The mythic attributes of Caf can be found in Maurice, *Indian Antiquities*, 1:235; Bailly, *Letters Upon the Atlantis of Plato*, 2:143; William Franklin, *The Loves of Camarúpa and Cámalata: An Ancient Indian Tale* (London, 1798), p. 278; and Guillaume, Baron de Saint-Croix, *A Critical Inquiry into the Life of Alexander the Great, by the Ancient Historians . . . with Notes and Observations, by Sir Richard Clayton, Bart.* (Bath, 1793), p. 366. In a draft for the Preface to *Prometheus Unbound*, Shelley alludes to his spirit choruses of Act I: "I am not conscious of having deviated from the <custom> of antique mythology—The Spirits indeed belong under various names to every system of supernatural agency, it is a generic name including Genii, Lamiæ, elementary powers Angels fairies, ghosts, demons" (Lawrence John Zillman, *Shelley's "Prometheus Unbound": The Text and the Drafts*, p. 44). Compare the note in Peacock's first published poem, *The Genius of the Thames*: "Beings, similar to the Genii of classical mythology, may be found in almost every other mythological system. Their importance in that of the Hindus is evident from what has been said above: there are some traces of them in various parts of the *Zend-Avesta*: and many authorities concur to show that they entered into the religious tenets of the disciples of Confucius" (*Works*, 6:374).

[48]Anquetil du Perron, *Zend-Avesta, Ouvrage de Zoroastre* (Paris, 1771), 2 vols. in 3

parts. For Albordj as the mountain of life, see 1^2:88; 2:177-78; as Mithra's home, 2: 206; as the same as Caucasus, see "A Brief Account of a Voyage to India undertaken by M. Anquetil du Perron, to discover and translate the works attributed to Zoroaster," *Annual Register*, 1762, Part 2, 117n. A section of the *Zend-Avesta* is appended to the first edition of Bryant's *New System* (3:588-98).

[49]Thomas Maurice's *Indian Antiquities* begins, "In the year 1785, a singular phœnomenon made its appearance in the world of literature, under the title of BHAGVAT-GEETA . . ." (1:7). By 1790 a number of important texts were available: *The Code of Gentoo Laws*, trans. Halhed, 1776; *Ayeen Akbery* [The Mirror of the Emperor Akber], trans. Gladwin, 1783; the *Bhagvat-Geeta*, trans. Wilkins, 1785; the *Heetopades*, trans. Wilkins, 1787; and *Sacontala, or The Fatal Ring*, a drama by Kalidasa, trans. William Jones, 1788.

[50]The terms for the dispute over the authenticity of the *Zend-Avesta* can be found in John Richardson, *A Dissertation on the Languages, Literature, and Manners of Eastern Nations*, 2nd ed. (Oxford, 1778), pp. 11-20. It is summarized from the perspective of time by Faber, *Origin of Pagan Idolatry*, 2:61-63. Anquetil du Perron was also attacked by Volney, who thought that he had Christianized the Zoroastrian mythology: *New Researches on Ancient History*, trans. Colonel Corbet (London, 1819), 2:52-53. The cited Peacock annotations occur in *Works*, 6:191, 423, 425. On the latter occasion Peacock also notes the recognized authority before Anquetil du Perron, Thomas Hyde's *Historia Religionis Veterum Persarum* (1700). References to Zoroaster in Peacock's works begin as early as *The Genius of the Thames* (see note 47 above), and his Zoroastrian ode, "The Spirit of Fire," is especially significant, inasmuch as it promises a volcanic eruption to overthrow modern tyrannies and corruptions. One should take into account the fact that almost any work on mythology or comparative religion published in the half century after the appearance of the *Zend-Avesta* devotes considerable attention to Zoroastrianism.

[51]Dio Chrysostom, *Discourses*, XXXVI. 40; Boccaccio, *Genealogie*, 1:30-31. Others also record that the sun touched the mountain peak: Philostratus, for instance, in giving details of the Prometheus legend, reports that "the peaks of the Caucasus are so lofty that the sun is cloven asunder by them" (*The Life of Appolonius of Tyana*, II. 2; trans. Conybeare, 1:119). Fabre d'Olivet assumes that this is a poetic commonplace about Mount Caucasus (*Lettres à Sophie sur l'Histoire*, 1:290). As for the actual height, Elphinstone reported peaks as high as 20,493 feet, affirming that "the peaks of Hindoo Coosh are higher than those of the Andes" (*Account of the Kingdom of Caubul* [London, 1815], p. 95), a supposition supported by mythologists (see, for instance, Bailly, *Letters Upon the Atlantis of Plato*, 2:173), but quickly displaced by William Moorcroft in his *Journey to Lake Mánasaróvara in Ún-dés* (*Asiatic Researches* 12 [1816], 375-534): he measured peaks as high as 25,669 feet in the Himalayas. For purposes of comparison, the leader of the second successful expedition to climb Mont Blanc reported its height as 15,662 feet, that of Teneriffe as 15,396 feet, and that of Chimboaço in the Andes as 20,608 feet (Horace Benedict de Saussure, *Sketch of a Tour through Swisserland* [London, 1788], p. 91).

[52]To the Jews he was considered a disciple of Abraham or identical with Nimrod, Seth, or Balaam; early Christians thought him one of the three wise men who attended on Christ (Joseph Bidez and Franz Cumont, *Les Mages Hellénisés* [Paris: Société d'editions "Les Belles Lettres," 1938] 1:41-54); the Greeks reported that the Manicheans believed Zoroaster, Manes, Buddha, Christ, and the sun all the same (Beausobre, *Histoire Critique de Manichée*, 1:254); and Anquetil du Perron develops numerous biographical parallels between Zoroaster and Christ (*Zend-Avesta*, 1^2:12ff.). The Christian Neoplatonist, Francesco Patrizi, saw affinities between Zoroaster and Japhet, the son of Noah (*Magia Philosophica, hoc est Francisci Patricii summi Philosophi*

Zoroaster et eius 320 Oracula Chaldaica [Hamburg, 1593], p. 2a). Noah himself was identified with Fohi or Buddha by Shuckford (*Sacred and Profane History*, 1:102-03, 236), and Buddha was in turn identified with Zoroaster by Volney (in *The Ruins: or, A Survey of the Revolution of Empires*, 5th ed. [London, 1807], p. 286n) and by the Abbé Foucher (*Historische Abhandlung über die Religion der Perser, seit dem Ursprung dieses Volks bis jetzt* [published with a German translation of the *Zend-Avesta*, Leipzig and Riga, 1781], 1^2:66-67n). Wilford notes parallels with Buddha, Belus, and Nimrod ("Of the two TRI-CU'T'A'D'RI," *Asiatic Researches* 10 [1811], 137-38); and Faber volunteers others (*Origin of Pagan Idolatry*, 2:76-77). As is customary with such conflation, every principal figure of the ancient world is sooner or later made identical with every other.

[53]Six Zoroasters are listed by Thomas Stanley in *The History of the Chaldaick Philosophy* (pp. 2-3), published with *The History of Philosophy: Containing the Lives, Opinions, Actions and Discourses of the Philosophers of Every Sect*, 3rd ed. (London, 1701). Diogenes Laertius in his *Lives and Opinions of Eminent Philosophers* (I. 2) gives the date of 5000 years before the fall of Troy. For a view of these vagaries by a contemporary of Shelley's, see D. G. Wait, "Wherefore have the ancients recorded a variey of men, under the name of Zoroaster?" *Classical Journal* 7 (March 1813), 220-26. Modern researches have established Zoroaster's dates as roughly from 628 to 551 B.C.

[54]Elphinstone reports that the Asians distinguished Balkh by the title of "mother of towns" (*Account of the Kingdom of Caubul*, p. 464), and Maurice emphasizes its proximity to India and legends that Zoroaster was accompanied on a visit to the Indian sages by the Persian emperor Darius Hystaspes (*History of Hindostan*, 2:270-72; *Indian Antiquities*, 2:130-35). Shuckford claims that it was Abraham who reformed the Persian religion and established his residence in Balkh (*Sacred and Profane History*, 1:306-07; also, *Universal History*, 5:154). Beausobre, noting strong affinities between Magian and Pythagorean concepts, summarizes the authorities for the meeting of Pythagoras and Zoroaster and claims that through his instruction Pythagoras communicated Magian ideas to Plato (*Histoire Critique de Manichée*, 1:30-31, 313 [misnumbered 393]). Voltaire takes the visit to India for granted in one of his responses printed in Bailly's *Letters Upon the Atlantis of Plato* (1:44); J. Z. Holwell sees this relationship as crucial to the dissemination of knowledge throughout the ancient world (*Interesting Historical Events, Relative to the Provinces of Bengal, and the Empire of Indostan . . . also the Mythology and Cosmogony, Fasts and Festivals of the Gentoo's* [London, 1766-71], 2:24-27); and Maurice uses the visit to India to suggest that Pythagoras and Zoroaster communicated Judaic conceptions to their hosts, since he finds them everywhere in Indian thought (*History of Hindostan*, 2:268-69). Humphrey Prideaux, Dean of Norwich, terming Zoroaster "the greatest imposter, except Mahomet, that ever appeared in the world," claims he was a servant in Daniel's house during the Babylonian captivity (*The Old and New Testament Connected*, 16th ed. [London, 1808], 1:263). For more on the relationship of Judaism and Zoroastrianism, see note 71 below. Zaehner ends the introductory chapter of his *Dawn and Twilight of Zoroastrianism* with a sentence summarizing the thrust of the Persian religion: "Zoroaster is the Prophet of life, and of life ever more abounding" (p. 61). That understanding, though emphasized by modern religious scholars, was also common in the eighteenth century. The *Universal History*, in its long account of Zoroaster, remarks that "of all virtues, he esteemed what the Greeks called *philanthropy*, and the apostles *brotherly love*, the greatest" (5:401). Volney notes the prevalence of aqueducts throughout the Persian empire and asserts they were built "in order to multiply, according to the precepts of Zoroaster, *the principles of life and of abundance*" (*Travels through Syria and Egypt, in the Years 1783, 1784, and 1785* [London, 1787], 2:164.

[55]*Zend-Avesta*, 1^2:364-71. Animated stars and planets figure in Plato's *Timaeus*,

and Maurice asserts that the Indians appoint astral deities (*History of Hindostan,* 1:117).

[56]Herodotus, *History,* I. 131; trans. Godfrey, 1:171; a similar description is in Strabo's *Geography,* XV. 3. 13-14. These accounts, though limited, are largely accurate: for a catalog prayer in general accord with Herodotus' description, see Anquetil du Perron, *Zend-Avesta,* 1²:113.

[57]*Zend-Avesta,* 2:254; R. C. Zaehner, *The Dawn and Twilight of Zoroastrianism,* pp. 81, 150.

[58]A definite analogy, a meeting with one's double in a garden, has been noted in the seventeenth-century compendium of folk superstitions, John Aubrey's *Miscellanies,* by Margaret and Ralph Arthur Ranald ("Shelley's Magus Zoroaster and the Image of the Doppelgänger," *Modern Language Notes* 76 [1961], 7-12). The possibility of Shelley's acquaintance with Aubrey's *Miscellanies* is stronger than the authors contend, for after its initial publication in 1696 it was reprinted in 1721 and 1784 and was sufficiently current for Byron to refer to it familiarly in his notes to *The Vision of Judgment.* Still, the analogy is at best superficial, since Aubrey's account of such apparitions defines them as portents of death, which is certainly not the case in *Prometheus Unbound.* The distinguished scholar of eastern religions Jacques Duchesne-Guillamin—in *The Western Response to Zoroaster* (Oxford: Clarendon Press, 1958), p. 16—comments on this scene of *Prometheus Unbound:* "I have searched in vain for a definite source for this particular episode: unless I am mistaken, it is of Shelley's own invention. He appears to have freely combined the account of Zoroaster's visions with that of the faithful soul's encounter with the Daēnā after death. In order to convey what he thought essential in the Zoroastrian message, namely, a secret correspondence and attraction between visible and spiritual realities, he fashioned a new Zoroaster." In this passage, it is significant to note, Duchesne-Guillamin does not in the least doubt Shelley's purposeful use of a Zoroastrian context. If Shelley did not derive this episode from Aubrey's *Miscellanies,* it is likely that he elaborated upon a similar scene, the enigmatic 'Vision of Hystaspes' that forms the appendix to Chapter 7 of the treatise by the "Scotch philosopher" Shelley teasingly alludes to in his preface. Hystaspes, of course, is famous as the royal patron of Zoroaster. In this allegorical vision, he is walking in his garden in Babylon, reflecting on the sorrows of human life, when he is confronted by a divine messenger in the form of a pillar of mist. This Angel of Instruction takes Hystaspes into the air, like Ianthe, to contemplate the earth and promises immortality to those devoted to the growth of the intellect and spirit. This parable, strongly suggesting that the true and simple religion of man, the veneration of spirit, is inimical to the interests of church and state, would naturally have appealed to one with a "passion for reforming the world." See Robert Forsyth, *Principles of Moral Science* (Edinburgh, 1805), pp. 504-20, and for the chapter, "Of the Passion for Reforming the World," pp. 283-94.

[59]*Zend-Avesta,* 2:263, 276.

[60]*Zend-Avesta,* 2:4. The harsh sentence of Zoroastrian law for defiling the dead bears a striking similarity to the terms of Prometheus' imprisonment. The criminal is chained to a mountainside, in peril of attack from carrion birds, until he repents of his acts, at which point he is released and reassimilated to society (*Zend-Avesta,* 1²:282-83). Even without knowledge of Zoroastrian doctrine, of course, one can discern the essential nature of the Phantasm of Jupiter: Volney, for instance, claims that in various traditions phantoms, composed of ether, are "the image or idol of the soul" (*The Ruins,* p. 304).

[61]Bryant, *A New System,* 1:217-18, 222; see Peacock, *Works,* 6:257. This Mithraic cavern is not in Shelley's writings unique to *Prometheus Unbound:* it is also a significant context for the cave of Cythna in *The Revolt of Islam* and for that in which

the Witch of Atlas lives. *The Witch of Atlas,* indeed, shares many of the same mythological contexts as *Prometheus Unbound.*

[62]Kathleen Raine and George Mills Harper, eds., *Thomas Taylor the Platonist: Selected Writings* (Princeton: Princeton Univ. Press, 1968), p. 301. Both Thomas Maurice (*Indian Antiquities,* 2:133-35, 178-83, 242-56, 395-96) and George Stanley Faber (*A Dissertation on the Mysteries of the Cabiri* [Oxford, 1803], 2:357ff.; *Origin of Pagan Idolatry,* 2:412-14, 3:215) devote considerable attention to the symbolic properties of the Mithraic cavern. Among the many quotations of Porphyry's account are a number easily accessible to Shelley: Anquetil du Perron, "Vie de Zoroastre," in *Zend-Avesta,* 1^2, 27-28; Banier, *Mythology,* 2:122; Dupuis, *Origine de Tous les Cultes,* 2^2:204, and Volney, *The Ruins,* p. 297. Anquetil du Perron maintains that the likely location of this cave was on Mount Albordj: since he also identifies this mountain as Caucasus, the original Mithraic cavern is thus the same as the Promethean cave (*Zend-Avesta,* 1^2:28).

[63]That Zoroaster received the *Zend-Avesta* within a cave is maintained by Maurice, *Indian Antiquities,* 2:40-41, and is mentioned in a review of J. Taylor's translation from the Sanscrit of two dramas, *The Rise of the Moon of Intellect* and *The Knowledge of Spirit,* in the *Edinburgh Review* 22 (January 1814), 400.

[64]Diodorus Siculus, *Library of History,* XVII. 83. 1; Arrian, *Anabasis Alexandri,* V. 3. 2; Faber, *Origin of Pagan Idolatry,* 1:334-35, 352-53. The statues and cave at Bamiyan are discussed in George Sale's "Preliminary Discourse" to *The Koran* (p. 19), Anquetil du Perron's "Discours Preliminaire" to the *Zend-Avesta* (1:ccccviii-xin), Maurice's *Indian Antiquities,* in connection with Porphyry's description of the Zoroastrian cave (2:134-35), Moor's *Hindu Pantheon,* pp. 247-48, and Faber's *Origin of Pagan Idolatry,* 1:322; 2:469-72. Maurice, like Wilford, emphasizes a third cave containing the image of a child: in reality there are only the two great statues, which are Buddhist, not Zoroastrian.

[65]"On Mount Causasus," *Asiatic Researches* 6 (1801), 455-536. Bamiyan and its environs are discussed in particular on pp. 467-91; the passage on the oracle of the earth occurs on p. 515. Wilford reports that the legendary Promethean cave is "near the pass of *Sheibar* [Shibr or Shabar], between *Ghor-band* and *Bamiyan*" (p. 495). Two years before, in a masterful display of the offhand, Wilford referred to that Prometheus "who lived near Cabul" ("On the Chronology of the Hindus," *Asiatic Researches* 5 [1799], 289). What pleasure the residents of that city might take from their illustrious ancestor is somewhat mitigated by Wilford's assurance that "when *Satan* was ejected, or *kicked,* as they say, out of the garden of *Eden,* where he first lived, he leaped over the mountains, and fell on that spot, where *Cabul* now stands" (*Asiatic Researches* 6, 492). "On Mount Causasus" was of sufficient importance to warrant an extensive critique in the initial number of the *Edinburgh Review* (1 [1800], 39-42). It should be noted here that Wilford was forced to retract some of his early oriental researches when he found that his enterprising pundit was inventing links between eastern and western myths to please his patron. Edward B. Hungerford uses this information in *The Shores of Darkness* in order to dismiss all of Wilford's work: Wilford, however, in his lengthy confession, invalidates only his very early work, specifically excepting all but some trifling details of the essay "On Mount Caucasus" and the whole of his major effort, "An Essay on the Sacred Isles in the West": for this retraction, see *Asiatic Researches* 8 (1809), 247-62. This same information was conveyed by E. H. Barker in "Prometheus Vinctus," *The Classical Journal* 4 (September 1811), 221-22.

[66]Maurice, *Indian Antiquities,* 3:157; see also 188-90. Maurice distinguishes the Monoptere from the Hypaethron, a circular edifice with two rows of columns, the second raised above the first, and without a dome. Writing to Peacock from southern

Italy early in 1819, Shelley discourses on the ruins of Greek temples which, he says, "were mostly upaithric" (*Letters*, 2:74). Cythna likewise compares her island prison to a "hupaithric temple" (*Revolt of Islam*, l. 2935). The term is not a coinage, as Frederick L. Jones asserts in his note to the 1819 letter, but Shelley's adjectival rendering of a precise architectural term which is inexplicably omitted from the *Oxford English Dictionary*. Carl Grabo may be right in asserting that the Spirit of the Hour's description of the imaginative sun temple derives from Shelley's Italian tour (*"Prometheus Unbound": An Interpretation* [Chapel Hill: Univ. of North Carolina Press, 1935], p. 120), but, since Shelley's description of the sun temple effectively dissociates it from hypaethric models, it seems equally clear that he was aware of the distinction between a hypaethron and a monoptere.

⁶⁷Boccaccio, *Genealogie*, 1:14.

⁶⁸*Origine de Tous les Cultes*, 2²:208. Mithraic ritual forms the substance of Thomas Maurice's *Ode to Mithra*, published with *Grove-Hill* in 1799.

⁶⁹The following brief example should suffice to demonstrate their similarity:
Respond, Ormusd, with truth to what I ask of you.
How was the celestial world composed in the beginning? How did you fashion the good beings and good productions, O you who are pure, absorbed in excellence, raised above all else, Ormusd, friend of the two worlds?
Respond, Ormusd, with truth to what I ask of you.
Who was the primal father who engendered life? Who brought forth from himself the fixed stars? How did you make the moon whose phases are created and destroyed? Teach me, Ormusd, these things that I desire to know.
Respond, Ormusd, with truth to what I ask of you.
Who made the earth which preceded man and will follow him? Who made the water, the trees...? (*Zend-Avesta*, 1²:190)

⁷⁰*Lettres à Sophie sur l'Histoire*, 1:136-63, 253.

⁷¹*Origine de Tous les Cultes*, 3:1. Dupuis also notes that Christmas comes at the time of the great celebration of Mithra's birth (3:44-45), and in the accompanying "Explication des Planches" further documents their similarities: "In effect, Mithra and Christ are born the same day, in a grotto or stable; Christ and Mithra regenerate the universe by the blood of a lamb or of a bull; they die at the moment of the rebirth of light, as they were born in the season of darkness. Both, finally, have secret initiations, purifications, baptisms, and even confessions... (p. 12). In his "Précis de la Cosmogonie et de la Théologie des Perses," which is mainly derived from the *Zend-Avesta*, Dupuis remarks a number of Zoroastrian sources for the Revelation of St. John (3:273-85). Dupuis's assertion that the Zoroastrian duality, derived from seasonal cycles, is basic to all religions of Europe and the Near East (3:10-20) earned him this opening sentence of an essay by Joseph Priestley: "This work of M. *Dupuis's* is certainly the most extraordinary production of the present, or of any preceding age, and the *ne plus ultra* of infidelity" ("Remarks on M. Dupuis's *Origin of all Religions*," in *The Theological and Miscellaneous Works, &c. of Joseph Priestley*, ed. J. T. Rutt [London, 1815-32], 17:320-59). Maurice's Indian researches are openly directed against the atheistical tendencies of "Mr. Dupuis' long-threatened work, the baleful fountain from which Mr. Volney's was only a rivulet" (*History of Hindostan*, 2:vii). A rivulet, perhaps, but with a strong current: "Jews, Christians, Mahometans, however, lofty may be your pretensions, you are, in your spiritual and immaterial system, only the blundering followers of Zoroaster" (*The Ruins*, p. 159). The tendency to derive the Judaeo-Christian religion from Zoroastrianism began with Voltaire's claim that Zoroaster's writings antedate and influence all western religions ("Essai sur les Mœurs et l'Esprit des Nations," in *Oeuvres Complètes de Voltaire* [Paris, 1877-83], 11:34). He was

sarcastically, if ineptly, attacked by Bishop Warburton in *The Divine Legation of Moses Demonstrated* (in *Works* [London, 1788], 2:654-55).

[72]Mallet, *Northern Antiquities; or A Description of the Manners, Customs, Religion and Laws of the Ancient Danes, including those of our own Saxon Ancestors*, trans. Bishop Thomas Percy, 2nd ed. (Edinburgh, 1809), 2:20, 98, 130-33; Bailly, *Letters Upon the Atlantis of Plato*, 1:203; Vallancey's researches, published in Nos. 12 and 14 of *Collectanea de Rebus Hibernicis* (1770-1804), 3:ii (1783), and 4:ii (1786)—the second of which dissertations, *A Vindication of the Ancient History of Ireland*, is wholly devoted to proving the Irish and Persians of the same race—Maurice, *Indian Antiquities*, 2:40, 121; 6: passim; 7:672-77; Faber, *Origin of Pagan Idolatry*, 2:77-78, 352-54; Wilford (who especially supports Asia's assertion, basing his "Essay on the Sacred Isles in the West" on the supposition that England was settled by Brahmans), *Asiatic Researches*, 11 (1812), 11-110; Sale, *The Koran*, p. 72, 89-94; Drummond, *Origines*, 1:386; Dupuis, 1:224-28. The claims for connections between the Brahmans and Druids are briefly rehearsed in Edward Moor's *Hindu Pantheon*, p. 46.

[73]Plutarch's *Moralia*, "Of Isis and Osiris," 46; trans. Babbitt, 5:111.

[74]Theopompous claimed that the struggle between Ormusd and Ahriman lasted just 3000 years (*Bell's New Pantheon*, 1:92) : Shelley, of course, may simply be varying the number of years (30 or 30,000) traditionally mentioned as spanning the imprisonment of Prometheus.

[75]Although a few commentators, following the accurate description of Zurvan (Ζαρουαμ) by Theodore of Mopsuesta, tried to fit him into the known facts of Zoroastrianism (e.g. Beausobre, *Histoire Critique de Manichée*, 1:171-74), Anquetil de Perron was the first to give him prominence. His Zurvanite monotheism was accepted as the true Persian mode by Gibbon (*Decline and Fall*, ch. 8) and in Sir John Malcolm's *History of Persia* (London, 1815). See Jacques Duchesne-Guillamin, *Western Response to Zoroaster*, pp. 16-17; and for a detailed account of Zurvan's place in the Persian scheme, see R. C. Zaehner's *Zurvan, a Zoroastrian Dilemma* (Oxford: Clarendon Press, 1955). Dupuis's term, "an eternity of time without end" (*Origine de Tous les Cultes*, 1:94), nicely defines the balance of time and the timeless achieved in the fourth act of *Prometheus Unbound*.

[76]Shelley could have found accounts of Ahriman's being created from Doubt in Pierre Bayle's *A General Dictionary, Historical and Critical*, trans. J. P. Bernard, T. Birch, J. Lockman, et al. (London, 1734-39), 5:636; Beausobre, *Histoire Critique de Manichée*, 2:253-54; *Bell's New Pantheon*, 1:92; the *Universal History*, 5:159; and in the Chevalier Andrew Michael Ramsay's *Discourse upon the Theology and Mythology of the Pagans*, continually printed with the numerous editions of his *Travels of Cyrus* (e.g. 8th ed. [London, 1752], p. 290). The implications of Doubt for *Prometheus Unbound* are considered more fully in the following chapter.

[77]"Voltaire's or Diderot's attitude was to survive essentially unchanged: to a Goethe in his *Parsee Nameh* (*West-östlicher Divan*, with *Noten* on the Ancient Persians), to a Byron in *Childe Harold*, to a Wordsworth in *The Excursion*, the Persian religion remained the model of a natural, reasonable religion, later corrupted by priestly fanaticism" (Jacques Duchesnes-Guillamin, *Western Response to Zoroaster*, p. 15). The references in Byron are to Canto III, stanzas 14 and 91; in Wordsworth, to *Excursion*, IV.671-80. The summary of Zoroastrian ideals is from the Marquis de Pastoret's *Zoroastre, Confucius et Mahomet*, pp. 66-68.

[78]Campbell, *The Masks of God: Occidental Mythology* (New York: Viking, 1964), p. 191. Campbell notes, too, that Zoroastrianism was the first progressive, rather than cyclical, religion of which there is documentation (p. 192). Although ethically dualistic, Zoroastrianism did not divorce flesh and spirit, but, emphasizing happiness on earth, even disapproved of chastity: Baron de Saint-Croix, *Recherches Historiques et Cri-*

tiques sur les Mystères du Paganisme (1784), pp. 470-71 [1817: 2:143]. ". . . the material world only has reality as seen against the background of the spiritual; yet it is this very interdependence of the two worlds that gives the battle between the followers of Truth and the followers of the Lie its eternal actuality here on earth. The earth, then, and all it brings forth, is holy. . ." (Zaehner, *Dawn and Twilight of Zoroastrianism*, p. 62). The duality of matter and spirit is Greek, alien to the Persian temperament, asserts Duchesnes-Guillamin, *Ormazd et Ahriman: L'Aventure Dualiste dans l'Antiquité* (Paris: Presses Universitaires de France, 1953), p. 107.

[79]*Dawn and Twilight of Zoroastrianism*, p. 41. See also Duchesnes-Guillamin's *Ormazd et Ahriman*, pp. 47-49. More pertinent to Shelley's knowledge is the identification of "free will" and "Magian" in the very passage of Sale's "Preliminary Discourse" to *The Koran* from which he quotes in *Queen Mab* (*The Koran*, pp. 163-64).

[80]"Indeed if any person, deeply skilled in the principles of both systems of theology, were minutely to examine and compare them together, I am convinced, that, except in the dreadful instance of that incestuous commerce allowed his disciples by the Persian legislator, and some peculiar local superstitions practised by the Indians, no very material differences would be found between them" (Maurice, *Indian Antiquities*, 2:121). Such an attitude assumes that the Persian Ahriman is identical with the Indian Siva, which, wrong though it is, has interesting repercussions for Shelley's drama. In his renowned syncretic essay, "On the Gods of Greece, Italy, and India," which inaugurated the Asiatic Society of Bengal, Sir William Jones asserted at some length the identity of Siva and Jupiter (*Asiatic Researches* 1 [1799], 248-49; *Works* [1807]—owned by Shelley—3:358-59). The characteristic weapon of Indra, god of war and chief of the malevolent Devas, is the thunderbolt.

[81]Peacock, *Memoirs of Shelley*, in *Works*, 8:71-72. Many scholars have puzzled over Newton's system, concerned with its sources as well as its impact on Shelley. The most extreme view is taken by Ross Woodman: "To view all life as symbolically congealed upon the Hindu Zodiac or to view all poetry as a single, cyclic work is to stand outside the ages, beyond rather than within the circumference of life-in-time. Newton did not convert Shelley, the man, to Hinduism; rather he converted the poet to an archetypal mode of perception preserved in the Hindu Zodiac, but applicable to all religions and to all poetry. The Zodiac, therefore, enters Shelley's poetry not as Hinduism, but as pattern" (*The Apocalyptic Vision in the Poetry of Shelley* [Toronto: Univ. of Toronto Press, 1964], p. 100). Professor Woodman has contributed valuably to our understanding of symbolic and mythic ideas in Shelley, but this statement has no basis in historical fact and wholly distorts Shelley's attitudes. Newton used the Hindu zodiac printed in *Philosophical Transactions* 62 (1772), 353, as his point of departure for a syncretic rhapsody on the Eleusinian mysteries that connected only superficially with Indian religion. His *Three Enigmas attempted to be Explained*, published by the friend of Shelley and Peacock, Thomas Hookham, in 1821, pays fulsome tribute to Faber's *Origins of Pagan Idolatry* in its preface, but is derived without acknowledgment from Dupuis, particularly from the French scholar's learned and far more successful attempt to construct a system consolidating all known zodiacs into a syncretic form, *Mémoire Explicatif du Zodiaque Chronologique et Hiéroglyphique* (Paris, 1806). Dupuis asserts that the Indian zodiac and the circular planisphere discovered at Dendera during the French Egyptian campaign of 1798-99 are the most ancient of all zodiacs and basically comparable, as are subsequent forms in European, Asian, and African cultures. Peacock's version of Newton's system furnishes details absent from his pamphlet, particularly the emphasis on the zodiac of Dendera and on the form of the cross. One suspects that so careful a scholar as Peacock is accurate in his report, however, for Newton's eccentric pamphlet abounds with shrewd hypocrisy. Adapting Dupuis but giving credit to the Christian Faber, piously asserting

religious orthodoxy as if unaware that his cosmology denies it, concluding his disquisition with an unwarranted panegyric on the coronation of George IV, Newton seems determined at all costs to avoid the attack that had greeted a previous attempt to adapt Dupuis in English, Sir William Drummond's *Oedipus Judaicus* (a title derived from the great storehouse of mythological arcana, Athanasius Kircher's *Œdipus Ægyptiacus* [1652-54]). A minor pamphlet war was aroused by Drummond's publication in 1811: his major disputant, George D'Oyly— in *Letters to the Right Honourable Sir William Drummond, relating to his Observations on Parts of the Old Testament, in his Recent Work, Entitled Oedipus Judaicus* (London, 1812)—excoriates the work in terms applicable to Newton's *Three Enigmas:* "You have taken not only the foundation of it, but many of the particular details from a French infidel writer, Dupuis. . . . Dupuis again is a plagiarist, for Volney had made most of these happy discoveries before him" (pp. 16-17). Newton's reticence about the zodiac of Dendera is thus easily explained, for Dupuis in 1806 had lent his support to previous scholars who asserted that the position of the constellations on the zodiac predated the Judaic genesis and implicitly disputed Scripture. His "Observations sur le Zodiaque de Dendra," *La Revue philosophique, littéraire et politique,* 1806, no. 2 (11 and 21 May), 257-73, 321-38, gained wide currency through being reprinted in subsequent editions of *Origine de Tous les Cultes.*

The zodiac of Dendera became a *cause célèbre* during the first quarter of the nineteenth century. In 1821 Louis XVIII purchased the planisphere and had it returned to France for prolonged study. It was exhibited in the Louvre amid much fanfare, then later moved to the Bibliothèque Nationale, where, now a mere curiosity, it still reposes. The controversy was resolved in 1822—though prolonged through the ingenious devices of scholars for many years—when the great French Egyptologist, J. F. Champollion (*Lettre à M. Dacier*), deciphered the names of several Roman emperors on the zodiac. (For accounts and further bibliography, see Dacier, "Notice Historique sur la Vie et les Ouvrages de M. Dupuis," *Histoire de l'Academie Royale des Inscriptions et Belles-Lettres* 5 [1821], 127-29; J. H. H. Greppo, *Essay on the Hieroglyphic System of M. Champollion, Jun, and on the Advantages which it offers to Sacred Criticism,* trans. Isaac Stuart [Boston, Mass., 1830], pp. 177-86; *Quarterly Review* 28 [1822], 59-97, 191-92; and the dialogue of essays collected by Charles Hippolyte de Paravey under the title *Illustrations de Astronomie Hiéroglyphique et des Planisphères et Zodiaques retrouvés en Egypte, en Chaldée, dans l'Inde et au Japon* [Paris, 1835]. It is worth noting that the copy of Newton's *Three Enigmas* in the Library of Congress is bound with John Cole's *A Treatise on the Circular Zodiac of Tentyra, in Egypt,* which dates the zodiac about 100 years after the flood and was published—with, one presumes, orthodox relief—by Longman and Co. in 1824.)

Shelley refers to this (or a comparable) Egyptian zodiac in *Alastor,* ll. 118-20, and one certainly can ascertain Newton's specific influence in Peacock's *Ahrimanes.* The jotted annotations on that manuscript cite Drummond's *Oedipus Judaicus,* as well as what Peacock terms the "astronomical mythologists," mainly Dupuis and Volney (*Works,* 7:422-27). But Shelley is not Peacock, and he testified to Hookham in 1813, "I do not think that Sir W Drummonds arguments have much weight. His Œdipus has completely failed in making me a convert" (*Letters,* 1:350). And one might assume that, as Shelley moved increasingly away from his early materialism, his conversion would be even less likely. The essential difference between Peacock's epic and *Prometheus Unbound,* indeed, illustrates the fallacy of using Newton to gloss Shelley. Whatever Derassah and Kelasris attempt, they are foiled by a deterministic universe that promises no relief from the struggle between Ormusd and Ahriman. They endure in a closed, inhumane cosmos. Shelley's open-ended skepticism cannot rely on a zodiacal pattern. Peacock's portrait of Newton in *Nightmare Abbey* as Mr. Toobad, the Manichean Millenarian, suggests his awareness of the true religious roots of

Newton's ideas and represents as well, perhaps, an exorcism of the closed, dark vision of *Ahrimanes* that he never brought to fruition.

[82]Voltaire appears to have given primacy to the Indian race, as quoted by Bailly in *Letters Upon the Atlantis of Plato*, 1:42, as well as in his "Essai sur les Mœurs et l'Esprit de Nations" (*Oeuvres Complètes*, 11:46), where he derives both Abraham and Ibrahim from Brahma. The French translator of the Sanscrit *Hitopadesa*, Langles, also argued that the Indian mythology and learning were the first developed in the ancient world: he is quoted by Priestley in *A Comparison of the Institutions of Moses with Those of the Hindoos and Other Ancient Nations* (1799), in *Works*, 17:139-40. Faber notes of the Indian mythologists that "an enormous number of successive worlds is believed to have existed" and, emphasizing his Noachian thesis, remarks that "at every renovation of the world, the same events take place; the same heroes reappear upon the stage; and the same Sama, Cama, and Pra-Japati, are born again to every Menu" (*Origin of Pagan Idolatry*, 1:112). Maurice quotes from the Abbé Raynal to the effect that the caste system "betrays marks of the most ancient system of slavery" and himself suggests that feudalism first developed in India (*History of Hindostan*, 1:78; 2:514).

[83]Woodman's contention in *The Apocalyptic Vision in the Poetry of Shelley* is that the poet's central ideas are Orphic. He does not, however, base the conclusion on solid historical evidence and too easily embraces the duality betwen spirit and matter that Orphism introduced to Greece. His Orphism, via Thomas Taylor, leads directly into Neoplatonism. Although one doubts Shelley's allegiance to so circumscribed a view, his knowledge of Orphism is indisputable, confirmed not only by numerous allusions in the poetry, but by the direct citation of the *Hymns* found in the earliest holograph of *A Defence of Poetry*. As for attitudes of Shelley's time, Faber equates Dionysus and Noah as primal father in *Origin of Pagan Idolatry*, 2:272; Bailly comments extensively on Orpheus as "poet legislator" in his posthumous *Essai sur les Fables*, 2: chs. 14-17; Volney claims that Zoroaster's doctrine "is found entire in that of Orpheus, Pythagoras, and the Indian Gymnosophists" (*The Ruins*, p. 286n). Other general accounts of the Orphic theology are contained in Bryant, *A New System*, 2:126-38, and in Maurice, *Indian Antiquities*, 4:332-34. Dio Chrysostom's fable of the chariot occurs in *Discourses*, XXXVI. 55-58; trans. Crosby, 3:469-73:

> . . . when the mind alone had been left and had filled with itself immeasurable space, since it had poured itself evenly in all directions and nothing in it remained dense but complete porosity prevailed—at which time it becomes most beautiful— having obtained the purest nature of unadulterated light, it immediately longed for the existence that it had at first. Accordingly, becoming enamoured of that control and governance and concord which it once maintained not only over the three natures of sun and moon and the other stars, but also over absolutely all animals and plants, it became eager to generate and distribute everything and to make the orderly universe then existent once more far better and more resplendent because newer. And emitting a full flash of lightning, not a disorderly or foul one such as in stormy weather often darts forth, when the clouds drive more violently than usual, but rather pure and unmixed with any murk, it worked a transformation easily, with the speed of thought. But recalling Aphrodite and the process of generation, it tamed and relaxed itself and, quenching much of its light, it turned into fiery air of gentle warmth, and uniting with Hera and enjoying the most perfect wedlock, in sweet repose it emitted anew the full supply of seed for the universe. Such is the blessed marriage of Zeus and Hera of which the sons of sages sing in secret rites. And having made fluid all his essence, one seed for the entire world, he himself moving about in it like a spirit that moulds and fashions in generation, then indeed most closely resembling the composition

of the other creatures, inasmuch as he might with reason be said to consist of soul and body, he now with ease moulds and fashions all the rest, pouring about him his essence smooth and soft and easily yielding in every part.

And having performed his task and brought it to completion, he revealed the existent universe as once more a thing of beauty and inconceivable loveliness, much more resplendent, indeed, than it appears today.

Nothing could be more apt to Shelley's drama than the ancient philosophical idealism of this song of the Magi.

[84]Peacock, *Works*, 7:245-46. The similarity of Zoroastrianism and Orphism as humane religions is emphasized by Plutarch: "those persons have resolved more and greater perplexities who have set the race of demigods midway between gods and men, and have discovered a force to draw together, in a way, and to unite our common fellowship—whether this doctrine comes from the wise men of the cult of Zoroaster, or whether it is Thracian and harks back to Orpheus, or is Egyptian, or Phrygian" (*Moralia:* "The Obsolescence of Oracles," 10; trans. Babbitt, 5:377-79).

[85]*The Mystical Initiations; or HYMNS OF ORPHEUS. . . with a Preliminary Dissertation on the Life and Theology of Orpheus* (London, 1787), p. 190.

[86]Faber, *Origin of Pagan Idolatry*, 1:267. Wasserman's arguments for identifying Prometheus as the One Mind are summarized in *Shelley: A Critical Reading*, pp. 255-57.

Chapter 3. Sceptical Idealism and the Physics of Paradise

[1]It is curious that Mercury has elicited such sympathetic judgments from otherwise shrewd critics. Both Lawrence Zillman—*Shelley's "Prometheus Unbound": A Variorum Edition* (Seattle: Univ. of Washington Press, 1959), pp. 326-27—and Earl Wasserman —*Shelley: A Critical Reading* (Baltimore: Johns Hopkins Univ. Press, 1971), 286*n*—are taken in by his craven speech. One suspects that a Renaissance reader would have been more suspicious: not only was Mercury traditionally identified with lust and venery, but, more important for Shelley's conception, he embodied the spirit of selfish capitalism. See, for example, Stephen Batman, *The Golden Booke of the Leaden Goddes* (London, 1577), p. 4: "By Mercurie Marchauntes be ment. His wynges at head & feete betoken the expedition of Marchauntes, which to gett worldly pelfe, post through all corners of the World: the whyte & blacke coloured Hat, signifieth their subtilty, which for greedines of gaine, spare not to face white for blacke, & blacke for white. By his Fawlchon is signified, goodes gotten by violence, when subtiltie cannot comprehend." To translate this figure into a culture closer to Shelley's, Mercury stands for what Bunyan execrates as Mr. Worldly Wise-man, an amoral servant of selfish interest and the established powers.

[2]The last words of Asia and Prometheus in the drama represent a culmination of this pattern of diction, as Prometheus quietly assimilates Asia's language with the arrival of the Spirit of the Hour (III. iv. 96-97):

> *Asia,* Listen! look!
> *Prometheus.* We feel what thou hast heard and seen: yet speak.

[3]This metaphorical pattern is complemented by mythological contexts. Asia's journey into the primeval takes her first into the verdant realm of Pan, first-born of Demogorgon, and beyond to Demogorgon's cave. She follows the echoes of her dreams and is accompanied by a rare, ineffable music heard as well by the fauns of scene 2. Echo was Pan's wife, and Syrinx, the nymph he doted on to the point of tragedy (as in Shelley's *Hymn of Pan*), is commonly understood to represent the music of the spheres. Complicated and illusive as is Shelley's rendition of the myth, his large de-

sign is easily grasped: no division exists necessarily between the natural and spiritual. The echoes of Asia's soul are in harmony with the perfect balance of celestial bodies: the same power drives both. (For mythological contexts, see Boccaccio, *Genealogie Deorum Gentilium* [Bari: Laterza, 1951], 1:21-25, the section immediately following the account of Demogorgon; and [Thomas Blackwell], *Letters concerning Mythology* [London, 1748], pp. 54-58.) Just as clearly, the realm of Pan recalls his fellow divinity of the living earth—Bacchus, or Dionysus—whose origin was the fertile country below Caucasus traversed by Asia and Panthea.

[4]Thomas Maurice, *Indian Antiquities*, (London, 1800), 7:706. Further ramifications of the *akass* are discussed in chapter 5.

[5]*Siris: A Chain of Philosophical Reflexions and Inquiries*, sect. 200, in *The Works of George Berkeley, Bishop of Cloyne*, ed. A. A. Luce and T. E. Jessop (London: Thomas Nelson, 1953), 5:100.

[6]Ibid. (sect. 152), 5:82.

[7]Shelley derives this metaphor, as Tennyson (in "Now sleeps the crimson petal") did after him, from Virgil's brilliant conceit in the second *Georgic*:

> Then Ether, the omnipotent father, in fecund rain
> Showers the lap of his happy wife,
> And engenders great life throughout her great body.
> (ll. 325-27)

In *The Sacred Theory of the Earth* (6th ed. [London, 1726], 1:248-49, 270-71), Thomas Burnet expounds upon the traditions of ether as a universal male sexual force, a commentary reproduced by Thomas Blackwell in *Letters concerning Mythology*, pp. 106-08. Shelley carefully enlarges this conception, imaging both earth and moon as androgynous, both giving and receiving, in the dispersal of light in the universe. The dual sexual nature of the earth is represented by Gaia, Pan, Demogorgon, and the youthful Spirit of the Earth through the first three acts of the drama. Alexander Ross notes that the moon also has dual sexual natures (*Mystagogus Poeticus, or The Muses Interpreter*, 3rd ed., [London, 1653], p. 242); and Thomas Maurice remarks that in India the moon is considered a male deity (*Indian Antiquities*, 2:107). For gentile conceptions of the moon as the abode of the gods and of the preexistent souls of men, and as the parent of a renewed earth, see George Stanley Faber, *The Origin of Pagan Idolatry ascertained from Historical Testimony and Circumstantial Evidence* (London, 1816), 1:209, 379.

[8]Volney, *The Ruins: or, A Survey of the Revolutions of Empires*, 5th ed. (London, 1807), pp. 302-03. An excellent summary (with extensive bibliography) of eighteenth-century conceptions of electricity is to be found in chapter 2, "Electricity: The Soul of the Universe," of Philip C. Ritterbush, *Overtures to Biology: The Speculations of Eighteenth-Century Naturalists* (New Haven and London: Yale Univ. Press, 1964). The source for Shelley's conception of elemental contraries, as for Blake's, is the physics of Sir Isaac Newton; but more immediate to Shelley is the extensive elaboration of such a principle in Erasmus Darwin's *The Temple of Nature; or, the Origin of Society: A Poem, with Philosophical Notes* (London: Joseph Johnson, 1803). Among the "philosophical notes" is a thirty-page dissertation on the "Chemical Theory of Electricity and Magnetism," which proposes that there are two etherial fluids, analogous to male and female, from whose attraction and repulsion all motion derives. The further implications of Darwin's analogy will be treated in the fifth chapter: it suffices for the moment to observe that in his theory electricity, magnetism, and gravitation all operate by the same principle. William H. Hildebrand, emphasizing Coleridge's conception of polarity in chapters 12 and 13 of the *Biographia Literaria*, points to the realism of Shelley's paradise as depicted in such passages as IV. 406-11. His interpre-

tation, which appeared when this book was in press, accords in many respects with that offered here. See *Shelley's Polar Paradise: A Reading of "Prometheus Unbound"* (Salzburg: Universität Salzburg Institut für Englische Sprache und Literatur, 1974).

[9]Matthews' phrase occurs in his indispensable essay, "A Volcano's Voice in Shelley," *ELH* 24 (1957), 215. Also of central importance for the study of Shelley's scientific knowledge, of course, is Carl Grabo's *A Newton Among Poets: Shelley's Use of Science in "Prometheus Unbound"* (Chapel Hill: Univ. of North Carolina Press, 1930), especially chapters 7-9.

[10]An Observer, "Why are there so few excellent Poets?" *The Reflector* 2 (1811), 249-74: the passage occurs on p. 254n.

[11]"Lawlessness" is the distinguishing characteristic of the masque, as Leigh Hunt views the genre in his essay "Some Account of the Origin and Nature of Masks," which prefaces *The Descent of Liberty* (p. xxi). Further considerations of the masque, and of the specific relationship of *Prometheus Unbound* to *The Mask of Anarchy*, are examined below, in chapter 6. Shelley's generic term for *Prometheus Unbound*— "lyrical drama"—is technically a synonym for opera (see, e.g., *The New British Theatre* [London, 1814], 3:303), a form greatly loved by Shelley and clearly of influence on this work. Jupiter exits through the same trapdoor as Don Giovanni. However, the opera that might most have justified the ritualistic conception of *Prometheus Unbound*, Mozart's *Magic Flute*, was unknown to him and, indeed, not produced in England until some years after he left.

[12]*The Transcendental Masque: An Essay on Milton's "Comus"* (Ithaca and London: Cornell Univ. Press, 1971), p. 116.

[13]Ibid., p. 134.

[14]For "lyrical drama" as a generic description of the Miltonic brief epic, see my essay "The Mental Pinnacle: *Paradise Regained* and the Romantic Four-Book Epic," in Joseph Anthony Wittreich, Jr., ed., *Calm of Mind: Tercentenary Essays on "Paradise Regained" and "Samson Agonistes"* (Cleveland: Press of Case Western Reserve Univ., 1971), pp. 139-60.

[15]*Letters*, 2:94 (6 April 1819). To his publisher Charles Ollier (6 September 1819) Shelley claimed that *Prometheus Unbound* "is in my judgement, of a higher character than any thing I have yet attempted; and it is perhaps less an imitation of any thing that has gone before it" (*Letters*, 2:116).

[16]Mont Blanc, like Mount Caucasus, is merely a monumental form of barren rock: it is the human mind that transforms it into a symbol whereby to organize a 'reality':

> And what were thou, and earth, and stars, and sea,
> If to the human mind's imaginings
> Silence and solitude were vacancy?
>
> (*Mont Blanc*, ll. 142-44)

The unconditional, if rhetorical, answer to Shelley's question—"Nothing"—returns the responsibility for meaning to the mind mistakenly looking outward for its source.

[17]In *A Defence of Poetry* Shelley offers his own fine commentary on *Prometheus Unbound* and on the character of the revolution it dramatizes: "We want the creative faculty to imagine that which we know; we want the generous impulse to act that which we imagine; we want the poetry of life: our calculations have outrun conception; we have eaten more than we can digest. The cultivation of those sciences which have enlarged the limits of the empire of man over the external world, has, for want of the poetical faculty, proportionally circumscribed those of the internal world; and man, having enslaved the elements, remains himself a slave. To what but a cultivation of the mechanical arts in a degree disproportioned to the presence of the creative faculty, which is the basis of all knowledge, is to be attributed the abuse of all inven-

tion for abridging and combining labour, to the exasperation of the inequality of mankind? From what other cause has it arisen that these inventions which should have lightened, have added a weight to the curse imposed on Adam? Thus Poetry, and the principle of Self, of which Money is the visible incarnation, are the God and Mammon of the world" (*Prose*, 7:134).

[18]*Ahrimanes*, II, Stanza 3, in *Works*, 7:278.

[19]Though unnoted by Shelley critics, there is probably no more thoughtful and penetrating study of the implications of *Prometheus Unbound* than a work that never mentions Shelley by name but seems to have him by heart. I refer to Herbert Marcuse's *Eros and Civilization*, written many years ago as a counterstatement to the fatalistic pessimism of Freud's *Civilization and Its Discontents*.

[20]Shelley's note to *Queen Mab*, VIII, 203-07, provides an appropriate context: "If . . . the human mind, by any future improvement of its sensibility, should become conscious of an infinite number of ideas in a minute, that minute would be eternity." In perceptual theory as in physics, Shelley had a remarkably modern conception of relativity.

Chapter 4. The Rule of Ahriman

[1]'Hope' (or its derivatives) is employed nineteen times in *Prometheus Unbound*: eleven of these occurrences come near the end of acts (I. 706, 775, 808; II. iv. 24, 59, 160; III. iv. 136, 145, 185, 192; IV. 570-73). Conversely, nine of the eighteen references to the term in *The Cenci* occur in the final scenes (V. ii. 53, 122, 131; V. iii. 97; V. iv. 88, 98, 121).

[2]Both Jupiter and the Count speak with a common diction and rhetoric: compare *Prometheus Unbound*, III. i. 70-71, with *The Cenci*, IV. i. 26-27.

[3]*Boun-dehesch*, section iii, in *Zend-Avesta, Ouvrage de Zoroastre* (Paris, 1771), 2:350-55.

[4]This is probably one of the several traditional sources from which Shelley draws in his portrayal of the regeneration of the moon in *Prometheus Unbound*, Act IV. Dupuis, who sees the moon as governing all generative life and emphasizes her role as Isis, suggests that vernal rebirth is symbolized in the coition of Isis and Osiris, representing moon and earth: *Origine de tous les cultes*, 1:167-75, 396-401. Also, Dupuis renders an exact conflation of this myth with the Zoroastrian legend of the great bull in 1:375, and again in 2:114. For Proclus' hypothesis, based on ancient Egyptian traditions, "that the summit of the earth is ethereal, in order that it may unite with the orb of the moon," see Thomas Taylor's note to his translation of Pausanias' *Description of Greece* (London, 1794), 3:255-56. Shelley ordered this work in the summer of 1817.

[5]See Isaac de Beausobre, *Histoire Critique de Manichée et du Manicheisme* (Amsterdam, 1734), 1:244-45; 2:386-88, 395-96. The account derives, among other sources, from Augustine's anathema, *Contra Faustum*.

[6]When Savella orders the family removed to Rome, Beatrice condemns the double standard of justice in the world as a "two-edged lie" (IV. iv. 115); and during her trial Beatrice argues that were she a common parricide, she would not have left Marzio as a "two-edged instrument / Of my misdeed" (V. ii. 97-98).

[7]For an extensive analysis of this casuistry, see my *Shelley's "Cenci": Scorpions Ringed with Fire* (Princeton: Princeton Univ. Press, 1970), pp. 138-40. Simply put, the argument is that, since suicide is a mortal sin and since allowing oneself to incorporate evil is a blasphemous treachery against God, Beatrice sees her father's murder as the single self-defence, a sin she will rely upon God to forgive.

[8]In *Queen Mab* see the footnote to VII. 135-36, "I will beget a Son. . . ." In the fragment "On the Moral Teaching of Jesus Christ," which Forman printed at the end of the *Essay on Christianity*, Shelley emphasizes the radical implications of Christ's teachings: "The doctrines indeed, in my judgment, are excellent and strike at the root of moral evil. If acted upon, no political or religious institution could subsist a moment" (*Prose*, 6, 255).

[9]For the nature of these dynamics in *The Cenci*, see *Shelley's "Cenci": Scorpions Ringed with Fire*, pp. 131-36.

[10]Carefully marshaling evidence, G. M. Matthews submits that only the first thirty lines of the poem were written at Este in September 1818 and that substantial work was done in March 1819. See "'Julian and Maddalo': The Draft and the Meaning," *Studia Neophilologia* 35 (1963), 57-84, esp. 65-66.

[11]Ibid., p. 83.

[12]*Paradise Lost*, II. 565.

[13]Compare with *Lines Written Among the Euganean Hills*, ll. 327, 332-34: "And the soft dreams of the morn . . . / Pass, to other sufferers fleeing, / And its ancient pilot, Pain, / Sits beside the helm again."

[14]The poet of *Alastor* "seeks in vain for a prototype of his conception," while the error of the fictive poet imagined in the draft preface to *Epipsychidion* is " θνητος ὡν μη θνητα φρονειν "—being mortal to yearn for the immortal.

[15]This is the only controversial section in Earl Wasserman's otherwise exemplary analysis of the poem: *Shelley: A Critical Reading* (Baltimore: Johns Hopkins Univ. Press, 1971), pp. 80-81.

[16]"Resolution and Independence," ll. 48-49.

[17]Keats's brilliant phrase occurs in his letter on the poetical character, addressed to Richard Woodhouse (27 October 1818).

[18]"As from a centre, dart thy spirit's light / Beyond all worlds, until its spacious might / Satiate the void circumference": *Adonais*, 418-20. The idea is central to Shelley's "intellectual philosophy," as is manifest in the fragment "On Life": "Each is at once the centre and the circumference, the point to which all things are referred, and the line in which all things are contained" (*Prose*, 6, 194).

[19]"*Bocca bacciata non perde ventura, / Anzi rinnuova come fa la luna*"—the kissed lip does not lose its value, but rather renews itself like the moon. Arrigo Boito, apparently as fond of these lines as Shelley, inserted them into the love duet of Fenton and Nanetta in Verdi's *Falstaff*.

[20]Shelley's admiration for *The Dunciad* is suggested in a cancelled passage for the preface to *Prometheus Unbound*: see Lawrence Zillman, ed., *Shelley's "Prometheus Unbound": The Text and the Drafts* (New Haven: Yale Univ. Press, 1968), p. 38 (ll. 94-118).

[21]Shelley's friends and contemporaries satirize Wordsworth as turncoat, as vague metaphysician, and as pompous versifier. Shelley's deepest charge is moral. Among the satirical attacks with which he would have been most familiar are Peacock's ex·tended scene with the Lake Poets at Mainchance Villa in *Melincourt* and Byron's jibes both in the first canto of *Don Juan* and, earlier, in *English Bards and Scotch Reviewers*. Reynolds' parody of *Peter Bell* is essentially stylistic, and Shelley practices a brilliant parody upon his parody, transposing lame doggerel into a powerful, insistent vision. The first of the following passages, from Reynolds' satire, was quoted in *The Examiner* notice; the second passage reproduces lines 217-21 of Shelley's poem:

. . . But Peter Bell he hath no brother.

Not a brother owneth he,
Peter Bell he hath no brother;
His mother had no other son,
No other son e'er called her mother;
Peter Bell hath brother none.

And this is Hell—and in this smother
All are damnable and damned;
Each one damning, damns the other;
They are damned by one another;
By none other are they damned.

The meter employed in both satires, of course, is that of the original *Peter Bell.*

[22]The review is reprinted in Newman Ivey White, *The Unextinguished Hearth: Shelley and His Contemporary Critics* (Durham: Duke Univ. Press, 1938), p. 152.

[23]F. W. Bateson's restoration of two unpublished stanzas from the poem reveals Shelley's knowledge of Wordsworth's adolescent "Don Juanism" and insinuation of an incestuous relationship between William and Dorothy. Shelley's suppression of the stanzas does, perhaps, suggest a concern that Wordsworth's private life be excluded from the poem, but the references to his frigidity are borderline at best. For the suppressed stanzas, see F. W. Bateson, "Exhumations V. Shelley on Wordsworth: Two Unpublished Stanzas from 'Peter Bell the Third,'" *Essays in Criticism* 17 (1967), 125-29.

[24]In quoting from this poem, I have used the more complete text of Ingpen and Peck (*Complete Works*, 4:65-66). For Forman's description of this fragment, see *Notebooks of Percy Bysshe Shelley* (St. Louis, 1911), 1:139-56.

[25]Beatrice thus confronts her father in the banquet scene: "Father, never dream / Though thou mayst overbear this company, / But ill must come of ill" (I. iii. 149-51). A similar accent is placed in *Lines Written Among the Euganean Hills:* "Men must reap the things they sow, / Force from force must ever flow, / Or worse" (231-33).

Chapter 5. Purgatorial and Prophetic Odes

[1]For an extended discussion of links between "On the Devil, and Devils" and the poems of 1819 see my essay, written with Joseph Wittreich, "The Dating of Shelley's 'On the Devil, and Devils,'" *Keats-Shelley Journal* 21-22 (1973), 80-102.

[2]This is intimated by Kenneth Cameron in *The Young Shelley: Genesis of a Radical* (New York: Macmillan, 1950), pp. 306-07.

[3]Plutarch's *Moralia*, "Of Isis and Osiris," 46.

[4]This is printed by H. Buxton Forman in *The Notebooks of Percy Bysshe Shelley* (St. Louis, 1911), 1:146.

[5]Ibid., p. 155.

[6]"Limbo," l. 38.

[7]The scientific accuracy of Shelley's description, long a subject of critical haggling, seems at last to have been definitely proved by F. H. Ludlam in "The Meteorology of Shelley's Ode," *Times Literary Supplement*, 1 September 1972, pp. 1015-16.

[8]A notebook fragment, employing imagery Shelley converted into his ode, begins "'Twas the 20th of October": see Forman, *Notebooks*, 1:170. The last day of Libra, the Balance, is 23 October.

[9]I adopt the term of German theology—*zwischen die Zeit*—as applied to prophetic literature by Ronald L. Grimes. See "Time and Space in Blake's Major Prophecies," in

Stuart Curran and Joseph A. Wittreich, Jr., eds., *Blake's Sublime Allegory: Essays on "The Four Zoas," "Milton," and "Jerusalem"* (Madison: Univ. of Wisconsin Press, 1973), 59-81.

[10]Bailly derives the Zoroastrian and Indian idea of two principles from the operations of nature: "It is . . . in all cases Nature that acts: she has energies that create; she has also energies that destroy. She has, then, two principles in herself, which balance and contend with each other, without the destruction of either" (*Letters Upon the Atlantis of Plato*, trans. James Jacque [London, 1801], I, 80-81), Bailly goes on to relate this natural rhythm to the yin and yang of Chinese philosophy. Dupuis analyzes Zoroastrian thought from the same naturalistic basis: "They fix the epoch of the duration of man's well-being from the Lamb or from the sign of the vernal equinox, to the sign of the Balance, which occupies the autumnal equinox. Then, if we follow them, evil is introduced into the universe" (*Origine de Tous les Cultes* [Paris, 3 (1795)], 1:234). Dupuis converts the 12,000-year struggle between Ormusd and Ahriman into one lasting 12 months.

[11]Boccaccio, *Genealogie Deorum Gentilium* (Bari: Laterza, 1951), 1:210. Spence, *Polymetis: or, An Enquiry concerning the Agreement Between the Works of the Roman Poets, and the Remains of the Ancient Artists* (London, 1747), p. 204.

[12]*Histoire Critique de Manichée et du Manicheisme* (Amsterdam, 1734), 2:228. The second statement, according to Beausobre, derives from Joannes Franciscus Buddeus, *Introductio ad historiam philosophiae Ebraeorum* (1702), p. 454. In this same passage Beausobre remarks that the Valentinians conceived the wind as "plastic nature," a demiurgic force throughout the created universe.

[13]Zaehner, *Dawn and Twilight of Zoroastrianism* (London: Weidenfeld and Nicolson, and New York: Putnam, 1961), pp. 149, 148. In translating the *Zend-Avesta*, Anquetil du Perron appears to have lacked the last several *Yashts*: he breaks off with the fourteenth, thus not printing the *Yasht Ram*, the fifteenth, devoted to Vayu. There are elsewhere, however, several references to the "victorious wind": see also, note 22 below.

[14]Beausobre, *Histoire Critique de Manichée*, 2:258. Augustine's assertion is reported also by Nathaniel Lardner in *Credibility of the Gospel History: Works* (London 1788), 3:462.

[15]Rieger's essay on the *Ode to the West Wind*, among the best treatments, emphasizes the union of form and content and illuminates many elements through Pythagorean numerology. For the wind as *quinta essentia*, see *The Mutiny Within: The Heresies of Percy Bysshe Shelley* (New York: George Braziller, 1967), p. 171. For the Manichean original man and the elements, see Beausobre, *Histoire Critique de Manichée*, 1:242, 2:311. Volney notes that the ancient Egyptians conceived of five elements also: *The Ruins: or, A Survey of the Revolution of Empires*, 5th ed. (London, 1807), p. 296. For the *akass*, see Volney, *Ruins*, pp. 216-17, and Maurice, *Indian Antiquities* (London, 1800), 7:705-06: both Volney (pp. 302-03) and Maurice (7:708) connect the *akass* with electricity. Sir William Jones, whose works Shelley owned, goes so far as to assert, on the basis of the *akass*, that "the whole of [Newton's] theology, and part of his philosophy, can be found in the *Védas* and even in the works of the *Súfis*" (Discourse the Eleventh . . . On the Philosophy of the Asiatics," in *Asiatic Researches* 4 [1799], 176; *Works* [1807], 3:246). For Berkeley's *Siris*, see Berkeley, *Works of George Berkeley, Bishop of Cloyne*, ed. A. A. Luce and T. E. Jessop (London: Thomas Nelson, 1953), 5:82.

[16]Jones, "On the Gods of Greece, Italy, and India" (1784), in *Asiatic Researches* 1 (1799), 249-50; *Works* (1807), 3:360. Jones's sentence is repeated not only by Maurice, *Indian Antiquities*, 2:163, but also in Edward Moor's *Hindu Pantheon* (London, 1810), p. 47. Other references are to Maurice, *History of Hindostan* (London, 1795), 1:59;

and Wilford, "Essay on Vicramaditya and Salivahana," *Asiatic Researches* 9 (1809), 218.

[17]Charles Wilkins, trans., *The Bhagvat-Geeta, or Dialogues of Kreeshna and Arjoon* (London, 1785), p. 80.

[18]One of the main purposes of the enormous labor Thomas Maurice put into his *Indian Antiquities* was to prove the Indian triple godhead a corruption of the Christian trinity. The missionary spirit preyed on many other scholars as well. Shelley's knowledge of the Hindu godhead, however, probably derived immediately from a more dependable work, Edward Moor's *Hindu Pantheon*, which was in his library. Moor has extensive commentary on Brahma (pp. 5-14), Vishnu (pp. 15-34), and Siva (pp. 35-71).

[19]"The Fourth Element in the *Ode to the West Wind*," *Papers on Language and Literature* 3 (1967), 328.

[20]*Lettres à Sophie sur l'Histoire* (Paris, 9 [1801]), 1:42. See also chap. 3, n8, above.

[21]Mary dates this poem in 1818. Neville Rogers, pointing to adjacent materials in the notebook (Bod. MS Shelley adds. e. 8) and an apparent reference to critics in the figure of the woodman, suggests the period of *Adonais*, 1821: *Shelley at Work*, 2nd ed. (London: Oxford Univ. Press, 1967), p. 263.

[22]The Zoroastrian wind appears in Anquetil du Perron's *Zend-Avesta*—(Paris, 1771), 1^2:180—as "the wind called Vadjeschte, the fire of Ormusd." The relationship of fire and wind in the *Ode to the West Wind* is complicated by Shelley's attempt, for dramatic purposes, to separate elements that are traditionally joined. Simply stated, the wind that voices the sense of loss of the first three stanzas must be charged with the fire of Shelley's self-sacrifice to become an internal equivalent of that ether which is the agent of life throughout the universe.

[23]It is, perhaps, unfair to Wordsworth to leave him thus stifled. *The Excursion* is obsessed with the impact of contraries on human life, but tends to resolve them too easily. The Solitary surely no longer views the world with the eyes of his youthful self, but the recollection of his former rhapsodic attitude goes unchallenged, even by him:

> "Blow winds of autumn! let your chilling breath
> Take the live herbage from the mead, and strip
> The forest of its green attire,—
> And let the bursting clouds to fury rouse
> The gentle brooks!—Your desolating sway,
> Sheds," I exclaimed, "no sadness upon me,
> And no disorder in your rage I find.
> What dignity, what beauty, in this change
> From mild to angry, and from sad to gay,
> Alternate and revolving! How benign,
> How rich in animation and delight,
> How bountiful these elements. . . ."
>
> (III. 307-18)

[24]*Clairmont Journals*, pp. 194-95. Hogg's remarks occur in his commentary on the rarity of a poet such as Shelley: "The primary object, great final cause, and last and most important result of the poetical faculty and temperament is to make, to create; but the incidental consequences are also to destroy: a poet is a maker, but he is likewise a marrer" (Thomas Jefferson Hogg, *The Life of Percy Bysshe Shelley* [London, 1858], 2:48).

[25]*Paradise Lost*, I. 19, 21-22.

[26]"Rhetoric as Drama: An Approach to the Romantic Ode," *PMLA* 79 (1964), 67-79.

[27]See the comment to Ollier (*Letters*, 2:258), quoted as epigraph to this chapter.

Chapter 6. The Poet as Legislator

[1]For a succinct formulation of this thesis, see E. P. Thompson, *The Making of the English Working Class* (New York: Vintage, 1963), pp. 671 ff.

[2]To be accurate, the concerns of the political poems are personalized in the later odes, where Shelley places his own life within the context of the struggle.

[3]I am grateful to Karl Kroeber for pointing out that Shelley's portrayal of the main figures in the procession bears a marked, if independent, similarity to details of Cruikshank's designs for William Hone's *The Political Showman—at Home!* exhibiting his cabinet of curiosities and Creatures—All Alive!, a radical attack on the Sidmouth government in 1821. Shelley's use of iconography, great and small, is a subject deserving greater attention than it has received.

[4]Writing to Ollier in March of 1820, Shelley hypothesized that *Prometheus Unbound*, though "my favourite poem, . . . cannot sell beyond twenty copies" (*Letters*, 2:174). To Hunt in May he confided that the drama "will not sell—it is written for the elect" (*Letters*, 2:200).

[5]Leigh Hunt, *The Descent of Liberty. A Mask* (London, 1815), p. xix.

[6]Ibid., p. v. Throughout the masque Napoleon is called "the Enchanter."

[7]Angus Fletcher has perceptive observations on the political dimensions of the masque in the opening chapter of *The Transcendental Masque: An Essay on Milton's "Comus"* (Ithaca and London: Cornell Univ. Press, 1971). This paragraph is, however, particularly indebted to his expansion of these concerns in the as yet unpublished paper, "Masque, Person, and Authority," delivered at the 1973 Newberry Library Renaissance Conference.

[8]Hunt, inexplicably reducing the original blank verse to prose, prints this passage on pp. xxxiv-xxxv.

[9]Ibid., p. xxi.

[10]Ibid., pp. xxii-xxiii. The triumph was a literary form long before the fifteenth century, the time of Lorenzo de Medici. Hunt's point seems to be that until that time it had not been a dramatic form.

[11]Shelley read Petrarch's *Trionfo della Morte* on 19 September 1819, but it would appear by so late a date that Shelley was drawn to the poem by his employment of the triumph conventions in his own masque. The stage directions for the third and fourth triumphs (Of Death, Of Time) in Beaumont and Fletcher's *Four Plays, or Moral Representations, in One* are much closer in spirit and form to Shelley's masque. "The Triumph of Death": "*Enter Musicians; next them, Perolot, with the wound he died with; then Gabrielle and Maria, with their wounds; after them four Furies with bannerets, inscribed,* Revenge, Murder, Lust, *and* Drunkenness, *singing; next them, Lavall wounded; then a chariot with Death, drawn by the Destinies.*" "The Triumph of Time": "*Enter Delight, Pleasure, Craft, Lucre, Vanity, &c. dancing (and masqued) towards the rock, offering service to Anthropos. Mercury from above. Musick heard. One half of a cloud drawn, singers are discovered; then the other half drawn. Jupiter seen in glory. . . . Enter the Triumph. First, the Musicians: then Vain-Delight, Pleasure, Craft, Lucre, Vanity, and other of the vices: then a chariot with the person of Time sitting in it, drawn by four persons representing Hours, singing.*" *The Dramatic Works of Beaumont and Fletcher: Printed from the text, and with the notes of the late George Colman, Esq.* (London, 1811), 3:603, 607.

[12]August Wilhelm Schlegel, *A Course of Lectures on Dramatic Art and Literature*, trans. John Black (London, 1815), 2:290. Francis Bacon emphasizes the grotesqueness of the antimasque in his short essay "Of Maskes and Triumphs," commonly reprinted in collections of his works.

[13]Hunt quotes extensively from the stage directions for these antimasques (*Descent of Liberty*, pp. xxxviii-xxxix). Shelley seems equally conscious of the prosodic conventions of the masque. Though the meter of *The Mask of Anarchy*, divided into quatrains, recalls the ballad, it is the same acephalic tetrameter employed with such noted success in the couplets of *Lines Written Among the Euganean Hills*, a local-descriptive pastoral. Hunt thus comments on the meter of the masque: "the heptasyllabic measure which Fletcher rendered so attractive in his Faithful Shepherdess, and which from its adoption by succeeding writers, particularly Milton, has almost become appropriated to the rhyming speeches of the Mask and Pastoral Drama, as distinguished from their songs and dialogue" (*Descent of Liberty*, p. xlviii).

[14]As a dramatic model *Comus* is pertinent to *The Mask of Anarchy*. Milton also integrates formal conventions and themes, bringing the main figure of the antimasque, the sorcerer Comus, directly into the action, and weaving from the confrontation of the grotesque and the virtuous a ritual drama of tyranny and liberty. The passive resistance by which the Lady withstands the assaults of Comus also has its strong counterpart in Shelley's political masque.

[15]The similarity of this cycle to what Northrop Frye has termed Blake's "Orc cycle" is obvious, but Shelley's concentration on its economic basis goes beyond Blake's depiction and looks forward to the later concerns of Marx and the British socialists.

[16]*Escape from Freedom* (New York: Farrar & Rinehart, 1941), p. 172.

[17]The phrase appears in the preface to *The Revolt of Islam*. The most useful study of Shelley's interest in Drummond is that of C. E. Pulos, *The Deep Truth: A Study of Shelley's Scepticism* (Lincoln: Univ. of Nebraska Press, 1954).

[18]These phrases are taken from the preface to *Prometheus Unbound* and from the preface and dedication to *The Cenci*.

[19]Shelley's devotion to these writers lasted through his maturity. It is noteworthy, however, that he and Mary were reading heavily in both during 1819, particularly during the month of August.

[20]*Letters*, 2:30.

[21]John Black, *Life of Torquato Tasso; with An Historical and Critical Account of His Writings* (Edinburgh: John Murray, 1810), 2:132-34. (This is not the John Black who translated Schlegel's *Lectures* and was later associated with Dickens.) For Shelley's probable knowledge of Black's *Life*, see Donald H. Reiman, ed., *Shelley and His Circle* (Cambridge, Mass.: Harvard Univ. Press, 1973), 6:591. For a modern translation of this passage, see Mariella Cavalchini and Irene Samuel, trans., *Discourses on the Heroic Poem* (Oxford: Clarendon Press, 1973), pp. 77-78.

[22]*Letters*, 2:122.

INDEX

Abel, 217-18 *n*35
Abominable Snowman, 61
Abraham, 78, 221-22 *n*52, 222 *n*54, 229 *n*82
Action, 136, 161
Adam, 14, 77, 120, 163, 219 *n*44, 219-20 *n*45
Adonais, 147, 172, 193, 200, 218 *n*36, 237 *n*18
Aeneas, 38, 53, 79
Aeolian harp, 169
Aeschylus, 45, 60; *Oresteia*, 34; *Prometheus Bound*, xvii, 34-35, 38, 44; compared with *The Cenci*, 130-33
Afghanistan, 61
Ahasuerus, 20-21, 24, 41, 42, 211 *n*29, 213 *n*10
Ahriman, 33, 71, 84, 85, 86, 88, 91, 116, 127-28, 149, 150, 155, 226 *n*74, 227 *n*80, 227-29 *n*81
Ahura Mazdah, 87. *See also* Ormusd
Air, 39, 161
Akass, 106, 108, 162-63, 236 *n*15
Alastor: meaning, 21
Alastor, 4, 20-21, 24, 25, 26, 27, 34, 37, 64, 140, 143, 227-29 *n*81, 234 *n*14
Albordj, Mount, 67, 69, 77, 224 *n*62
Alexander, Czar of Russia, 61
Alexander the Great, xvii, 61, 77, 218 *n*39, 219 *n*42
Allegory, 29, 42-43
America, North, 63-64
Anarchy, 109, 117, 125, 162, 174, 175, 176, 177, 185, 187, 188, 190, 191, 192, 195, 200, 232 *n*11
Androgyny, 46, 237 *n*7
Anquetil du Perron, Abraham Hyacinth, 68, 73, 80, 84, 85, 128, 224 *n*62, 226 *n*75, 236 *n*13
Antichrist, 12, 171, 182, 185, 192
Antimasque, 189, 190-91, 192, 239 *n*14
Antinomianism, 115
Apocalypse, 10, 12, 15, 31, 158-60, 171, 181-82, 183, 185, 191-92, 199

Apollo, 88, 102; in Keats's *Hyperion*, 114; in *Prometheus Unbound*, 47, 59-60
Apollodorus, 47
Ararat, Mount, 63-65, 67, 218-19 *n*41, 219-20 *n*45
Archimedes, 5-6
Argos, 132
Ariosto, 9, 212 *n*7
Aristophanes, 39
Armaggedon, 159
Ark, of Noah, 63, 219-20 *n*45
Arrian, xvii, 77, 218 *n*39, 219 *n*42
Art, 43, 77, 81; perversion of, 148-49; principles of, 186; relation to society, 188-89, 198-99
Asia: in *Prometheus Unbound*, 36, 38-53 passim, 58, 60, 71, 75, 78, 80, 81, 83, 91-106 passim, 110, 112, 116, 117, 123-30 passim, 197, 209 *n*1, 213 *n*10, 215 *n*20, 217 *n*32, 230 *n*2, 230-31 *n*3
Asiatic Researches, xviii, 78
Astrology, 70, 87, 88
Athens, 119, 175, 176
Atlantic Ocean: as symbol, 158, 167
Atlantis, 63, 219 *n*43, 219 *n*44
Atlas, 77
Atomic principles, 15, 18, 19, 117, 165-66
Aubrey, John, 223 *n*58
Augustine, Saint, 161, 233 *n*5
Austria, 155, 179, 200
Authoritarianism, 196
Avernus, 53

Babylon, 69, 223 *n*58; Whore of, 182
Bacchic ritual, 49
Bacchus. *See* Dionysus
Bacon, Francis, 47, 196-97, 238 *n*72
Bailly, Jean Sylvain, 63, 83, 88, 91, 211 *n*31, 219 *n*42, 219 *n*43, 219-20 *n*45, 236 *n*10
Baker, Carlos, 212 *n*32
Balaam, 221-22 *n*52

Index

Index

Index

Index

Index

Index

Mithraism, 53, 79-80, 81, 82, 92; influence on Christianity, 225-26 *n*71. *See also* Mysteries

Monarchy, 27-28, 36, 175, 177, 182, 183, 188, 199

Monoptere, 79, 224-25 *n*66

Monotheism, 85

Mont Blanc, 221 *n*51

Mont Blanc, 4, 15, 35, 232, *n*16

Moon, 49, 51, 107, 117, 128, 215-16 *n*24, 231 *n*7, 233 *n*4

Moor, Edward, 211, *n*31, 226 *n*72, 236 *n*16, 237 *n*18

Moore, Thomas, xviii

Moses, 53, 69, 199, 219-20 *n*45

Mountains, 71, 75, 221 *n*51

Mozart, Wolfgang Amadeus, 232 *n*11

Music, 105-06, 125, 142, 169, 230-31 *n*3

Mutability, 65, 93, 101, 111, 115, 140

Mysteries, 53, 79-80, 81, 92, 93, 217 *n*32, 225-26 *n*71, 227-29 *n*81. *See also* Mithraism, Orphism

Myth, significance of, 43-44, 103, 198

Mythography: Christian, 55, 219-20 *n*45, 221 *n*50, 221-22 *n*52, 225-26 *n*71, 237 *n*18; English, 95-96, euhemerist, 44-45, 51, 81, 213 *n*9, 213-14 *n*14; French, 45, 52, 88, 95-96, 115, 165, 236 *n*10; Judaic, 221-22 *n*52; skeptical, 219-20 *n*45

Mythology: Buddhist, 63; Celtic, 83; Christian, 40, 41, 50, 51, 95, 153-54, 185, 217-18 *n*35, 231 *n*7, 237 *n*18; Greek, 38-40, 43, 46, 47, 49, 50, 93, 114, 160-61, 222-23 *n*55; Indian, 41, 46, 47, 67, 68, 78, 81, 87-91, 162, 216 *n*27, 220 *n*47, 222-23 *n*55, 227-29 *n*81, 229 *n*82, 236 *n*15, 237 *n*18; Judaeo-Christian, 45, 54-65, 69-70; Judaic, 58, 82, 119-20, 219-20 *n*45; Manichean, 68, 127, 128, 161, 163, 165, 171, 221-22 *n*52; Mohammedan, 45-46, 63, 83, 236 *n*15; northern, 82-83; occidental, 90, 95, 213 *n*12; oriental, 7, 46, 47, 50, 61, 63, 68, 82-83, 87, 90, 95, 161-64, 212 *n*13; Phoenician, 161, 165; syncretic, 39, 43-94, 95, 111, 112-13, 117, 196, 201, 205, 213 *n*12, 221-22 *n*52, 227 *n*80, 227-29 *n*81; zodiacal, 227-29 *n*81; Zoroastrian, 46, 47, 67, 68, 70, 73-74, 78, 81, 85, 87, 116-17, 128, 161, 165, 175, 221 *n*50, 233 *n*4

Mythopoeia, 37

Naples, Kingdom of, 155, 173, 179, 200

Napoleon Buonaparte, 10, 12, 29, 37, 45, 61, 177, 182, 187, 197

Napoleonic Wars, 10-11, 12, 19-20, 27, 182, 218 *n*39

Natural cycles, 156, 157, 225-26 *n*71, 236 *n*10, 237 *n*23

Natural law, 95, 103-110, 111, 116-17, 174, 197, 200, 205. *See also* Science, physical

Nature, 35, 45, 75, 77, 86, 93, 100, 104, 115-16, 141, 145, 147, 148, 178, 230-31 *n*3, 236 *n*10, 236 *n*12

Necessitarianism, 18, 19, 35

Necessity, 104, 109, 110, 216 *n*28

Necessity of Atheism, The, 205

Necromancy, 70

Neoplatonism, 45, 229-30 *n*83

Neptune, 51

Nereids, 47, 51

Neurosis, 116, 196

"A New National Anthem," 183

Newton, Isaac, 11, 165, 231-32 *n*8, 236 *n*15

Newton, John Frank, 36, 88-90, 227-29 *n*81

Nightingale, 169

Nimrod, 69, 221-22 *n*52

Noah, 45, 60-65, 69, 77, 91, 159, 214 *n*15, 217-18 *n*35, 218 *n*40, 218-19 *n*41, 219-20 *n*45, 221-22 *n*52, 229-30 *n*83

Nonnus, 91

North pole, 211 *n*31

Norton, xviii

Nous, 45, 93

Nymphs, 50-51

Nysa, 77, 91, 214 *n*18

Ocean: in *Prometheus Unbound*, 39, 42, 46-47, 59-60, 213 *n*9

Oceanides, 47, 130, 132

Ode: as genre, 155, 202; Romantic, 179

Ode to Liberty, 155, 172, 174-75, 176, 177-78, 181, 193, 196, 198, 204

Ode to Naples, 155, 172-73, 174, 175, 176, 178-79, 181, 192

Ode to the West Wind, 27, 155, 156-72, 173, 181, 186, 191, 192, 195, 196, 204, 237 *n*22

Oersted, Hans Christian, 108

Ogden, James, 210 *n*16

Ogilvie, John, 210 *n*16

Ollier, Charles, 151, 232 *n*15, 238 *n*4

Index

Index

Pompeii, 173, 179

Pope, Alexander, 149, 151, 200, 234 n20

Porphyry, 75

Potentiality, 30-31, 73-74, 97, 101, 111, 120, 123, 138, 173

Pottinger, Henry, 218 n39

Power, 100, 115

Pramathesa, 78

Preserver, the, 86, 87, 88, 155, 156, 157, 158, 162, 163, 167-68, 169, 171

Prideaux, Humphrey, 222 n54

Priestley, Joseph, 19, 217-18 n35, 225-26 n71, 229 n82

Prince Athanase, 37

Prince Regent. *See* George IV

Prison, 23, 121-22, 134-35

Proclus, 93, 233 n4

Prometheus, 35-39, 44-47, 49, 51-61, 64, 65, 67, 69-71, 73-75, 77-78, 81-86, 91-111, 115-33 passim, 139, 140, 145, 149, 155, 164, 196, 197, 205, 213 n9, 213-14 n14, 214 n15, 217 n32, 218-19 n41, 219 n43, 225 n65, 230 n2; and Christ, 54, 55, 57, 58; as creator, 45, 47, 76, 119-20; curse of, 41-42, 55-58, 71, 73-74, 97, 99, 101, 102, 105, 116, 126-27; as Dionysus, 91; as egotist, 57-58, 96-98, 127, 145, 146, 152; as Jehovah, 58; journey of, 64; as Jupiter, 74, 83-84, 85, 93, 102, 127, 152; as Noah, 45, 60-65; as principle of civilization, 44-45, 46, 86; as revolutionary, 34, 36, 37, 40, 41; as Romantic emblem, 34, 35, 43; and Satan, 54-59; as Zoroaster, 70, 85-86

Prometheus Unbound, xiv, xviii, 35, 36-118, 119-30, 137, 145, 146, 150, 153, 166, 171, 174, 186, 189, 191, 197, 199, 200, 205, 209 n1, 213 n10, 213 n12, 223-24 n61, 232 n15, 232-33 n17, 233 n1, 233 n2, 233 n4, 233 n19, 238 n4; and *Ahrimanes*, 227-29 n81; compared with *The Cenci*, 120-30; conceived in 1817, xvii; draft of, 220 n47; as drama, 38, 42-43, 44, 53, 55, 61, 96, 103, 117-18; genre of, 111, 112-13; Judaeo-Christian context, 54-65; as psychodrama, 96-103, 114; radical nature of, 110-11, 117; structure of, 39, 43, 70, 81, 92, 102-03, 111, 117, 212-13 n8; and Zoroastrianism, 68-87

Propaganda, 28, 30, 176, 186, 191

Prophecy, 113, 158, 159, 160, 171, 172, 173, 175, 177, 179, 199

Psellus, 216 n27

Puranas, 63, 211 n31

Purgatory, 152, 155, 169, 171, 172, 178, 179, 205

Pye, Henry James, 210 n16

Pyramid, 25, 28

Pyrrha, 45

Pythagoras, 69, 222 n54; principles of, 15, 39, 91, 161, 229-30 n83, 236 n15

Quarterly Review, 6, 65, 218 n39

Queen Mab, xvi, 4, 10-11, 13-20, 20-21, 23-24, 25, 26, 29, 30, 31, 32, 34, 41, 45, 55, 65, 82, 90, 108, 110, 134, 136, 151, 176, 199, 211 n23, 211 n31, 213 n10, 233 n20; failure of, 5-6, 18-20; metaphorical structures in, 14-17, 18; social vision of, 13, 14, 18-20

Quevedo Villegas, Francisco Gomez de, 190

Quietism, 11

Quintus Curtius. *See* Curtius Rufus, Quintus

Raben, Joseph, 218 n38

Raleigh, Sir Walter, 63

Ranald, Margaret and Ralph, 223 n58

Rape, 124, 128-29, 130, 135, 139, 171-72, 182

Reality, mental formulations and, 96, 111, 114, 115, 154, 232 n16. *See also* Idealism

Rebirth, 173, 174, 197, 233 n4

Relativity, 233 n20

Religion, 42-43, 44, 54, 77, 223 n58; natural, 104, 111; unity of all, 63, 95

Religious persecution, 193

Religious poetry, 205

Renaissance, ideals of, xx, 26, 134, 135. *See also* Humanism

Republicanism, 29

Resurrection, 168

Revelation, Book of, 159, 182, 185-86; Zoroastrian influence on, 225-26 n71

Revolt of Islam, The, 20, 24-32, 34, 36, 37, 38, 54, 65, 67, 81, 82, 84, 108, 134, 136, 151, 176, 186, 195, 199, 211 n31, 212 n33, 218 n36, 223-24 n61; failure of, 5-6, 29-32; narrative structure of, 28-29

251

Index

Index

Index